NC

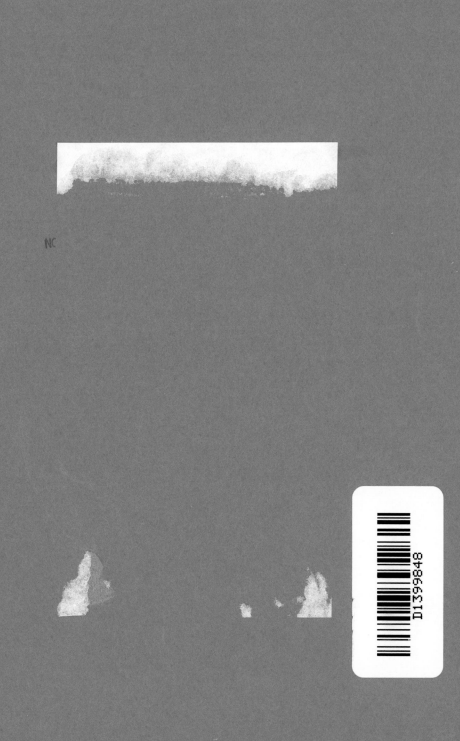

Principles of Modern Soccer

Principles of Modern Soccer

George Beim

WORLD CUP SPORTS, INC.

Houghton Mifflin Company   Boston

ATLANTA   DALLAS   GENEVA, ILL.   HOPEWELL, N.J.   PALO ALTO   LONDON

To my wife Caterina, children Kimberly and Pamela,
and all those who made this book possible.

Cover and title page photograph Terry McKoy. **Chapter opening photographs:** *Chapters 1, 6, and 9:* By arrangement with Newcastle Chronicle and Journal Limited, England. *Chapters 2, 3, and 7:* Courtesy The Press Association Limited. *Chapters 4 and 5:* Courtesy St. Louis University and The Athletic Institute. *Chapter 8:* Soccer Associates Photo.

Library of Congress Catalog Card Number: 76–11986
ISBN: 0-395-24415-3

Contents

Preface

Soccer is *the* sport of the world. It is a game of constant action and requires continuous adaptation to changing situations by the team as a whole as well as by individual players. Although it is a team game, there is ample room for players to display their brilliance through individual performance with the ball as well as through team play involving improvisation and tactical knowledge. It is a game that sends people from all over the world into a frenzy, creates national heroes and millionaires, and has even sent countries to war.

Individual soccer games have drawn upward of 200,000 spectators; an estimated 800 million people viewed the 1974 World Cup on television sets around the world. The game is fast, unpredictable, exciting, and beautiful. Is it any wonder that it is rapidly becoming one of the major sports in the United States and that in many areas of the country it has already achieved this prestigious position of popularity?

More and more people are playing soccer. It has grown by leaps and bounds at the youth, schoolboy, college, amateur, and professional levels here in the United States. As a result, there is a constantly increasing demand for more knowledgeable and better-qualified people to coach the game. This book was written to give a better understanding of the principles of modern soccer to those coaches and players who would grow with the success of the game.

Coaches are charged with the responsibility of teaching their players soccer techniques and tactics to develop teams who perform at the maximum level of effectiveness. Unfortunately, there are no magic formulas for transforming limited-skilled players into world-class champions. However, through the implementation of a well-planned training program and coaching that utilizes the principles of modern soccer, coaches can provide the best possible opportunity for improvement.

The two biggest problems that confront coaches in planning training sessions are "what to coach" and "how to coach it." By knowing and adhering to accepted principles, coaches can reduce the amount of guesswork to a minimum.

This book is devoted to the principles of how modern soccer should be played and to how coaches go about preparing a team, composed of 11 different people, for match play. It is not a kick-the-ball manual, and it does not deal with the sequential steps necessary for performing elementary soccer techniques.

The book first provides a background to how the game is played by tracing the tactical development of soccer from the first signs of organized systems or formations to modern-day strategy. All tactical changes are carefully examined, and references are made to specific individuals and teams that were most influential in making the changes. Each step is analyzed progressively; in addition, the specific catalysts that prompted the implementation of new tactical ideas are explained.

Systems of play such as the 4–2–4 or the 4–3–3 cannot be effective if the players who are utilizing them fail to adhere to basic principles of play. Thus the next section deals with the necessary application of the principles of attack and defense by individual players and the team as a whole. Each basic principle is comprehensively analyzed and diagrams help clarify the discussion.

Organization and detailed planning are essential elements of successful training sessions. Therefore the book gives special attention to the principles that coaches should follow in their training sessions. Since every team is composed of individual players, tactics must necessarily be coached at three different levels. This section thoroughly explains the principles that need to be followed in coaching individual, group, and team tactics. In addition, the methods needed to teach the numerous techniques to be effective and successful are clearly explained.

Particularly valuable to coaches is the coverage devoted to restart, or "still-ball," situations. The defending and attacking responsibilities of players are detailed explicitly, and a variety of set plays are diagrammed and explained for each specific type of restart.

Chapter 6 provides scientific principles of conditioning for soccer with diagrams and exercises that can develop the endurance, speed, strength, and mental fitness that are necessary to play the game.

A special feature of the book is the detailed coverage of training games that may be used to add variety to training sessions. The rules and descriptions of numerous training games that can be a great deal of fun, as well as illustrations of many of these games, are found in Chapter 4. The chapter is divided into four sections and provides specific games to help coaches achieve various objectives. Games for warm-up purposes, fitness, technique development, and tactical coaching can be enjoyed by players while still accomplishing specific purposes.

The final section of the book deals with the principles of coaching. The knowledge of any man can be wasted to a great extent if he is unable to establish a proper rapport with the players on his team. This section is devoted to the psychological principles that coaches can apply to bring out the potential inherent in their players.

Every coach has a personal coaching style simply because every person is unique. The best coaches in any sport are the ones who listen and learn from everyone they come in contact with, take the best that everyone else has to offer, and then improve on it by adding the best they have themselves. This book is not designed to provide all the answers to the problems of coaching soccer. It is designed to present certain accepted principles of soccer as well as some ideas on coaching the sport, that will stimulate the reader to develop his own methods to serve his particular needs best. The final test of coaching is in the results of the match. Not necessarily in the final score, but in how effectively a team utilizes its talent and potential.

I have been extremely fortunate to have had the opportunity to come in contact with many extremely knowledgeable people in the game of soccer from the United States as well as other parts of the world. As a result, I have learned a great deal through countless discussions about the game with them and from the soccer clinics they have conducted. Many of the ideas, tactics, and exercises that appear in this book will reflect my exposure to and appreciation of the thinking and philosophies of men such as Dettmar Cramer, Charles Hughes, Alan Wade, Walter Winterbottom, and many others too numerous to list. My knowledge has been influenced greatly by all my associates and friends in soccer as well as by many fine players that it has been my privilege to coach.

In addition, I would like to express my gratitude, for their assistance in reviewing the original manuscript, to Jerry Yeagley, Indiana University; Bill Hughes, State University of New York, Brockport; Mickey Cochran, Bowling Green University; and Mel Lorbach, West Chester State College.

I would like to give special thanks to three men who have played a major role in my soccer career: Frank Nelson of Nyack, New York, who initially triggered much of my interest in the game; Whitey Burnham of Dartmouth College who helped speed up the progress of my career; and Don Yonker of Drexel University who contributed more to my soccer development and career through his assistance and guidance than any other single person. Without the influence of these men, this text would not be a reality.

A special note of thanks is due to Rhonda Martin for her time, effort, and efficiency in preparing the manuscript. Also, to my family for bearing with me during the many hours spent away from them in preparing this text, I owe a special debt. I should also like to acknowledge all those who so kindly supplied photographs and other materials that were used in this text and gave their permissions for their reproduction.

George Beim

Diagram Key

⟶   Path of the ball

- - - - -▶   Path of a player without the ball

wwwwwww▶   Path of a player dribbling the ball

1	Goalkeeper
2	Right wingback
3	Left wingback
4	Right midfielder
5	Right center back
6	Left center back
7	Right wing
8	Right striker
9	Left midfielder
10	Left striker
11	Left wing

1

The Development of Systems

THE ORIGINS of soccer have never really been pinpointed. The data reveal traces of similar games played thousands of years ago in various parts of the world, but the sport did not really begin to take its present form until the nineteenth century.

THE BEGINNING OF THE MODERN GAME

On Monday, October 26, 1863, a group of men met in Freemason's Tavern in London, England, to form the first football association. This was one of the most important developments in the history of soccer because it was here that the game's first real laws were set down. Since 1863 most countries have established their own soccer associations, and more than 140 countries now belong to the Federation Internationale de Football Association (FIFA), the world governing body of soccer. The U.S. affiliate of FIFA is the U.S. Soccer Federation (USSF).

The early laws of association football in England were in some instances similar to the laws of rugby. For example, a player could catch the ball with his hands. Also there was no provision for a goalkeeper; the field of play was established at 200 yd long maximum, but no minimum existed; and the goal posts were 8 yd apart, but they had no crossbar on the top.

Before 1866 the offside rule in soccer was the same as in rugby. A player was considered offside if he was ahead of the ball. In 1866, however, the law was changed: A player was now considered offside if he was ahead of the ball and near his opponent's goal with fewer than three opponents between him and it.

Because of the existing offside law, dribbling dominated the game. Player positioning was crude at best, and players tended to bunch around the ball. Combination play and teamwork were virtually nonexistent.

By the early 1870s the laws of the game had changed considerably. The rules now prohibited field players from using their hands, and a goal-keeper had appeared who could use his hands to stop the ball. The length of the field was still 200 yd, but the width was now set at a maximum of 100 yd. The goal dimensions were set at 8 ft high with a tape stretched across the top acting as the crossbar. Later, in 1882, the tape was replaced by a real crossbar.

The throw-in from the touchline also came into being during the 1870s. The players were allowed to throw the ball in with one hand, and

Figure 1.1 An impression of soccer in the early days when the crossbar was a tape. (From Tony Pawson, *100 Years of the F.A. Cup*, William Heinemann Ltd., London, 1972. By permission of The Football Association.)

the throw was awarded to the player who first touched the ball after it had gone over the touchline. The throw-in rule was later changed to give possession of the ball to the opponent of the team that last played it before it went out of bounds. In 1882 the two-handed throw we know today replaced the one-handed throw-in from the touchline.

The penalty kick first appeared in 1891. At that time it was taken from 12 yd out as it is today, and a 12-yd line stretched the width of the field. This line designated not only the place from which players took the penalty kick but also the boundaries of the penalty area itself within which fouls committed by defenders resulted in penalty kicks.

A line 18 yd from the goal line designated the spot behind which all players except the goalkeeper and the player taking the penalty kick had to position themselves until the kick was taken. Also an area 6 yd from the goal line was marked off beyond which the defending goalkeeper could not go.

In 1902 the penalty area as we know it today came into being. The only difference was that it did not have the arc at the top center of the area. This arc, 10 yd from the place where the penalty kick is taken, was added in 1937. It was designed to keep all players except the one kicking at least 10 yd from the ball until the kick was taken.

The first international soccer match was played in 1872 between Scotland and England. The game was played in Glasgow, Scotland, and typified the dribbling game of the times. Tactically speaking, the Scottish team was a bit more advanced than the English since the Scottish utilized a goalkeeper, two backs, two what we would call "midfielders," and six forwards. The English played with a goalkeeper, one back, one midfielder, and eight forwards. However, since all the players tended to congregate around the ball and since the 1866 offside rule was still in effect, dribbling predominated, and there was little indication of any formations or systems being used during the match. Because of the emphasis on dribbling, the forwards tended to follow the ball all the way back on defense, and the game ended in a 0–0 draw.

The passing game and combination play began to develop out of the necessity to avoid bunching around the ball. This in turn changed the shape of team formations, or systems, and gave more balance to attack and defense. As attackers found weaknesses in the opposition's defense, defenders began to change their tactics to eliminate these weaknesses.

BIRTH OF THE PASSING GAME

The Scots have been credited with putting the pass into use. The Scottish team Queen's Park, the first to introduce any real tactics, brought the first true passes into the game. Realizing that the players all bunched around the person with the ball to prevent him from penetrating the opposition, the Scots began to pass the ball, forcing many defenders out of position and unable to prevent the attackers from penetrating the defense.

The Scottish team that played against the English team in 1872 was the first to show signs of a true team formation when they fielded two backs, two midfielders, and only six forwards. Later the Scots dropped one of their center forwards back behind the forward line in an attempt to strengthen their overall play; their formation now resembled a 2–2–1–5.

In the early 1870s the passes were generally quite short since both the attacking and the defending players still tended to mass around the ball. However, teams soon realized that they could increase the speed of the game by passing, and that by utilizing the full width of the field they could create better and more frequent opportunities to penetrate the opposition's defense.

In 1883 the soccer team from Cambridge University in England adopted a system of play that for the first time created a numerical balance between attackers and defenders. They further modified the Scottish 2–2–1–5 formation by withdrawing the player directly behind the forwards, thus creating the 2–3–5 formation, sometimes referred to as the *Pyramid system*. Other teams soon adopted this system, and a new tactical trend began.

At first, since dribbling and short passes still dominated the game, the three halfbacks generally played well upfield to support the five forwards. Attackers soon realized, however, that quick long passes to a teammate near the touchline could frequently produce effective fast breaks. The opponent's five forwards and three halfbacks, playing far into their own attacking end of the field, could be left completely out of position by long passes.

As the long pass found its way into the game more frequently, it became obvious that teams had to protect themselves against it. They began using the two fullbacks to guard the middle area in front of the goal, two wing halfbacks to mark the opponent's wing forwards and prevent long passes to them, one center halfback to defend the middle of the field and to act as an attacking player in supporting the forwards, and five forwards. This formation became extremely popular and lasted for many years.

Since most of the teams in England adopted the 2–3–5 system, this was the way that soccer was introduced around the world. Many countries still number their players according to their positioning in the 2–3–5 formation.

The English took Association Football with them to many parts of the world and were the influential force behind the game's widespread adoption. By 1870 the Germans were playing according to English rules, and at the same time the game was catching on in Portugal. British residents introduced soccer to Denmark around the mid-1870s, and during the 1880s the game spread to countries as far away from England as Canada, Australia, and Uruguay.

The Scotch had changed the game greatly by introducing the pass. The English further changed it by introducing the offside trap. Until 1925 the offside law required a player to have at least three men between himself and the opposing goal prior to receiving a forward pass, if he wished to be onside. Attacking forwards were usually so concerned about the play itself that they would not notice one of the two fullbacks moving upfield past them which put the forwards in an offside position. The English fullbacks became very adept at anticipating the long pass and playing the opponents offside, and soon the defensive offside tactic dominated the game.

As the opposition's attack developed, one fullback would position himself to defend the middle of the field while the other quickly moved up to the midfield line, leaving all the opponent's forwards behind him in offside positions. This offside tactic was developed by two fullbacks, Morely and Montgomery, of the Notts County club. However, it was McCracken, the Irish international player, and his fellow fullback at Newcastle United, Hudspeth, who exploited the offside trap to the fullest during the 1920s.

The offside tactics of McCracken and Hudspeth were copied throughout England so frequently that spectators grew weary of matches that were so heavily dominated by the offside trap. By the early 1920s professional soccer had already become big business, and the interest of the spectators was important to the clubs supported by them. As a result, the four British football associations that made up the International Board of Laws changed the offside law.

FIFA

At this time it is important to note the formation of the international association that governs soccer. Federation Internationale de Football Association, commonly referred to as "FIFA," was founded in 1904. Originally composed of only 7 members and now claiming more than 140, FIFA sets down the laws by which soccer is played.

The laws of the game govern how it is played. As a result, the laws directly affect the tactics and formations or systems utilized by soccer teams. As the laws of the game change, so does the game itself since the laws directly affect strategy and systems.

After some experimentation, the International Board of Laws changed the offside law in the summer of 1925. The new law reduced from three to two the number of defending players necessary to keep an attacker onside. As long as an attacking player had two defenders between the goal and himself at the time the ball was last played, he was onside. The new law took away the defensive advantage of the old offside trap and gave rise to a flurry of goal scoring. With the center halfback still playing very much of an attacking role, the two fullbacks found themselves unable to handle the opponent's attack. Teams began to seek out ways of strengthening their defenses, and the "stopper" center half or third back was born.

Chapman and the *WM*

Several people have claimed credit for this change, but generally Herbert Chapman, manager of the Arsenal FC in the English First Division, is credited as the inventor of the third back. He moved the fullbacks out of the middle to the flanks where they now marked the opponent's wingers and played in a diagonal around the center half so that each back had cover when necessary. The center half was withdrawn from his old attacking position to fill the gap in the middle between the two fullbacks, marking the opponent's center forward. The halfbacks were given the responsibility of marking the attacking inside forwards, thus forming an M-formation in defense.

Chapman was aided in developing the stopper by Charlie Buchan, the inside right and captain of the Arsenal team. Buchan, an experienced manager in his own right, suggested to Chapman that the center half be withdrawn to mark the opponent's center forward when the offside law was changed. To fill the gap left by the center half's moving back, Buchan suggested that one of the inside forwards be withdrawn to play behind the forwards.

It was evident that control of the midfield area was essential to the attack's build-up. Therefore, the other inside forward was also withdrawn to help in midfield. This left the two wingers and the center forward as the principal strikers and thus gave rise to the W-formation in attack.

Chapman believed that to play the *WM* system properly, players had to be specialists with strictly defined responsibilities. Since he did not feel

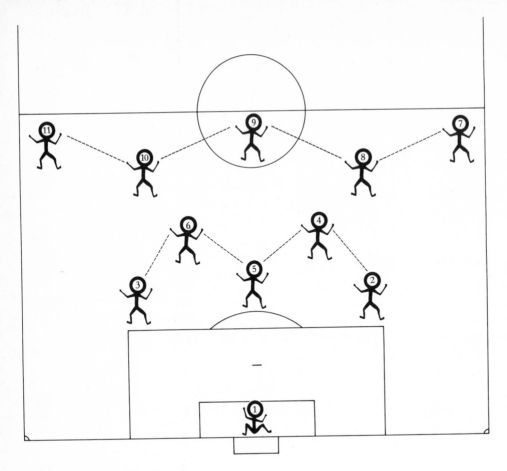

Diagram 1.1 *WM* formation.

that he could use the current Arsenal players in this way, he went out on a spree of signing players who would play the positions in the *WM*-formation to his liking.

The key to the *WM* defense was the stopper. He had to be tall, strong, and an especially good header to clear out high dangerous balls that came into his area. Chapman found this type of player in red-haired Herbie Roberts. Roberts was satisfied with a defensive role, and his outstanding heading and sure tackling often enabled him to greatly limit the effectiveness of the opponent's center forward.

Most teams who played the *WM* system were concerned first with stopping the other team's attack. Although this is also true of Chapman's

Arsenal team, he must also be given credit for building a most capable attacking side. He wanted attacking players who could score goals, and he was not concerned whether the goals came as a result of sheer strength and speed or as a result of especially artistic play. He merely wanted his team to score enough goals to win matches.

To develop a winning attack, Chapman looked for wingers who had speed and at the same time the ability to move in towards the goal and score. He filled these spots with Joe Hulme, one of the fastest forwards of the time, and Cliff Bastin, a youngster from Exeter. Between them they managed to score 53 goals during one season, and Bastin's scoring of 33 goals in 42 league matches is still a record for goals in one season by a First Division winger.

The center forward of the *WM* system was selected to counteract the stopper back. He had to be big and powerful, with the ability to give punishment as well as take it. As long as the center forward could score one or two goals every match, even if it were through sheer strength, most people did not worry whether he had a great deal of finesse.

One of the great *WM* center forwards who fit the stereotype was Dixie Dean who played for Everton in England. Dean had 37 hat tricks during his 18 seasons of top-class soccer, and during the 1927–28 season set a record that stands to this day by netting 60 goals in one season.

Chapman's initial center forward was Jack Lambert who was later replaced by Ted Drake, a prime example of the "tank-type" center forward. Drake was the kind of player who would go through a brick wall to get a goal, and in 1935 he set a First Division record by scoring seven goals in one match against Aston Villa.

In Chapman's plan, one inside forward had to play farther upfield than the other. The one playing upfield followed the three principal strikers and was there to finish the play if the other three had not been successful. To play this role, Arsenal bought David Jack from Bolton for a very high fee.

The other inside forward had to be the schemer of the team. He linked up the defense and the attack, and played back as the center half of pre-1925. The initial thrust of most of the Arsenal attack on their opponent's goal came from him. He had to understand his position well, have tremendous stamina to cover large areas of the field, and be able to distribute penetrating passes to his forwards. To perform these difficult tasks, Chapman used Alex James, who played a key role in Arsenal FC's success during the 1930s.

Chapman used the *WM*-formation to shine the limelight on Arsenal.

Figure 1.2 Dixie Dean of Everton, one of the great *WM* center forwards. (Courtesy Central Press Photos Limited, London)

When he took over the team in 1925, it was a mediocre club compared to the other teams in the English First Division, but with his tutelage and his use of the *WM* system Arsenal went on to achieve great success.

In 1927 Arsenal reached the FA Cup Final only to lose to Cardiff City of Wales by a score of 1–0. In 1930 they were once again finalists in the FA Cup, but this time they were successful, beating Huddersfield Town 2–0. In 1931 Chapman took Arsenal to their first League championship, which they won in a most impressive fashion. When the season was over Arsenal had accumulated a total of 66 points, having lost only 4 of their 42 League matches. They were finalists once more in the FA Cup in 1932, losing to Newcastle United by 2–1, and then winning two more League titles in 1933 and 1934. Herb Chapman died in 1934, but the team he left behind went on to a record-tying third consecutive League title in 1935.

When Chapman first introduced the stopper back, the other teams in Britain were far from convinced that this new tactical maneuver would work. At first many attributed the initial success of Arsenal to mere luck, and some even nicknamed them "Lucky Arsenal." However, by the

Figure 1.3 Arsenal, 1929–30: back row, Baker, Lambert, Preedy, Seddon, Hapgood, John; middle row, Herbert Chapman (Manager), Jack, Parker, James, Whittaker (Trainer); front row, Hulme, Bastin. (From Tony Pawson, *100 Years of the F.A. Cup*, William Heinemann Ltd., London, 1972. By permission of The Football Association.)

early 1930s no one could dispute that Arsenal's success was far more than luck, and soon almost all the teams in the British Isles converted to the three-back game.

While many teams were converting to the *WM* system during the 1930s, Karl Rappan, an Austrian who coached both club teams and the national side in Switzerland, designed the *Swiss Bolt*, or *Verrou*, system. This system was a forerunner of the English *sweeper* and the *libero* of the Italian *catenaccio* system. The system provided a team with a number of defenders equal to the opponent's attackers and gave the defenders an extra back, the *bolt*, to provide the necessary cover in defense and to protect the open space in front of the goal.

Diagram 1.2 Swiss Bolt system.

Rappan believed that if a team was weaker than its opponent, it had to concentrate on defense, and even a strong team could benefit from a "free" back. As a result of his system, his Swiss teams were successful for many years.

Rappan used three backs, as was the trend of the times, but he added a man behind the last line of defense to provide cover and pick up any attacker who beat one of the defenders. In the Swiss Bolt system, the wing halfbacks marked the opponent's wingers, one fullback played in the middle of the field, marking the opponent's center forward, while the other fullback became the free back or "bolt." One of the insides was withdrawn to mark one of the opponent's inside forwards, while the center half marked the opponent's other inside. Whenever a defender was beaten by an attacker, the free back would pick up the attacker and the beaten defender would assume the role of the bolt to provide defensive cover.

In attack, the Swiss Bolt system relied mostly on counterattacking strategy. As soon as possession of the ball was regained, the defending inside forward and the center half went on attack, and the wing halfbacks were also encouraged to press forward. Ideally, they would play the ball quickly and move it into the opponent's penalty area as quickly as possible so that they could take a shot on goal. Once they lost possession of the ball again, all the defensive players had to sprint back to their positions.

This system was extremely demanding physically since it required players to work very hard and cover great areas of the playing field. In addition, the players had to be intelligent and able to adapt to various roles if the system were to prove successful.

4-2-4

The stopper center back dominated the game for more than 25 years. Naturally teams tried to conceive ways in which their attack could destroy this defensive alignment, but a breakthrough did not occur until the early 1950s. This breakthrough, referred to as the 4-2-4 system, initiated a new system of play. Although the Brazilians are frequently given credit for introducing the 4-2-4 system around 1958, it actually originated in Hungary in the early 1950s.

Origin of the 4-2-4

During the time of the *WM* system's popularity, the center forward was generally a big, strong player, not necessarily very skillful, but one who had a strong shot, a good head, and was able to muscle his way to one or two goals every game. In 1951 Martin Bukovi was the manager of the Budapest Club Voros Loboga, now known as the Club MTK. He had a typical *WM* center forward in a player named Hoffling. When Hoffling left MTK in 1951 to join an Israeli club, Bukovi, unable to find another tank-type center forward to replace him, decided to change the attacking style of MTK.

He gave Peter Palotas, one of his midfielders, the No. 9 shirt of the center forward. However, instead of playing the regular spearhead role of the *WM* center forward, Palotas was withdrawn from the front line while continuing to play the midfielder role. He collected passes from his defense and then redistributed them to the forwards. Since he was now duplicating the job of one of the present two midfielders, one of them was withdrawn from midfield to play a more defensive role. This was probably the initial conception of the 4–2–4 system. Some people refer to this system as the *withdrawn center forward* formation, but for all practical purposes it can be referred to simply as the first 4–2–4.

The Magic Magyars

During the early 1950s the national coach of Hungary was Gusztav Sebes, and his chief assistant was Marton Bukovi of MTK. For the 1952 Olympic games in Helsinki Sebes selected four very goal-minded forwards in Zoltan Czibor, Sandor Kocsis, Ferenc Puskas, and Laszlo Budai. Because he was faced with the problem of not having a strong center forward, Sebes adopted Bukovi's system for the national team and selected Peter Palotas as his center forward.

After a preliminary round against Rumania in Helsinki, which Hungary won by a narrow margin of 2–1, Sebes decided to make a change since he was not satisfied with Palotas' play. He selected Nandor Hidegkuti to play instead. Now he had Budai and Czibor on the wings with Kocsis and Puskas playing as the inside forwards and principal strikers. Hidegkuti withdrew to the left midfielder's position; beside him on the right was an excellent midfielder, Joszef Bozsik. The left midfielder, Joszef Zakarias, was withdrawn into a defensive position and became the fourth back in the Hungarian defense. With this alignment the Hungarian team won the Helsinki soccer Olympics.

The Hungarians exploited the weaknesses of the three-back game to the fullest. Budai and Czibor, the wingers, operated close to the touchlines and dropped back slightly towards their defense. This forced the opponent's wing fullbacks either to move upfield, exposing a great deal of space behind them with only the center back remaining in defense, or to stay back and allow the Hungarian wingers to pick up passes from their defense and develop a strong attack from there. While the wing fullbacks played tightly on Budai and Czibor, Puskas and Kocsis roamed about in the opponent's defense picking up passes from midfielders Hidegkuti and Bozsik. The six Hungarian attackers moved about

Figure 1.4 Hidegkuti scores Hungary's sixth goal during their 6–3 win over England at Wembley in 1953. (Courtesy Central Press Photos Limited, London)

freely, gracefully and with their extremely high degree of skill, were able to destroy their opponent's defense.

In 1953 the Hungarian team gained international prominence when they played England's National team at Wembley Stadium in London. The English came into the match never having lost against a foreign team in Wembley Stadium. The Hungarians, however, with their exceptional skill and their new system, picked apart the English defense and won handily by 6–3.

The return match was held in Budapest in May 1954, and the Hungarians left no doubt as to their superiority by once again defeating the English team, this time by 7–1. From 1951–1955 the Hungarian

Figure 1.5 Puskas, on the ground, scores for Hungary at Wembley in 1953. (Courtesy Syndication International Ltd., London)

National team dubbed as the "Magic Magyar's" played 47 matches of which they won 40, drew 6, and lost only 1, the World Cup Final, to Germany in 1954. As a result of their resounding success, a few people began to take note not only of the great individual players on the Hungarian National team but also of the system they used. Clearly, the old *WM* formation had many flaws, and the end of its use at the international level was rapidly approaching.

4–2–4 in England

In England the triumph of the "Magic Magyars" at Wembley and their success during the World Cup Final in 1954 in Switzerland was viewed with interest by Les McDowall, the manager of Manchester City. He was so impressed by the Hungarians' play that he decided to adopt their tactics at Manchester. During the 1954–55 season, McDowall used Don Revie, Alf Ramsay's successor as the manager of the English National team, in the role of the withdrawn center forward. Manchester City had a most successful campaign in the League and reached the FA Cup Final in 1955, where they lost to Newcastle United by 3–1.

After the Hungarian Revolution in 1956, the Hungarian National team relinquished its claim to international supremacy. At that time another great team opted for the 4–2–4, Real Madrid of Spain.

Real gathered players from all over the world to form a team that had a phenomenal winning streak during the late 1950s and the early 1960s. They used the withdrawn center forward to perfection, and many people consider them the best club team ever put together. They had outstanding personnel and, as a team, did so many things well and could attack effectively in so many ways that they were practically unbeatable.

In 1955 the first European Cup Championship that was open to the League Champions of every country in Europe was inaugurated in Paris. Real Madrid played and beat Reims, the French champions, in the first final and then went on to win the European Cup for an amazing string of five consecutive years. Their most impressive win in the finals came in 1960 when they defeated Eintracht of Germany by a score of 7–3.

The key man in the Real Madrid team was the great player Alfredo Di Stefano. He wore the No. 9 shirt and withdrew into the midfield area as Hidegkuti had done. However, Di Stefano played a much greater role in the success of Real than any other withdrawn center forward ever did for his team.

Originally from Buenos Aires, Di Stefano played for River Plate in Argentina and the Milionarios club in Bogota, Colombia, before joining Real in 1953. Tall and blond, he possessed unbelievable stamina, which allowed him to cover far greater areas on the field than most players could. He was a fantastic dribbler, extremely accurate passer, could head well, and the number of goals he accumulated testified to his ability to finish. During the 1960 European Cup competition, Di Stefano scored in every round, sometimes getting more than one goal in a game. It was not a rare occurrence to see this man make a tackle in his own penalty area, involve himself a moment later in a passing combination at midfield, and then finish the attack himself by driving the ball into the opponent's net. A complete and remarkable player, he was unquestionably the key in making the Real Madrid's 4–2–4 work so well.

Because of Di Stefano and the other outstanding players on the Madrid team, Real was able to add a new facet to the 4–2–4 system. Di Stefano was able to control the play at midfield by utilizing short passes. When the defenders were finally tempted out into the midfield area to challenge for the ball, Di Stefano would hit long accurate passes, especially to the extremely talented and fast outside left Gento, who would leave his fullback behind after a few strides and attack the goal.

The beauty of the Real attack was that it could take on so many different forms. It might be the long pass from Di Stefano to the quick Gento, or it could be a cannonlike shot from far out coming off the left foot of Ferenc Puskas, who joined Real in 1959, or it might be a series of quick rebound passes with Di Stefano popping up in the penalty area and driving the ball home.

With outstanding players like the center back José Santamaria, midfielder Vidal, and forward Del Sol, it is no wonder that Real played their version of the 4–2–4 system to perfection. They used the system, but most of all the players, to pile up records that may never be duplicated.

Brazil Shows the 4–2–4 to the World

The Brazilian national team, under coach Vincente Feola, used a 4–2–4 system to win the World Cup in 1958 in Sweden. The reason that many people attribute the invention of the 4–2–4 to Brazil is that by 1958 it was easily recognizable, and the Brazilians probably played it more rigidly than teams had previously. The Hungarians were very flexible in their play, and many people could not identify the system they were using. In fact, some thought they were still playing the *WM* system, which when looked at numerically could be called a 3–2–2–3 or a 3–4–3. In the Hungarian attack there were many outstanding players such as Kocsis, Puskas, Bozsik, and Hidegkuti. Because of their great play people often dismissed even thinking about the fact that the Hungarians had developed a new system. Also the Hungarian left midfielder Zakarias, who withdrew to play a defensive role, was not always recognizable as a center back; at times he still appeared to be a left halfback.

The 1958 Brazilian team played the system in such a positive way that the numbers 4–2–4 were easily placed and identified as their system. They used two wingers, Zagalo and Garrincha, and two distinct strikers, Vava and the great Pelé. Didi and Zito were definitely the midfield players, and there was no question that Orlando dropped back into the position between the center half and the left back, thus forming a definite double center back situation and a back line of four players.

Where the Hungarian system may not have been recognizable as a result of their place changing, the Brazilians held a fairly rigid formation.

Figure 1.6 Pelé, one of the greatest soccer players of all time. (Soccer Associates photo)

Vava and Pelé usually remained in the middle as the lead players of the attack, while Zito and Didi usually stayed in the midfield area.

People realized quickly that no one center back could contain both Vava and Pelé effectively since they always had a two-against-one situation. The old center back had a dual role: he either marked the opposing center forward or marked the space in front of the goal. Obviously he could not do both jobs. Now that two strikers were attacking him, it was impossible to handle the situation; therefore, the second center back evolved very quickly. Since one man was not enough to handle the midfield role, one player was withdrawn from the front line. This created the 4–2–4 arrangement. By 1959, just one year after Brazil won the World Cup, many major soccer teams around the world had adopted their 4–2–4 system.

One of the most important aspects of the Brazilians' game was their ability to make a smooth and well-balanced transition from defense to attack. When they went on defense, their forwards fell back, often quite deeply into their own half of the field. Thus when they regained possession of the ball, the forwards could give additional support to the player with the ball and make short passes as well as quick counterattacking long passes.

The primary objective of the 4–2–4 system is to give a team seven or eight players defending when the opponents have the ball, and six or seven players attacking when in possession of the ball. On defense at least one of the wingers retreats to assist the midfielders. When in attack the two midfielders, and often one of the wing fullbacks, should assist the four forwards.

Although the Brazilians were not the true innovators of the 4–2–4 system, they were responsible for making the rest of the world fully aware of it. It is primarily because of their play that this system was adopted by so many teams.

CATENACCIO

During the 1950s, while most soccer teams around the world were busy transforming the old *WM* system to the new 4–2–4, the Italians were devising the "super" defense, known as *catenaccio* (Italian for "bolt"). Initially this defensive game took the form of the old Swiss Bolt, but by the late 1950s the modern catenaccio defense had been established.

During the 1948 Olympic games in England, it became evident that there were quite a few top-quality soccer players in the Scandinavian countries. As a result, the more wealthy Italian teams went into Scandinavia to sign players. The Italians liked the idea of signing Scandinavian players because they were amateurs and a club did not have to pay any transfer fee. Juventus, A.C. Milan, and F.C. Internationale of Milan all bolstered their sides with Scandinavian players.

Juventus won the 1949–50 season with John Hansen and Karl Praest, both of Denmark, playing important roles. By the 1950–51 season, A.C. Milan had signed three players from Sweden, Nils Liedholm, Gunnar Gren, and Gunnar Nordahl; Nordahl went on to be the high scorer of the Italian professional league for many seasons. With the addition of these players, A.C. Milan took the title during the 1950–51 season. For the 1951–52 season Juventus added Karl Hansen of Denmark and regained

Diagram 1.3 The catenaccio.

the championship. Finally, F.C. Internationale of Milan won the championship during the 1952–53 and 1953–54 seasons with the help of Lennart Skoglund of Sweden and Hungarian Stefan Nyers.

As the wealthier clubs were able to build up their teams by buying top players from around the world, the managers of the poorer and weaker teams in Italy saw that something had to be done. When these coaches began to get sacked when they lost by a large margin, a panacea for tight defense evolved.

At first coaches felt that it might be enough to double-mark the opponent's top forward, and leave the center back (in the three-back defense) to play his normal stopper's game. Usually this relieved the center back from having to mark any particular players, and he could concentrate on covering the danger area in front of the goal.

Once the weaker teams adopted defensive tactics, they were able to lose by fewer goals and at times come up with a draw or even an occasional win against a top team. This convinced them of the necessity of defensive soccer. After all, every soccer game begins as a draw, and since a draw is worth one point, it is worthwhile to keep the game as it started.

The trend towards the defensive game is evidenced in Italian football during the 1950s by the number of goals scored by the league champion. In the two seasons between 1949 and 1951, the championship team had scored over 100 goals. However, by the 1952–54 seasons the championship team's goals had declined into the 60s.

At first the Italians adopted the Swiss Bolt defense used by Karl Rappan. However, by the late 1950s they had developed the true catenaccio, the super defense that allowed a team to draw, or even beat, an opponent with superior players. As a result, even the stronger teams like A.C. Milan who were playing the old *WM* also opted for stronger defensive soccer.

The principle behind the catenaccio defense is that a team will mark the opponent's attackers man-for-man and then leave one player to act as the bolt behind the defense. Since defenders do not have to worry about giving each other cover and only have to mark one opponent, the play is reasonably easy to execute. The last man in defense, known as the *libero, free back,* or *sweeper,* provides cover for his teammates in defense, and thus when an attacker has the ball, he is always double marked. The man marking him can mark him tightly and still be secure in the knowledge that the libero is providing cover.

The numbers attributed to the catenaccio defense depend on the formation used by the opposition. In other words, when a team using a catenaccio matches up against a team playing 4–2–4, the catenaccio formation is 1–4–2–3. However, when the opponent is playing a 4–3–3, then the catenaccio formation is 1–3–3–3. In addition, if a team is playing for a draw, it would play a 1–4–3–2 even against a team that uses the 4–2–4 system. In this case it takes away from the team's attack but puts even greater strength in the catenaccio defense by providing a third midfield player. Everything depends on the opponent's strength and the aim of a particular match. If a team playing a catenaccio defense is looking for a draw, they increase their numbers at midfield. If they feel they can win, they increase their numbers in the front line.

The attacking philosophy of a catenaccio defense is to get the ball out as quickly as possible from the defense to the strikers and then counter quickly against the opponent. With a catenaccio defense the amount of time the opponent has the ball becomes far less important since it is very difficult for the opposition to score. In addition, the opponent often becomes complacent because he has the ball so long in attack and his defenders tend to overcommit themselves. This leaves them very vulnerable to quick counterattacks. It frequently occurs that a team playing a catenaccio defense counterattacks just a few times during a game, scores one or two goals, and then sits back and defends until the match has been won.

Herrera and Inter-Milan

Helenio Herrera is generally given credit for perfecting the catenaccio system during the early 1960s while he was the manager of the F.C. Internationale of Milan. Born in Buenos Aires, Herrera came to F.C. Internationale in 1960 after managing teams in France and Spain and leading F.C. Barcelona to back-to-back championships during the 1958–59 and 1959–60 seasons. He is the only coach who has had the distinction of managing the national teams of three different countries. Although he was not an instant success at Inter, he eventually led them to several League championships, two consecutive European Cup Championships, and the World Club Championship.

One of Herrera's initial moves at Inter was to place the outside left, Mario Corso, into the midfield, where he felt Corso's talents could be used to better advantage. This left Inter without a left wing and created more space for the left back, Giacinto Faccetti, to make overlapping runs into attack and score many goals. There is little doubt that tactical maneuvers like this one and Herrera's great coaching ability were responsible for much of Inter's success, but there is equally little doubt that without his outstanding players Inter would not have been nearly so effective. For it was players like Corso and Faccetti as well as strikers Peiro and Mazzola, midfielder Suarez, and libero Picchi who performed so well on the playing field for Inter.

There is no question that there is a defensive advantage in playing catenaccio as opposed to a four-back game. In a four-back game the two

Figure 1.7 From left to right: Amarildo, Facchetti, and Mazzola, three of the highest-paid players to play in Italy, in action with their clubs. (Courtesy Fotocronache Olympia, Milano, Italy)

center backs still have to divide three duties between the two men. They must mark the opposition's central strikers, and at the same time one of them must provide cover for the dangerous space in front of the goal. In the catenaccio defense the defenders simply mark one opponent and the libero provides cover and protects the danger area by the goal.

4–3–3

During the 1962 World Cup the Brazilians once again won the championship and again displayed a new system that the world would later copy, the 4–3–3. In 1958 Mario Zagalo, the untiring outside left of Brazil, often

Figure 1.8 Mario Zagalo scores Brazil's fourth goal in their 5–2 win over Sweden in the 1958 World Cup Final. (Courtesy Central Press Photos Limited, London)

came back very deep into his defense to render assistance. In the final game against Sweden, Zagalo even headed a ball that would have been a certain goal clear from his own goal line after the Brazilian goalkeeper Gylmar had been beaten. For this reason Coach Feola was quoted as referring to the Brazilian system not as a 4–2–4, but as a "4–2½–3½."

In 1962, although he sometimes played as a striker, Zagalo spent most of his time as a midfielder. Thus Brazil actually played a 4–3–3 system during the 1962 World Cup.

Perhaps the most important reason why Brazil, now managed by Aymore Moreira, went to a 4–3–3 system was their loss of superstar Pelé.

In the second match of the competitions, Pelé pulled a thigh muscle and was unable to play in the remaining matches. Amarildo, who replaced Pelé at the inside left position, performed very well and scored several vital goals for the Brazilian side. However, Amarildo was no Pelé! Thus it was necessary for Brazil to use Zagalo more as a midfield player to give them more support in the middle. Because of his tremendous stamina, however, Zagalo still frequently ended up as a striker, thus really fulfilling a dual role for his team.

After the competition in Chile, managers throughout the world hurried to adopt the new 4–3–3 system. Unfortunately, few if any teams had another Zagalo playing for them, and most began to play with three midfielders at the expense of sacrificing one of their wingers.

The worldwide adoption of the 4–3–3 greatly changed the type of players that coaches looked for. Since the 4–3–3 requires constant fluid motion and position interchanging, managers now needed players who could do a good job on attack as well as on defense. They no longer wanted players who could play only one position. Thus modern soccer began to eliminate the specialists such as the great winger Sir Stanley Matthews of England. It is no wonder that in the 1970s it is very difficult to name more than one or two great orthodox wingers in the world.

In defense, the 4–3–3 formation used seven defenders in addition to the goalkeeper. Since most teams have at least four men in their back line and six men as the main attacking force, a team playing the 4–3–3 can have one more defender than the other team has attackers. As a result, one defensive player can be utilized as a free back.

One major reason why many teams have adopted the 4–3–3 system is that most teams have found it extremely difficult for two men to handle effectively the midfield role, which was necessary in the 4–2–4 system. By adding a third midfielder, the other team's attack could often be stopped by the midfield rather than the back line of defenders.

The 4–3–3 system also forces the use of midfielders in attack because the three lone forwards cannot adequately sustain a strong attack. Front-running players in modern soccer can create space in the opponent's defense, but because they are so closely marked, they can rarely use it. In the modern game it is the player coming from behind who can best utilize space created by the front-running players. As a result, many goals are now being scored by the midfielders and even by players coming through from the back line. A perfect example of this was the 1970 World Cup competition in Mexico where backs and midfielders scored over 60 percent of the goals.

In discussing the systems in soccer, it is extremely important to emphasize the fact that it is the *players* on a team that make a system work effectively. Systems are basically just numbers designating how many people on a particular team play their basic roles as forwards, midfielders, or backs. It has always been the players, not the system, that have made a particular team successful.

Team formations can also change during a match. For example, a team playing a 4–2–4 may switch to a 4–3–3, or even a 4–4–2, if they find that they are outclassed in midfield. The converse applies as well, and a team playing a 4–3–3 may change to a 4–2–4 if they find that the game is going their way.

A system also takes on various forms at different times during a game. A 4–2–4 looks like a 4–4–2 when the team is on defense and the wing forwards have withdrawn to assist, while it may also resemble a 3–3–4, or even a 2–4–4, when the team is in possession of the ball and the wing fullbacks have pressed forward into the attack.

The defensive back line may also often take on different forms. The four backs may play in a diagonal, just as the three backs played during the era of the stopper back, or three of the backs may play in front of a libero. There have been instances of teams moving the free back in front of the other three backs to act as a "front sweeper." Similar variations can be found in the forward line. Even though the Hungarians, the Spaniards, and the Brazilians all played a form of the 4–2–4 system, none of them played it in exactly the same way.

It is generally accepted that it is very difficult for a team to function properly with less than four backs to defend, two midfielders, and two forwards to attack. This leaves only two other field players who can be maneuvered to create a desired formation. Therefore it seems absurd to boggle the mind with different number combinations and spend a lot of time worrying where to place the remaining two players when it is the *tactical principles of play* that should receive the attention.

If a team coach could get players to adhere effectively to the principles of attack and defense, he would never have to mention systems. Systems are to a great extent designed to outline specifically the duties of particular players. However, if players disregard the principles of play in soccer on defense and attack, regardless of what system of play has been designed for them, they will not succeed.

Unless a team publicizes the system they use, spectators often cannot pinpoint the precise numbers in the front line, the midfield, or even in the back line. A good example of this is the 1966 World Cup team of England, coached by Sir Alf Ramsey.

Sir Alf Ramsey and the 4–4–2

Alf Ramsey left his post as manager of Ipswich Town to succeed Walter Winterbottom as the manager of the English team in 1962. Entering the 1966 World Cup games in England, Ramsey was planning to have his team play a 4–3–3 formation. However, he did not feel that there were any legitimate wingers available, and he wound up playing without any true wingers during the World Cup.

Ramsey wanted players of all-around ability, and especially those with the stamina to run all day long. A good example of this kind of player was Alan Ball from Blackpool whose tremendous work rate and stamina showed up vividly during the extra time of the 1966 final game.

During the 1966 World Cup Final in Wembley, Ball was positioned as a winger on the English front line alongside Hurst and Hunt. However, Ball withdrew to play a predominantly midfield role, thus forming a 4–4–2 formation for the English who won over West Germany. Even after the English had won the Cup, many people still thought that they had done so with 4–3–3 system. Both the 4–3–3 and the 4–4–2 formations require so much position interchanging that very often it is difficult to determine just where a coach has assigned a player.

Conclusions About Systems

Coaches should always remember to fit the system to the players. A coach must determine the strengths and weaknesses of the players on his team and then devise a system that is best for them. He cannot determine the type of system to use before he sees his players in action and evaluates them. There is no magic in systems, and a coach should not and cannot successfully force a particular system on his players.

When the Brazilians opted for the 4–3–3 in the 1962 World Cup in Chile, they were able to do so successfully because their left winger was Mario Zagalo. The reason they succeeded with the 4–2–4 system in the 1958 World Cup was that they had two outstanding midfielders in Zito and Didi, not to mention the great Pelé. The Hungarian 4–2–4 of the early 1950s was successful especially because they had two great midfielders in Hidegkuti and Bozsik. Certainly much of Real Madrid's success can be attributed to the amazing play of Di Stefano. Throughout the history of soccer it has been great players that have enabled managers to utilize particular systems of play. There has never been a system of play that has made a player great.

THE WORLD CUPS AND SYSTEMS

Soccer has been changing ever since it started, and every four years the play in the World Cup Finals depicts the game's latest developments and its progress throughout the world. The play at the World Cup Finals also tends to influence soccer's further development in countries all over the world. This was particularly clear after the 1958 and 1962 World Cups, when teams in many different countries decided to adopt the system of the World Champion Brazilians.

For some time soccer development moved steadily towards the negative defensive aspects of the game. The catenaccio defense in particular made the game less colorful. The emphasis was on preventing goals rather than on scoring them. More and more players were placed in the back lines and fewer in the forward line.

1966 World Cup

The 1966 World Cup did not seem to indicate much tactical progress. It left few glimmers of hope that world soccer would revert to an attacking style of play. Nevertheless, some overall positive trends emerged from the competition, primarily: increased standards of fitness of the players, greater displays of action at high speed, and players' willingness and determination to attain higher work rates.

The play of the vast majority of teams seemed not only to preserve the defensive trends in the game, but even to strengthen them. The popularity of the 4–3–3, 4–4–2, and the 1–4–2–3 systems is evidence of this. Clearly the majority of the teams in the competition placed greater emphasis on defending than on attacking.

The systems are not really to blame, however. After all, the players execute the systems, and their coaches assign the negative roles and functions to the players at fault.

The English, winners in extra time over West Germany, were certainly not the most entertaining team in the competition with their 4–4–2 formation. Nor did they have the best individual players, but they did win the Cup!

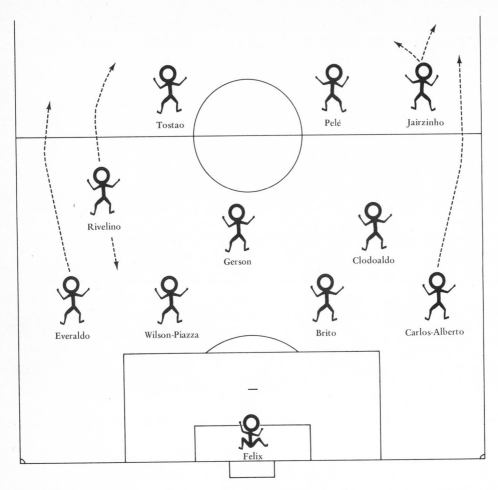

Diagram 1.4   Brazil's 4–2¹/₂–3¹/₂ formation of the 1970 World Cup.

1970 World Cup

During the 1970 World Cup in Mexico, a trend toward attacking soccer appeared, and with it came the hope that soccer would grow more entertaining. The number of shots taken, the beautiful and imaginative pass work as well as the quick combinations in attack, and some demonstrations of tremendous individual genius gave rise to the belief that creative soccer was on its way.

The Brazilians, who won the Jules Rimet Trophy for the third time and thus retired it, were a tremendously entertaining team to watch. They were also able to take the great individual skill of their stars and combine it with all their players into a collective team effort. Players like Pelé, the "king of soccer," worked hard with their teammates to help bring the championship home to Brazil.

With Mario Zagalo as their manager, the Brazilians played a mixture of the 4–3–3 and the 4–2–4 which was best described as a $4–2\frac{1}{2}–3\frac{1}{2}$ formation. The attack consisted of Clodoaldo and Gerson in the midfield, with Pelé and Tostao as the strikers, Jairzinho on the right wing, and Rivelino playing on the left side as a midfielder. In addition, both wing backs, Everaldo and Carlos-Alberto, moved up to play attacking roles.

The Brazilian team accounted for 19 of the 95 goals scored during the competition. In six games they averaged slightly over three goals per game, with their 1–0 win over England being the only time that they were held to fewer than three goals.

More position interchanging by players, increased overall mobility, and greater total involvement by all players are the kinds of trends that account for attacking soccer. In addition, backs and midfielders, given greater roles in their team's attack, steadily increase the number of potential attackers.

1974 World Cup

The 1974 World Cup in Germany once again showed that attacking soccer can be both entertaining and successful. Holland, with their bright orange colors, joyful philosophy, and total commitment to attack, caught the fancy of many. Their free-wheeling play was soon christened the "Dutch Whirl" since their players seemed to have no fixed positions, and individual players could be found in many different areas of the field assuming various roles in the course of the game.

The attacking style of the Dutch is often called "total football." Since about 1972 the term has been used frequently and at times perhaps even overused. After all, there is really no magic to total football. It means merely that every player on a team should be able to attack and defend as the circumstances of a given match dictate. It does stand for attack-oriented soccer and with luck will continue to dominate the world soccer scene, for it is certainly what the spectators were crying for.

The concept of "complete" players capable of performing different roles for their teams is not a new idea. In the 1950s, Dr. Willy Meisl introduced the concept in his book *Soccer Revolution*. Meisl predicted the arrival of the "Whirl," where players would interchange positions freely,

Figure 1.9 1974 Dutch National Team: back row, Jongbloed, Rijsbergen, Haan, Neeskens, Krol, Suurbier; front row: Rep, Cruyff, Resenbrink, Jansen, van Hanegem. (Courtesy The Press Association Limited, London)

taking up the roles of attackers or defenders as the match progressed and the needs of their team changed. It is from this idea that the term "Dutch Whirl" was adopted in describing the Dutch play in the 1974 World Cup.

Initially the play of Ajax of Amsterdam, who won the European Cup for three consecutive years, prompted the phrase "total football" to be used in describing their entertaining, attacking form of soccer.[1] They had tremendously skilled players who had absolute faith in their ability to attack, score goals, and overcome obstacles presented by their opponents. With players like the great Johan Cruyff,[2] Ajax dominated the European soccer scene.

[1]In 1971 Ajax won the European Cup 2–0 over Panathinaikos of Greece; in 1972 they won 2–0 over Inter-Milan; and in 1973 they won 1–0 over Juventus of Italy.
[2]Cruyff was transferred in 1973 to F.C. Barcelona of Spain, reportedly for $3 million.

Figure 1.10 Dutch superstar Johan Cruyff. (Courtesy The Press Association Limited, London)

The manager of the Dutch national team in 1974 was Rinus Michels of F.C. Barcelona, previously the manager of Ajax. With Michels at the helm and many Ajax players on the national team along with the other outstanding Dutch players, it is little wonder that their play greatly resembled that of Ajax when they were at their best.

The Dutch were not the only team in the 1974 World Cup competition who played attacking soccer. Other teams who played attacking soccer were the Champion West German team, and the fine team from Poland, although even the Polish did not play with such seeming disregard to specific roles as the Dutch.

For the Germans, managed by Helmut Schön, Gerd Müller was certainly a specialist as a striker, but no wing back in the competition played more of a dual attacking and defending role than Paul Breitner. Breitner played excellent soccer all over the field, and although he was a back he managed to score three times during the competition.

Another outstanding player was Franz Beckenbauer, the West German captain who played as the libero. While an excellent defender, Beckenbauer was probably the most liberated of all liberos, a truly "complete" player, as effective in attack as in defense. It was not unusual to see Beckenbauer make runs all the way into the attack and then finish them

Figure 1.11 Paul Breitner scores the first goal for West Germany on a penalty kick during their 2–1 win over Holland in the 1974 World Cup Final. (Courtesy The Press Association Limited, London)

off with shots on goal, as he did most noticeably in the match against Yugoslavia. Clearly, he brought a new dimension, never dreamed of by the Italians, to the libero's role through his brilliant and artistic play.

Even if some felt that the Dutch were better players and a better team, no one could question the character of the German team or its right to be the winner when it defeated the Dutch 2–1 after being a goal down a minute into the final match.

Comment on the attacking teams of the 1974 World Cup must include the team from Poland. Although considered amateurs because there was (and still is) no professional soccer league in Poland, they won the 1972 Olympic Games in Munich and then after eliminating England from the final 16 teams, returned to Germany in 1974 to put on a fine display of artistic and positive soccer.

Had it not been for the outstanding play of the West German goalkeeper Sepp Maier who made several brilliant saves in the semifinal

Figure 1.12 Franz Beckenbauer of West Germany. (Courtesy Horst Müller, Pressebilderdienst, Oststrare, Germany)

game against Poland, it might well have been Poland instead of West Germany in the final against Holland. As it was, Poland took third place with a young team that believed in a game played on principles of attack and scoring goals. Grzegory Lato ended the competition as the high scorer of the tournament with 7 goals, while teammate Andrezj Szarmach finished with 5. In addition, midfielder and captain Kazimierz Deyna and winger Robert Godocha played extremely well throughout the competition. Certainly the Poles proved to be one of the best and most entertaining teams.

It is interesting to note that as the concept of "complete" players and "total football" came in, the old system of numbering players by positions began to disappear. In 1974 the West Germans had 4 of their 11 players on the field with numbers above 11 (Müller No. 13, Hoeness No. 14, Overath No. 12, and Holzenbein No. 17), while Argentina and Poland had 6 starters with numbers above 11, and Holland had 7, some of the better known being Cruyff No. 14, Neeskens No. 13, and Rep No. 16. The numbers players now wear identify the individual and do little or nothing to represent his position.

Figure 1.13 Lato of Poland beats Sweden's goalkeeper Hellstroem to give his team a 1–0 victory in a second-round match during the 1974 World Cup competitions. (Courtesy The Press Association Limited, London)

The trends for the future from the 1974 World Cup seem to be positive. Increased standards of player fitness come from the application of scientific research. Emphasis is being placed on the development of the players' physical assets of speed, skill, and versatility. Players will have to have high work rates. They will have to be quick, skillful, and versatile enough to attack and defend effectively–"complete" players. There will be improvisation, and the game's tempo should increase with emphasis on attack.

REFERENCES

Batty, Eric. *Soccer Coaching the Modern Way.* Faber and Faber, London, 1969.

Cramer, Dettmar. *United States Soccer Federation "Coaches Manual."* Four Maples Press, Minisink Hills, Pa., 1973.

Csanadi, Arpad. *Soccer.* Corvina, Budapest, 1965.

Glanville, Brian. *Soccer A Panorama.* Eyre and Spottiswoode, London, 1969.

Greaves, Jimmy. *Soccer Techniques and Tactics.* Pelham Books, London, 1966.

Joy, Bernard. *Soccer Tactics.* Phoenix House, London, 1962.

Lodziak, Conrad. *Understanding Soccer Tactics.* Faber and Faber, London, 1966.

Signy, Dennis. *A Pictorial History of Soccer.* The Hamlyn Publishing Group, London, 1968.

Smith, Stratton and Eric Batty. *International Coaching Book.* Souvenir Press, London, 1966.

Wade, Alan. *The FA Guide to Training and Coaching.* William Heinemann, London, 1967.

2

Principles
of Attack

To win matches in soccer, a team must score more goals than the opposition. This is accomplished by coordinating the play of all 11 players into one collective effort through the development of attack and defense tactics based on accepted principles of soccer. Although the players' skill limitations must be a prime consideration in a team's tactical planning, all the players must be aware of and adhere to the principles of play regardless of their skill.

This chapter deals with the main principle of play, ball possession, and also with the importance of space, and with the six principles of attack: (1) support/depth, (2) width, (3) penetration, (4) mobility, (5) improvisation, and (6) finishing.

BALL POSSESSION

Goal scoring can be accomplished only by having possession of the ball. On rare occasions teams manage to accidentally score goals on themselves. However, as a general rule a team cannot score goals and win games if they do not have the ball, and conversely, their opponents cannot score goals if they have it. Thus the most important principle in soccer is to maintain possession of the ball as much as possible.

Generally we talk about soccer in the framework of attack or defense. However, another important aspect of the game is the *midfield preparation* for either attack or defense. Think of the field of play as divided crosswise into three equal sections, as shown in Diagram 2.1. The section nearest a team's own goal is their area of defense, the central section is the area for the midfield preparation, and the third section is the attack area.

The primary principle of play, ball possession, can be applied directly to this division. In the defensive third of the field, a team should take no chances that may result in the loss of ball possession. Losing the ball in this third of the field could result in an immediate shot on goal by an opponent. In the central third of the field a player can take some chances to penetrate the opposition's defense or to gain some other advantages in attack. However, losing the ball here is still dangerous because it could result in a quick, successful counterattack by the opposition. In the attacking third of the field, a team may gamble if the result might be a goal or a good shot. If a team can get 3 good shots on goal out of every 10 chances they take in the attacking third of the field, their gambling is successful. The number of chances players may take increases in direct

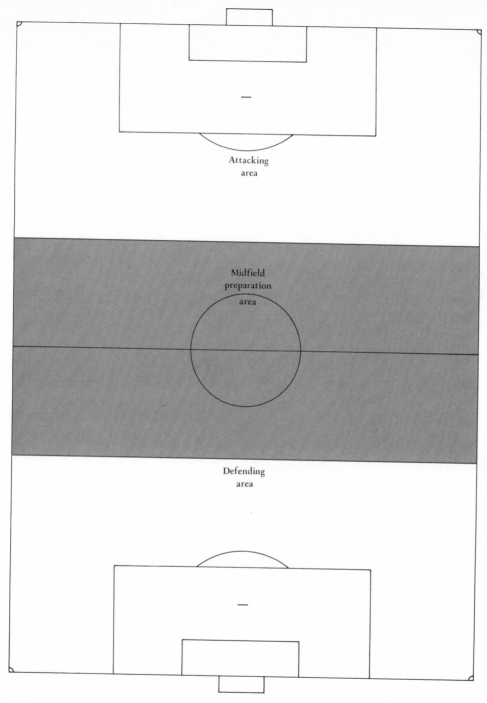

Attacking
area

Midfield
preparation
area

Defending
area

Diagram 2.1 The field of play should be thought of as divided into three equal sections.

proportion to how far away they get from their own goal and how probable that their gamble will result in a good shot at their opponent's goal.

IMPORTANCE OF SPACE

Understanding the importance of *space* in soccer is vital to both offensive and defensive tactics. If we break soccer down to its most fundamental form, we see that it is based on the concept of utilizing space. In attack players must make use of the space between and behind the defensive players, or they must create new space by forcing some defenders to move. The job of the defense is primarily to deny the use of that space to the opposition.

Space is extremely important in maintaining possession of the ball. The more space a player has to work in, the more time he has to control the balls passed to him, to analyze situations during the game, to serve good balls to his teammates, and generally to make fewer errors that result in losing the ball. Thus space and time are interdependent. The more a player has of one, the more he has of the other.

As attackers get closer to their opponent's goal the available space decreases. This, more than any other single factor, creates a need for the principles of attacking play.

SUPPORT/DEPTH

Every player must constantly analyze the game and prepare himself mentally to receive the ball. He must plan one or two moves in advance all the time and must know who is around him, as well as what his options will be if he gets the ball. When an attacking player receives the ball, he must immediately get maximum support from his teammates to give him several passing options and make his task easier.

Ideally, a player should receive support from all directions, but this is not always possible. Adequate support and depth in attack would involve a triangular formation with a minimum of three attacking players. The flatter the triangle formed by the player with the ball and his two teammates, the less depth is provided. As the players flatten out, they reduce the passing opportunities and force the player in possession to make increasingly squarer passes. This is dangerous because square passes are the most susceptible to interception.

Generally players should take up supporting attack positions about 10 to 15 yd from the player with the ball. This gives him opportunities for short passes and gives him space to work in. When supporting players come too close, they reduce the available space because they draw additional defenders with them into the area around the ball.

In certain situations deviation from the preferable supporting distance is necessary. The closer attacking players get to the opponent's goal, the more limited their playing space becomes. Attackers are then forced closer together, and supporting players may have to move as close as five yd away from the player with the ball.

The condition of the field may also influence the distance from which players provide support. Rough, bumpy surfaces may cause balls to bounce unexpectedly, and players may need to give themselves more time to control the ball. Thus on fields with poor playing surfaces supporting players may leave a little more space than usual between themselves and the player with the ball. On the other hand, when a team plays on a very true surface such as artificial turf the supporting players may reduce the distance between themselves and the ball and increase the tempo of the game.

The *angle* from which players provide support is also very important. Supporting players must always be in a position where they could be reached by a simple pass on the ground. The man with the ball should not be forced to pass over an opponent, and unless a clear direct line can be drawn from the ball to the supporting player, the supporting position is inadequate.

Some supporting positions are more advantageous than others. Support from behind the ball is very important since it provides the man with the ball an opportunity to play it back. The closer the attacking team gets to their opponent's goal, the more important this is.

Front-running players always tend to be marked more closely than those behind the ball. Therefore it is often difficult for them to receive a pass and even more difficult for them to play the ball forward when they do get it. Support from behind will give them at least one immediately available pass.

As a rule support should not be provided from directly behind the man with the ball. A position behind and to one side of the ball, as shown in Diagram 2.2, is much better. If a player positions himself directly behind the ball, it is very difficult to play it straight forward after receiving it. The only way to play it forward is to chip the ball over the teammate in front.

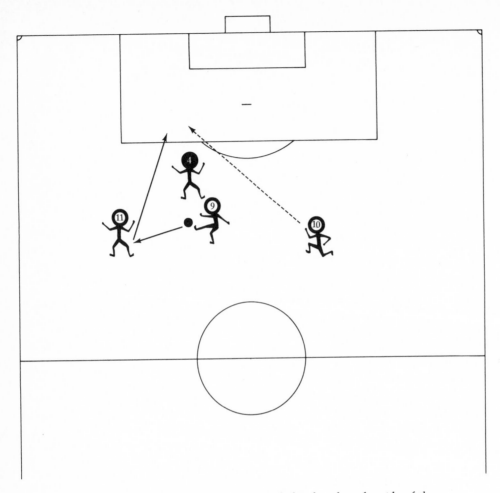

Diagram 2.2 By taking up a supporting position behind and to the side of the ball, a player can play the ball forward more easily.

By taking up a position behind and to the side of the ball, on the other hand, the supporter can play the ball forward more easily, as shown in Diagram 2.2.

Overlapping

Every team always wants to establish numerical superiority during a match, whether they are in attack or in defense. Attacking teams may sometimes accomplish this by bringing players forward from positions behind the ball. Since these players generally receive looser defensive marking, they can go on forward overlapping runs and, by thus producing numerical superiority, sometimes aid the attack.

The biggest dilemma that confronts players in making overlapping runs in advance of the ball is knowing when to make them. A supporting player must pick the proper moment to abandon his supporting role and go forward. He has to assess the situation, and if he feels that the man with the ball can do without his support, he may make a run in advance of the ball. It is very important to remember in what third of the field the attacking players are located, for as they near the opposition's goal the degree of risk involved in abandoning support decreases. As players make their runs, they should try to get into the most advantageous positions possible, from which they can receive the ball and utilize space behind their opponents where a favorable attack can further develop. Obviously, it is vitally important that players coordinate their runs so that they continue to fulfill defensive responsibilities.

How to Develop Support/Depth

The game Keep Away (see Chapter 4, page 133) is an excellent method of developing support and depth in attack. Players may be confined in an area perhaps 10 yd square to play two or three attackers against one defender, or small sides of five men to a team could play Keep Away with no boundaries to confine them.

Small-sided games with goals are another excellent way of developing support and attacking depth. These games force all the players to be more directly involved in the play and thus more aware of the need to support the man with the ball. By adding a restriction on the number of consecutive touches of the ball permitted each player, a coach can make the players even more aware of this necessity. Additional games for developing most of the principles of play appear in Chapter 4.

WIDTH

Since the primary objective of defending players is to deny space to their opponent's attack, attacking players must try to counteract this objective. This can be accomplished by applying the width principle. The playing field is too wide for the defenders to cover completely, and thus if attacking players use the full width of the field, they will have more space in which to develop their attack.

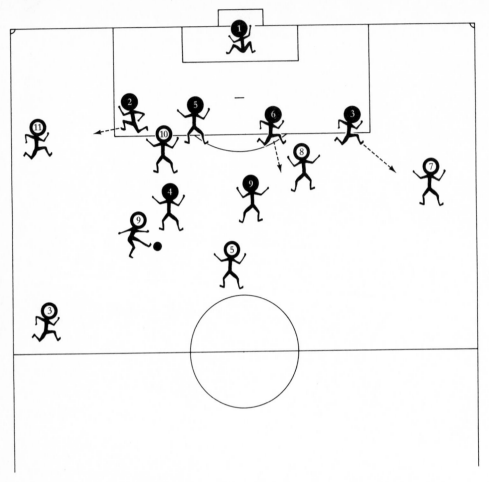

Diagram 2.3 By utilizing the whole width of the field, the attacking team will force the defense to spread out.

Width in the Attacking Third of the Field

One principle of defense, to be explained in Chapter 3, is *concentration*, or *funneling*. Defenders concentrate in the area immediately in front of the goal, from which most goals are scored, to limit the space available to their opponents. Attacking players must draw the defenders out of that area to get space into which they can run to receive the ball and take shots on goal. The only way they can do this is by utilizing the entire width of the field. As with modern tactical trends, teams play more and more with stacked defenses, the application of the width principle in attack has become increasingly important.

During a match all players are subjected to both physical and psychological stress. All players also make mistakes, but the mistakes in the defensive third of the field will generally prove more critical than those made in the attacking third. As a result the psychological stress is somewhat greater on a player defending his own goal than on one who is attacking his opponent's goal. One of the objectives of attacking players must be to subject the opposition's defenders to psychological stress long enough to make them commit errors.

When defenders are subjected to prolonged periods of psychological stress by the opponent's attack, they often become anxious, less confident in their ability to prevent goals, and they may be tempted to take unnecessary risks. This is precisely what attacking players should look for and take advantage of to score goals. They can do this by using width in attack since, again, width will provide them with more space and time. Attacking players have to be patient, however. Overanxiousness may make them take foolish chances, resulting in the loss of width as well as a breakdown in the entire attack.

When attacking players, especially those with responsibilities on the wings, come inside towards their opponent's goal, they make the space in their opponent's penalty area even more restricted. By utilizing the whole width of the field, as shown in Diagram 2.3, the attacking team will force the defense to spread out more to mark the attackers. As the defense spreads out, they will inevitably expose more space in front of their goal that the attackers can take advantage of.

Defensive Systems and Width

The more defense-minded a team's system of play is, the fewer players they place in their attacking front line. Teams that use only three or fewer forwards, with formations like the 4–3–3 or 4–4–2, cannot apply the principle of width in attack effectively without using their midfield players and backs.

Attacking players need first of all to be supported by teammates in order to maintain possession of the ball. It would be foolish for three forwards to spread out over the width of the field and forego the support principle. Obviously they cannot support each other when one of them

Diagram 2.4 Front-running players have to move to support one another and let players coming from behind them run into open spaces to provide the attack with width.

gets the ball if they are 25 or more yd apart. Front-running players have to support one another in such situations and let players coming from behind them run into the open spaces that are left to provide the attack with width, as shown in Diagram 2.4.

Width in the Midfield Third of the Field

In the midfield third of the field, moving all the front-running players to one side and clearing the other side is often a very good tactical maneuver. This will draw defenders over towards one side of the field and create space on the other side for a back to run into, providing width and initiating an attacking thrust.

The attacking left back in Diagram 2.4 can receive a ball from the forward and have a considerable amount of space to work in. Changing sides in an attack, as shown in the diagram, is a very effective way of initiating penetration into the opponent's defensive third of the field.

Width in the Defensive Third of the Field

Players are on the attack the moment they gain possession of the ball regardless of where they are on the field. Attack principles must be adhered to in a team's defensive third of the field as well as in the other two thirds. This certainly holds true with respect to the need for width in attacking play.

Since the defenders concentrate near their own goal to restrict space, when they win the ball they are in very poor attacking positions. They must therefore run immediately into support positions and spread out over the width of the field to give themselves space to initiate their attack.

As mentioned previously, one downfall of attacking players is their overanxiousness, which can destroy width as well as the attack itself. This is true regardless of where the players are on the field. In the defensive third of the field, players are often so eager to get the ball and themselves to the other end and away from their own goal that they sometimes take foolish chances and lose ball possession. This sort of play is foolhardy and inexcusable. Punishment often comes quickly when the opponents win the ball and score before the defense has time to reorganize.

One common error of defenders who gain possession of the ball is to push it back to their goalkeeper and then follow it. Pushing the ball back may be all right, but following it is not. Instead, as long as the pass from the defender to the goalkeeper is a good one, the defender should quickly run wide towards the touchline. The opposing players will usually follow the path of the ball, leaving the man who made the pass in a good position to receive the ball back from the goalkeeper and have both time and space to start the attack upfield.

Too frequently when possession of the ball is won near their own goal, players rush upfield, forgetting to create width. The correct thing for them to do is to try to achieve maximum width in their attack. They should spread out as quickly as they can, in positions that make use of

Diagram 2.5 After winning the ball in their defensive third of the field, the players must spread out to make use of the full width of the field.

the full width of the field, shown in Diagram 2.5. The wing fullbacks should run especially wide as soon as their team wins the ball and take up positions where they can receive it and have space to work in. The player who has the ball, particularly if it is the goalkeeper, should hesitate momentarily before making a pass so that his teammates can run and establish width. Good field players will anticipate plays in advance and will run into positions that establish width as the ball is in flight to the goalkeeper or another teammate, permitting him to release it without waiting.

By spreading out quickly and establishing width, opponents will be unable to mark tightly and still provide each other with adequate support. If the players on attack in their defensive third of the field use the entire width, they can create sufficient space to move the ball out of their defense safely, and start an effective attack.

How to Develop Width

Expertise in the use of width in the attacking third of the field can be developed by playing six versus four, six versus five, and six versus six over half a field with one full-size goal and a goalkeeper. The attackers should be given numerical superiority in the beginning to make maintaining possession of the ball easier for them. The coach should stress the importance of patience and should constantly remind the attacking players to maintain width and move the ball from one side to the other to spread the defense and create more space near the goal.

Creating and using width in the midfield preparation area can be improved by having front-running players practice clearing one side of the field and by sending backs into the space to provide the opportunity to change quickly the side from which a team develops their attack. Dummy situations like this can be most effective in getting players accustomed to various tactical maneuvers.

Players must be mentally alert and aware of the need for attacking width in the defensive third of the field. They have to be reminded of this during training matches, and they must practice taking advantage of it. A coach can use dummy situations to develop this awareness. Start the play by serving the ball to the goalkeeper and having the team play the ball up to their attacking third of the field against the opposition. The opposition should at first be passive and then progressively more realistic until the team trains under match conditions. Stop the play to correct tactical errors and make the players aware of what their errors are and how to avoid them.

PENETRATION

Whenever a team wins possession of the ball their primary objective is to get it into the defense of the opposition as quickly as possible and then through it to score goals. To realize this objective players must adhere to the principle of *penetration*, which requires them to move as deeply as possible into the opponent's defense with each pass while still maintaining possession of the ball.

The Importance of Forward Passing

Players should pass the ball forward whenever they can. Forward passes always achieve the deepest penetration as well as put the maximum number of defensive players temporarily out of the match. Defensive players can generally be effective only if they are between the ball and their goal. Diagram 2.6 shows how a long and accurate pass can put several opposing players temporarily out of the game since they end up on the wrong side of the ball to defend their own goal. No. 5 of the attacking side has two clear forward passing opportunities. The pass to No. 9 would be a safe one, but it would result in little forward progress and very limited penetration. On the other hand, the pass to No. 10 will go past five defensive players who are positioned between the ball and their own goal and will result in the deepest penetration of the opponent's defense. The dotted line across the width of the field in the diagram shows all the defensive players who are temporarily out of the match after No. 5 makes the pass.

Conversely, by playing the ball either back or square, a player may be putting some defenders back into the match. Square passes allow defensive players who were in ineffective positions time to get back into good defending spots. Back passes will put every defender they pass back into the game even if he was not trying to improve his position.

When to Pass Forward

To pass forward, a player must have space in front of him and a teammate who is in a position to receive the ball. Since both criteria are not always available, sometimes it is necessary to go back with the ball in order to play it forward.

Diagram 2.2 shows a situation where a forward pass is not available because of the position the defender took up. By playing the ball back, No. 9 enables No. 11 to pass the ball forward and behind the defender. When a player has a good opportunity to pass the ball forward, he must take advantage of it, but it is equally important for a player to realize quickly that when he cannot send a ball forward, he must pass it back to a teammate who can.

What constitutes a good passing opportunity depends on a player's position in relation to the three areas of the playing field. In the attacking

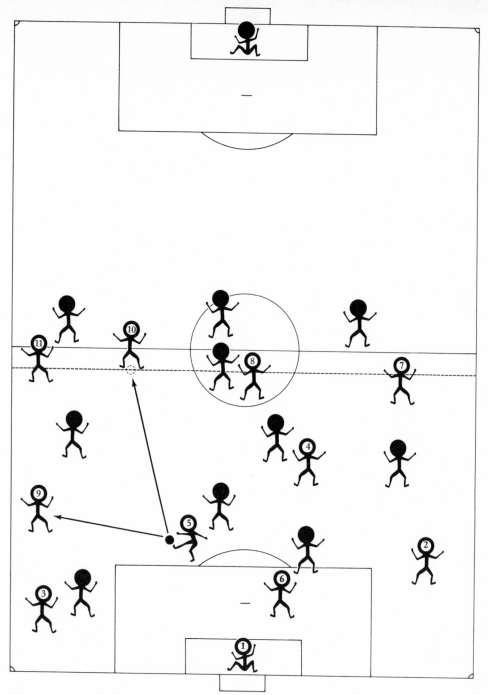

Diagram 2.6 A long, accurate pass can put several opposing players temporarily out of the game.

third of the field, a forward pass into a small space from a poor angle may very well be an excellent opportunity since it could result in a good shot on goal. In the defensive third, however, such a pass should not even be considered since the opposition might easily intercept the ball. The biggest dilemma for players is sorting out the good and bad passing situations in the middle third of the field, where some chance-taking is encouraged, but taking great risks is not.

Forward passes should be as long as possible to achieve the deepest penetration, but the attackers must not forget that the main principle of play is ball possession. If a player has two teammates in front of him who are in position to receive the ball, as in Diagram 2.6, the deepest penetration of the defense will result from a pass to the player farthest away. However, this is not a good passing opportunity if the man with the ball is not skillful enough to pass it accurately to the farthest man. Good passing opportunities are thus dependent not only on the attacker's position, but also on his skill limitations. If No. 5 in Diagram 2.6 is not skillful enough to pass accurately to No. 10, then the best passing opportunity for him would be to No. 9, even if he does not achieve a great deal of penetration.

Creating Space for Penetration

The more a team uses cross-field, or back, passes in their preliminary passing after winning the ball, the less effective their penetration will be. This sort of passing gives the opponents time to run back into good defending positions and establish a solid defense. Good forward passing opportunities are not always available, however, and for effective penetration, attacking teams must create space into which they can send players to receive penetrating passes.

Every time an attacking player goes on a run into space in front of the ball, he forces the defender to allow him one of two opportunities. Diagram 2.7 shows how the defender marking the player going on a run must either let him go, as in 2.7(a), and allow him to gain a position in which he can support the man with the ball and receive a pass, or stay with him, as in 2.7(b), in which case he can create attacking space for a teammate.

Remember that the space attacking players want to exploit is behind the defenders. In the defending and middle thirds of the field, attackers should create space behind defenders for the deepest and most effective

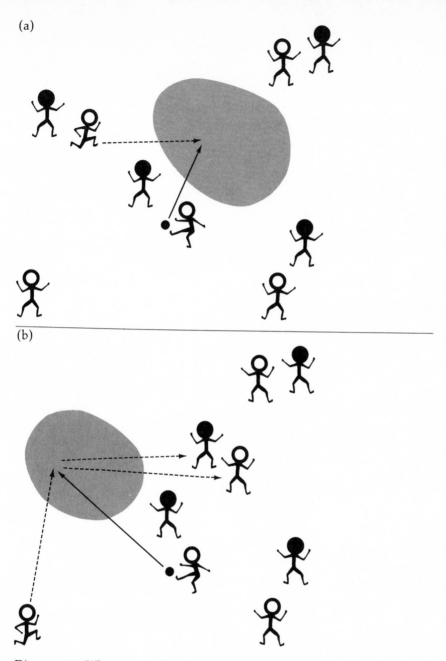

(a)

(b)

Diagram 2.7 When an attacking player goes on a run into space in front of the ball, he will either gain a position in which he can receive the ball as in (a), or draw a defender with him, thus creating attacking space for a teammate as in (b).

penetrating passes. In the attacking third of the field, players want to create and use any space from which they may take a good shot on goal.

How to Develop Penetration

Players must be able to recognize forward passing opportunities as well as create them. Small-sided games, such as four versus four in an area about 30 yd by 40 yd, will train for developing penetrating passes in the defensive and middle thirds of the field. The coach should instruct players to play the ball forward whenever possible and should stop the play to alert them of tactical errors and to demonstrate how to avoid them.

Playing six versus four and six versus five in half a field can develop penetration in the attacking third. Again, the coach should supervise the game and interrupt when necessary to assist the players.

Dummy matches of 11 versus 11 are also excellent for teaching penetration as well as all the other principles of play. The coach should increase the pressure from the defenders to match conditions only when he feels that the players have made sufficient progress in applying the principle they are concentrating on.

MOBILITY

It is easier for players to defend than it is for them to attack. Defending players are primarily concerned with preventing the opponents from scoring by breaking down their attack in any way they can, while the attacking players must be imaginative and creative to produce scoring opportunities. It is much easier to destroy something than it is to create, and in soccer it takes far less accuracy to simply kick a ball away than to work it through a defense and produce a good shot on goal. This can be demonstrated easily by having as many as eight players attack a goal with a goalkeeper and just four other defenders. The number of goals will be far fewer than the times the defenders break down the attack.

Even forwards who seem to have possession of the ball frequently rarely have it for longer than a total of about 5 min during a 90-min match. This fact emphasizes the great importance of each team member's play when he is not in possession of the ball, that is, during most of the match. Attacking players not in possession of the ball must concentrate on making the defenders' job as difficult as possible, and must try to provide the man with the ball the best penetrating and scoring opportunities. All these objectives require the application of the principle of *mobility*. Movement of players without the ball is essential for successful attacking soccer.

Disrupting the Opponent's Defenders

To make the defenders' job as difficult as possible, attacking players must interchange positions frequently. A defender's job is simplified when he is confronted by the same attacking player during the entire match, for the longer a good defender marks the same man, the more he will learn about his play and how to contain him. Also, if attackers remain in the same positions during the entire match, the defenders will always know where to find the men they are responsible for marking. When attacking players interchange positions, defenders are faced with the task of marking several different men during the match who may excel in different areas of the game; thus the defenders cannot easily anticipate what the opponent they are marking will do next.

The defenders' play can be disrupted also through subtle physical contact. Most defenders are bothered by the simple movement near them of the opponent they are marking. When that opponent begins to make physical contact occasionally by bumping or leaning slightly against the player marking him the defender may begin to concentrate more on the individual opponent than on the entire attack, thus making himself more prone to defensive mistakes.

Front-running players may also gain a needed step or two on the man marking them through the use of such tactics. By leaning slightly into the defender, the forward may catch his opponent momentarily off balance just prior to making a run. This way the attacker may gain a little more space to work in, which could make him free enough to receive a ball and shoot it.

Diagonal Running

Attacking players can create dilemmas for defenders by going on runs without the ball. An attacker's run can often force an opponent to leave a good defensive position for a poor one. This is most effectively accomplished through the use of diagonal running.

Straight forward runs at the opponent's goal must be tightly watched and marked by defenders because they could easily result in a goal. In these runs a defender does not have to make a decision, just stays with his man and falls back towards the goal. However, diagonal runs present a greater problem for defenders since the defenders are uncertain of whether to stay with the attacker. If the defender stays with the attacker, he may be forced to move across the field, thus spreading the defense. If he does not stay with the man making the run, he is leaving unmarked a man who could possibly get the ball and score.

Attacking runs will be most effective if they end up in space where the man making the run would be a threat if he received the ball. Players must keep this in mind even when they go on dummy runs intended as decoys for the actual thrust of the attack. This will make a defender's decision of whether to stay with his man more difficult because the defenders cannot know the purpose of each run.

Diagonal runs force defenders to move across the field, spreading their defense and creating more attacking space. They also create the best passing opportunities by presenting good passing angles to the man with the ball. Forward runs, although very successful if the man making the run can get the ball, present very poor passing angles since the players are usually running away from the ball. The nearer attacking players get to the opponent's goal, the squarer their runs will have to be to force defenders into making decisions of whether to stay with a man, to enable attackers to stay on sides, and to provide the best passing angles.

Mobility to Create and Use Space

Attacking players without the ball must do a lot of running to provide support for the man with the ball, to get themselves into good positions to receive the ball, and to provide the best penetrating or scoring opportunities for themselves and their teammates. They must be involved in the game all the time, ready to receive the ball at any moment by running whenever necessary to free themselves of defenders and by coming to meet it. Running off the ball is not just sprinting down the field towards the opponent's goal the moment that the attackers win the ball. It often requires a man to go on a run to create opportunities for teammates, and not just to run when he thinks the ball will be passed to him.

Diagram 2.8 shows how, through the use of mobility in the form of diagonal running, players create space for teammates to run into and produce excellent passing opportunities. Diagram 2.8(a) illustrates the runs of the players and Diagram 2.8(b) shows the passing opportunities that the runs create.

Diagram 2.8 (a) Diagonal running by players in attack creates space for their teammates and excellent passing opportunities.

The run by No. 8 creates space for both No. 11 and No. 7 to run into. It also puts him into an area with more space, in the event that the ball is passed to him. The run by No. 10 is meant primarily to draw the defender away from the path of No. 11's run, but it also puts him in a position to better support No. 4. The run by No. 11 is designed to take advantage of the space created. From here a goal may be scored, and this space provides the best penetrating pass opportunity. It also creates space that can be taken advantage of by No. 9.

Diagram 2.8 (b)

Diagram 2.8(b) shows the players in their positions after they have made their runs and developed the resulting passing opportunities for No. 4. The best pass is to No. 11 since he would have the best shooting and scoring chance. However, if the ball cannot go to him for some reason, several options still remain for No. 4. He can chip the ball to No. 9, pass it to No. 7, who could then push it through for a shot by No. 11, pass it to No. 10, who could also pass it on to No. 11, or send the ball wide to No. 8, who could continue the attack from the flank. Through mobility like this, even tightly marked front-running players may create and make use of space to score goals.

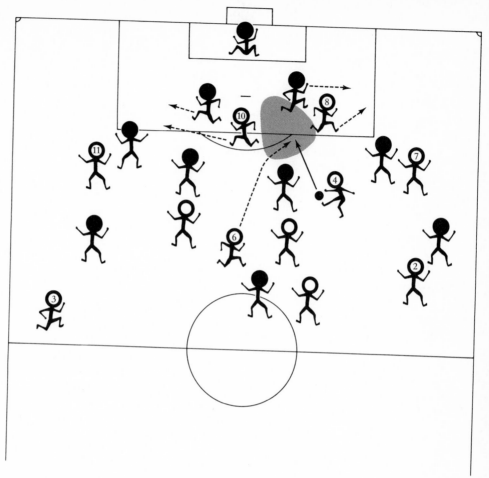

Diagram 2.9 Movement of tightly marked forwards can create space for team-mates to run into from behind.

Penetrating Runs by Backs

Because they are always so tightly marked, front-running players sometimes cannot move into good positions to receive the ball and score goals. In modern-day soccer more and more goals are being scored by backs coming from behind to take advantage of the space created for them by forwards.

Diagram 2.9 illustrates how the movement of tightly marked forwards may create space into which a player from behind may run to receive the ball and shoot on goal. As No. 8 goes on his run, the defender marking him must follow because he is going into a shooting position. The run of

No. 10 draws the other defender away, creating more space into which No. 6 can run to receive the ball. The movement of No. 6 triggers both runs. After he starts his run, the longest of the three, No. 8 and No. 10 move to create space for him. Number 4 passes the ball to No. 6's feet as soon as No. 6 gets to the penalty area where he could well make a goal.

Attacking players must be aware of their teammates' runs. One of the biggest problems of players with limited experience is that they do not know when to make their runs since they do not notice the runs made by their teammates that create space for them to use.

The two primary elements of good mobility are *timing* and *direction*. Players must seize the most effective moment for a run, and then execute it in the direction where it will create the greatest problem for the defenders, providing at the same time the best opportunities for penetrating the opponent's defense or attacking the opponent's goal.

Mobility and Fitness

Mobility is essential for success in attack, but it is also very taxing both mentally and physically. Players must constantly analyze the play to decide when a run will be helpful. They must watch the movements of the opponents as well as of their teammates and concentrate on the game constantly if they expect to be an asset to their team even when the ball is not at their feet. Such concentration can be very tiring.

Good support is essential to successful soccer, and players must be in position to receive the ball as soon as their team wins possession. This requires a great deal of running and is very demanding physically. On the average a good player will have to go on 15 runs where he does not receive the ball for every one where he does. This can be very frustrating as well as tiring, but nevertheless it must be done. Unless a player is prepared both mentally and physically for this type of running, he may stop going on runs as frequently as he should and will not be totally effective for his team. Mobility is essential to attacking soccer, but the constant mental concentration and physical stress require a high degree of player fitness.

How to Develop Mobility

Support in attack depends on the mobility of the attacking players. The development of this mobility has already been covered under the development of support and depth in attack.

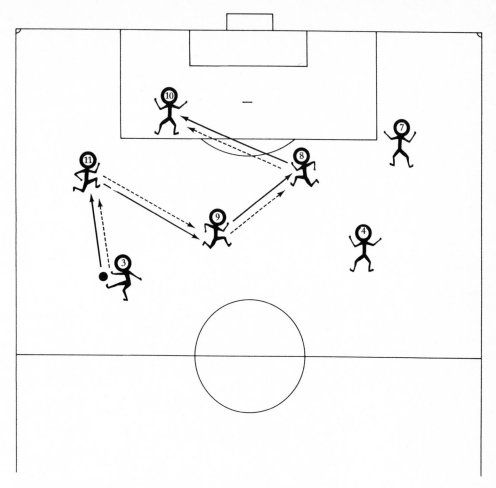

Diagram 2.10 By passing the ball and following it, attackers can interchange positions and still maintain width and depth in their attack.

However, to apply fully the principle of mobility in attack, players have to interchange positions. Interchanging positions can be introduced to players with limited experience by using an exercise where the players must follow the path of the ball after they pass it and take the position of the man who receives it.

Diagram 2.10 illustrates how, by passing the ball and then following it, attackers can continue to interchange positions and still maintain the width and depth of the attack. This exercise is performed best on an actual playing field as shown in the diagram. This way players can clearly see that they can interchange positions in attack without disrupting their basic system, or formation. The exercise can also be performed by having the attacking players actually try to score goals against a goalkeeper and four or five other defenders.

By playing six versus five or six versus six in a half-field with a goal, attacking players can practice various runs to create space for teammates and to make use of existing space between defenders. Training of this nature can also be done in the attackers' own defensive third of the field or in the middle third. Players should concentrate on their teammates' running as well as on their own. This way they will see how different runs often develop opportunities for someone else to go on a penetrating run or a run that may result in a good shot on goal.

IMPROVISATION

Soccer is a game of constant motion and continuous change. Although teams may have a general plan of attack, for the most part soccer does not lend itself to very organized set plays. The only time that set plays can be used really effectively is during restart situations. Too much organization in the attack will restrict it, make it more predictable and less effective than it might be otherwise.

Players must be able to adapt to all situations as they occur during a match, and to adapt like this, they must be able to improvise. Even though soccer is a game of percentages and usually players should do whatever will bring them the greatest chance for success, sometimes doing the unexpected and gambling on a low-percentage chance in the attacking third of the field may reap excellent results.

Improvisation is the ability of a player to rise to a given occasion and act on the spur of the moment. The three primary ingredients of performance in soccer are the *fitness* of a player, his *understanding* of the game, and his *skill*. The more a player has of these ingredients, the better able he is to cope with all situations that may arise during a match and thus the more prepared he is to improvise.

For a team to be successful, their methods of attack have to be limitless. This is not possible without a great deal of improvisation in their play. Modern soccer requires "complete" players, able to play almost any position on the field, understand modern tactics well, and have very high work rates.

The ultimate in improvisation is exemplified in the style of modern soccer dubbed "total football." Teams like Ajax of Amsterdam during the early 1970s and the Dutch National team of 1974 are good examples of this style. They often played with seeming total disregard for positions. The players moved about fluidly and appeared to improvise constantly according to how each new situation developed during the match. Their play was natural and spontaneous; in addition to being effective, this kind of soccer is exciting to watch.

Style of Attack

The *system*, or formation, of a team is the order of the 11 players or the number of players assigned to playing each role. A team's tactics are the manner in which they expect to defend and attack during a match with a particular opponent. The style of a team, on the other hand, is the way in which they play, with a lot of quick interpassing, perhaps, or with more individual dribbling.

A team's style is often dictated by the general psychological and physiological make-up of the players, which is in turn a product for the most part of their environment. Climate and the condition of home playing fields can also influence a team's style. The South American style of play is generally characterized by a considerable amount of individual dribbling and a fairly slow tempo. The European style, on the other hand, is characterized by more passing, greater work rates, usually more aggressive challenging for the ball, and a reasonably fast tempo. Some countries have a warmer climate than others, or are located at very high altitudes, and their players must pace themselves during a match, slowing down the tempo of the play so as not to become fatigued. These contrasts also reflect differences in the general character of the players as well as differences in the climates. Some people tend to be more aggressive than others, which is reflected in their games.

Even though styles of play differ, all players on the same team do not always play the game in the exact same manner and must still improvise as different situations dictate. Above all else, a team cannot afford to have a very predictable attack. They must make use of the type of passing, long or short, that a given situation calls for, and they must dribble or pass the ball depending on circumstances.

Midfield Preparation

Improvisation is very important in the midfield area. Here players must decide on one of two forms of attack when they win the ball. Either they must quickly counterattack or else they must build up the attack in a slower, more methodical manner.

When the team wins the ball in their defensive third of the field, their first and foremost objective must be to move the ball as quickly and safely as possible up the field towards their opponent's goal. When the ball reaches the midfield third of the field, or when a team wins possession there, players must decide on how they will attack and then proceed. They must now choose to attack with a quick counter or by methodically building up the attack, trying to take advantage of the defense's weakest area. The form of attack must be dictated by the positioning of the opponent's players in relation to the ball and the attacking players.

After winning the ball, if the attackers feel that a quick counterattack can break through the opponents' defense before they can reorganize, then most assuredly it is the best way to try to score. This will usually occur when the opponents are overcommitted to their own attack since that will leave large spaces between the defenders in the back line and between them and their goal.

To produce a successful counterattack, a team must make a very quick transition from defense to attack. The attack should be initiated within 10 seconds after a team wins possession of the ball. Players must rush into spaces that will permit deep, penetrating forward passes. The attackers cannot afford to wait to play the ball or to dribble since this wastes time. Remember also that any time a ball is passed square or back, it will help the opponents, giving them time to fall back and reorganize their defense. If a shot on goal cannot be taken within 25 to 30 seconds from the time a team wins the ball, then in all probability the counterattack will not succeed.

When the players feel that a quick counterattack will not work, they must build up their attack more slowly and systematically from midfield. They must maintain possession, change the speed and the direction of passes, and use or create space necessary for penetrating the opponent's defense and scoring goals. Usually players can use longer through passes to penetrate the opponent's defense in the midfield, but the closer they get to the opponent's goal, the shorter their passes will have to be because the defenders will leave little space to attack in. Players must always remember to improvise, however, as different opportunities develop, and to use either short or long passes depending on what the situation calls for.

Passing and Improvisation

Attacking players in possession of the ball have to concern themselves with attacking individual opponents. Improvisation plays a major role whenever attackers confront defenders one versus one. There are, however, only three general options open for the player with the ball: (1) He can pass the ball around the defender, (2) he can dribble around him, or (3) he can shoot the ball at the goal. Deciding on the appropriate method for a particular situation requires improvisation.

The easiest way to beat defenders is to pass the ball around them. This usually requires numerical superiority of attackers to defenders. As often as possible attacking players must try to establish two against one situations with defending players. This will greatly increase the odds of beating the defender and getting the ball into space behind him and closer to his goal.

There are only two ways to pass the ball to beat the defender: (1) Either the attacker pushes the ball past or over the defender into a space and an attacking teammate runs in after it, or (2) an attacking player runs into space behind the defender and the ball is then passed to him. Both methods are effective, and the given situation must dictate to the players which method will provide them with the best results. As a rule opponents will have more difficulty in intercepting a pass when the attacker goes on a run first and then receives the ball. In this situation the player making the pass can change his mind at the last second and hold the ball if he feels it may be intercepted. When the ball is passed first, this choice is not available.

Dribbling and Improvisation

The more proficient a player is at dribbling, the greater will be his repertoire of feints. As a result, his improvised feints will be less predictable and his success greater. Many of the world's great players, especially forwards like Sir Stanley Mathews, Alfredo Di Stefano, and Pelé, can attribute much of their success to their tremendous ability to dribble a soccer ball.

Dribbling is a useful method of gaining numerical superiority in attack and the player with the ball can use it to accomplish one of three goals:

(1) After he beats an opponent one against one, dribbling can free the attacker to take a shot on goal; or (2) it can free him to draw another defender towards him and thus release a teammate; (3) a player can also dribble to provide a teammate with time to run into a good position to receive the ball.

Unfortunately, dribbling is often overused, but it is still an essential ingredient to every successful attack. When used at the proper moments, it also adds a great deal of color and excitement to the game.

How to Develop Improvisation

Improvisation can be developed most readily by not stifling players' initiative and creativity. Some tactical organization for a team is obviously necessary, but coaches must take care not to regiment their teams too much. The best way to improve a player's ability to improvise is to encourage him to think for himself and to help him become a better overall and more complete player.

A player's greatest handicap in trying to improvise is a lack of understanding of the game and the inability to analyze, or read, the game while he is playing. Coaches must strive to make their players understand how to implement modern tactics and principles. This will help them understand the game better and anticipate the play of their opponents as well as of their teammates.

The technique of a player certainly determines what he can or cannot do with the ball. The more skillful a player is, the greater the variety of moves he can introduce into his improvisation. His technique and skill training helps him to improvise in match play, and his fitness training, vital to his overall ability to perform, ties in as well.

FINISHING

Too often teams control the play of a match because of their superiority in skill, but they fail to win the contest because they cannot score goals. Their attack works very well in the defensive third of the field and in the midfield third, but it breaks down in the attacking third before they can take a good shot on goal.

Goal scoring is really what soccer is all about, and all the beautiful midfield build-up and attacking play is meaningless if a team cannot finish and score goals. *Finishing* is developing an attack into shots on goal and eventually goal scoring. It is an essential principle of attack, for without it a team cannot score goals or win matches.

A team can get an opportunity to shoot on goal as a result of only two situations. (1) Either the defenders of the opposition make a mistake and provide the attackers with a chance to shoot, or (2) the attacking players create their own opportunity to shoot. Players must be aware of the type of defensive errors that most frequently result in good finishing chances, as well as how to create goals for themselves.

Goals from Defensive Errors

Many goals scored can be directly attributed to the errors made by defending players. Therefore attacking players must always be alert so that they can capitalize on their opponents' mistakes and, by scoring goals, punish the opposition for committing those errors.

Goals that result from defensive errors occur because the opponents fail to adhere to the principles of play. The four major causes of such goals are: (1) failure to mark and pressure the attacker who has the ball, (2) failure to mark attackers who go on penetrating runs, (3) failure to provide adequate defensive support and depth, and (4) failure to maintain possession of the ball after winning it, especially in the defensive third of the field.

The more pressure applied to an attacker with the ball, the less relaxed he will be and the more prone to making mistakes and poor services. Conversely, the less pressure the defenders apply, the more time the attackers have to analyze the situation and then serve a good ball. Lack of pressure on the attacker with the ball is probably the defensive error most often punished by the opponent's scoring goals. Leaving an attacking player with the ball without adequate defensive pressure is like giving the opponents a free kick.

Although front-running players are usually marked tightly, too often defenders allow attacking players to go on penetrating runs and do not pick them up and mark them. This is especially true when the attackers initiate their runs from behind the ball. The danger of such defensive errors is clear since they allow the opposing players to apply the principle of finishing by getting an unmarked attacker into a space where he can take a shot and score a goal.

Players must provide each other with support and establish depth in defense. This will enable one defender to move close to the ball to apply pressure and to restrict space behind the man marking the attacker with the ball to prevent forward passes. Failure to provide adequate defensive support and depth will allow attacking players who manage to dribble past a defender to have a clear, direct route to the goal or to pass the ball easily around and behind the defender pressuring the man in possession of the ball.

Failure to maintain possession of the ball after winning it is more prevalent with younger and less skilled players, but remember that it also occurs even at top, world class levels. Whether it happens as a result of carelessness or poor passing technique really does not matter. If it happens in a team's defensive third of the field, it gives the opponents an especially good scoring opportunity. Players must always keep in mind that the primary principle of play is maintaining possession of the ball, and if possession of the ball must be lost, it should be as far away from their own goal as possible.

Goals Through Creativity

Attacking players cannot always count on the opponent's making mistakes. They must be capable of scoring goals by creating their own opportunities. They must think of finishing primarily as creating shooting space within the opponent's defense, positioning an unmarked attacking player in that space, getting the ball to him, and finally having him get off a shot on goal that will score. This is accomplished by applying the principle of mobility to get an unmarked attacker into the space, and the principle of penetration to get the ball to him.

Forcing defensive mistakes is another way of creating scoring chances. Attacking players should capitalize on the weaknesses of the opponent's defense and try to force as many mistakes as possible. Runs to eliminate defensive support, use of psychological stress by maintaining possession of the ball for long periods of time, play upon the weaknesses of individual defenders, and pressure on the opponent's players as soon as possession of the ball is lost are effective means of forcing errors and creating finishing chances.

Remember that soccer is a game of percentages and should be played accordingly. Although surprising opponents with unexpected and unusual moves is effective at times, most of the time players should do the things they are best at and which afford them the best chances of success. Simple moves executed to perfection are far more efficient in the long run than complex moves performed in a mediocre way.

Set plays at restart situations greatly enhance the chances of scoring and in the attacking third of the field provide great opportunities for finishing. In modern soccer as many as 40 percent of all goals can be attributed to restarts. During these situations an attacking team has time to serve the ball with little or no defensive pressure, can place players in preplanned attacking positions, and can often gain some numerical superiority. All these factors can greatly aid attackers in creating excellent finishing chances. (Because of their great importance, Chapter 5 is devoted solely to restarts.)

Shooting on goal is the final step of finishing. Although the shooting range, or the distance from which goals can be scored, varies among individual players, usually good attacking players can score from as far away as 30 yd. Once the player with the ball gets into shooting range, he can do one of three things. (1) He can take a shot on goal, (2) he can dribble past the defender to get a closer shot, (3) or he can pass the ball around the defender. Which of the three choices a player makes must be dictated to him by each specific situation he finds himself in. As a rule, however, a player should shoot whenever he has the opportunity. It is especially unwise to try to get closer to the goal if the penalty area is very crowded. It is far better to get a shot off from 25 yd out than to lose possession of the ball while trying to get closer to the goal.

Shooting from outside the penalty area can be most effective. A shot from that distance could surprise the opponent's goalkeeper and find him unprepared to handle it, perhaps blocked by a player in the penalty area and unable even to see it. The ball could also hit one of the players in the penalty area on its way to the goal and score as a result of a deflection. In addition, enough shots taken from a long range may force the defenders to come out away from their goal, thus leaving more space in the penalty area that attackers could use.

The most important thing to remember is that shooting is the only way to score goals. If players don't shoot, they will not score. The average is one goal for every nine shots taken, so it is logical to take a great many shots.

How to Develop Finishing

Good finishing requires good shooting, and the more shooting players do in training, the better. Goal scoring is necessary for winning matches, and therefore finishing must be practiced frequently.

One way to develop finishing is through the use of full goals whenever possible in training sessions. Having several portable goals available can be a tremendous help in training since they can be moved around easily and placed wherever needed. Players have to get into the habit of shooting at the goal as the climax of every attack, and unless players can shoot at real goals the training is not realistic and does not duplicate match conditions as it should.

The other aspect of finishing, every bit as important as shooting, is the ability to create space for shooting opportunities. This can be practiced through the use of small-sided games, six versus four and six versus five half-field matches, or full 11 versus 11 matches. The important things to stress in these games are the movement of the players off the ball, awareness of runs both to use space and create space for teammates, and shooting whenever the opportunity arises.

REFERENCES

Cramer, Dettmar. *United States Soccer Federation "Coaches Manual."* Four Maples Press, Minisink Hills, Pa., 1973.

Csanadi, Arpad. *Soccer.* Corvina, Budapest, 1965.

Greaves, Jimmy. *Soccer Techniques and Tactics.* Pelham Books, London, 1966.

Hughes, Charles F.C. *Tactics and Teamwork.* E.P. Publishing, Wakefield, England, 1973.

Jones, Ken and Pat Welton. *Football Skills and Tactics.* Marshall Cavendish, London, 1973.

Wade, Alan. *The FA Guide to Training and Coaching.* William Heinemann, London, 1967.

Winterbottom, Walter. *Training for Soccer.* William Heinemann, London, 1960.

3

Principles
of Defense

THROUGHOUT the history of soccer, emphasis has periodically shifted back and forth between the attack and the defense. As soon as one started to dominate the other, coaches and players developed new tactical schemes or even changed the rules to counteract this inequality.

Defense, especially in the form of the offside trap, dominated the game prior to the offside rule change in 1925. When the offside law was changed, the attack took over. With the advent of the stopper, or third back, dominance reverted to the defense; then the withdrawn center forward gave rise to more goals and better attacking play.

Good defense is vital to a team's attack. A team can not score goals unless they have possession of the ball, and they can win possession of the ball from the opposition only through good defensive play.

A weak defense can work to frustrate its own attack. After all, any team that can score two or three goals in a match has had a good day attacking, but all this success is wasted if the defense has given up three or four goals, and the game is lost 2–3 or 3–4. Thus all players must think about defending their own goal as well as attacking the opposition's.

Total soccer, the balance between attack and defense, is the goal of most people involved in modern soccer. The play of some modern clubs like Ajax of Amsterdam and the national teams of Holland and Poland have given rise to the belief that perhaps this ideal blend of attack and defense is not far from being the rule rather than the exception.

PRIMARY OBJECTIVES OF DEFENSE

Whenever a team loses possession of the ball, its players must go on defense and should keep three primary objectives in mind: (1) It is vital, although not easy, to prevent the opponents from scoring. A team can ensure this only by denying the opponents the time and space necessary to work in, by exposing the goal to a minimum of danger, and by forcing the opponents to relinquish possession of the ball. So long as the opponents lose possession of the ball, it matters little whether a defender simply kicks it away, a crude but nevertheless effective method, or whether he wins it by intercepting a pass or with a successful tackle. (2) Then defenders must gain and maintain possession of the ball so that (3) they can initiate an attack.

To realize these three objectives of defense, a team must adhere to defensive principles of play. This chapter deals with the six defensive principles: (1) delay, (2) support/depth, (3) concentration, (4) balance, (5) pressuring, and (6) control. It explains how their implementation counteracts principles of attack and helps to prevent opponents from scoring.

FORMS OF DEFENSIVE STRUCTURE

Players in all matches must understand and apply the principles of defense regardless of the specific type of defensive structure a particular team uses. On the other hand, the exact type of defense a team uses has to be dictated primarily by the specific abilities and inabilities of the individuals that make up the team. Even then, no defensive structure should be so rigid that it stifles players from using their own judgment and improvising, depending on the situation of the moment.

Man-to-man Defense

Regardless of the specific defensive structure a team intends to use, in many instances the game eventually comes down to a confrontation of one defender and one attacker. Thus man-to-man defense appears to some extent in all matches.

Strict man-to-man defense is simple in that each defender is assigned only one opponent, whom he must keep from scoring and attacking effectively. The primary objective of a man-to-man defensive structure is to match up attackers with defenders to minimize the strengths of the opposition and maximize their weaknesses. Although this defensive structure is simple in principle and has its advantages, it also has some disadvantages.

Advantages of man-to-man defense

1. Defenders can be matched against attackers according to size, speed, and ability level to minimize the effectiveness of the opponents.

2. Each player's defensive responsibility is clearly defined and easily understood—to stop the man he is marking from being an effective attacker!

3. Some defenders look on marking a strong opponent as a personal challenge and thus put forth greater effort in this defensive structure

since personal achievement is more easily recognizable in man-to-man play than any other.

4. Flaws in the defensive structure, in the form of poor play by individuals, are easily recognizable and thus may be corrected, even in the midst of a match, more readily than in other defensive structures.

Disadvantages of man-to-man defense

1. Many even matchups between defenders and attackers are not possible if the opponents have superior players. Even when the opponents do not have many outstanding players, they may still have one or two top players that no defender can match.

2. It is difficult, if not impossible, to adhere always to defensive principles of play such as support/depth and balance since each defender must stay with the man to whom he is assigned. If the attackers all move to one side of the field, for example, then the defenders marking them must follow and their defensive unit becomes unbalanced.

3. Man-to-man marking is extremely taxing on defenders since it requires tremendous mental concentration throughout a match. A defender must constantly be aware of and react to every movement made by the man he is marking.

4. Cohesion among defenders and playing as a total defensive unit are at times very difficult since players can easily become engrossed in their personal defensive battles. It is small consolation for a player to know that the man he was marking was ineffective if his own team loses the match.

5. This form of defense will almost always require the use of a free back to provide cover as in a catenaccio defensive setup. In a strict man-to-man defense, it is virtually impossible to provide cover and protect vital space in front of the goal without the use of a free back or libero.

6. Man-to-man defense retards a team's attacking power. The transition from attack to defense is difficult, especially for the players caught up deep in the attacking third of the field, since each defender must locate and catch up to the man he is supposed to be marking. As a result, players become leery of overcommitting themselves in attack for fear of not being able to recover and mark their men when they lose possession of the ball. This is especially true of players in the defensive back line.

How to develop a man-to-man defense

Man-to-man marking can be developed first on an individual basis, then with small groups of players, and finally using the entire team. Individuals can practice simply by having an opponent walk, jog, and sprint around the field while a defender attempts to stay with him and react to all changes of speed and direction. To make it more interesting a coach can give the attacker a ball and the two players can play one against one with a target goal to shoot at.

Two groups of five players each can be assigned opponents to mark and then play Keep Away. A team receives a point each time they make five consecutive passes. This game can be made easier for defenders by restricting the playing area or the number of touches allowed per attacking player. To emphasize proper positioning a coach can restrict the defenders to winning possession only by intercepting passes, with no tackling permitted.

Finally small-sided games with goals and five or six players per side can be played with each man assigned an opponent to mark. This will be followed by full-sided matches with man-to-man marking assignments.

Zone Defense

In a zonal defensive structure each defender, instead of marking one specific opponent, covers a particular area of the field and marks any attacking player who enters his zone, regardless of the position that this opponent plays. The zones of adjacent defenders overlap, as shown in Diagram 3.1, and generally are not strictly defined, to allow for player flexibility.

It is generally accepted that on a regulation- or near regulation-size field, a minimum of four players is needed in the defensive back line to provide proper cover for the width of the field. Each man can usually cover an area with a radius of 10 yd; when a playing area 70–75 yd in width is divided by 20 yd (the width one man covers), it can be seen that a minimum of four players can cover the area. Thus when setting up zone responsibilities, a coach can start by dividing the defending third of the field into four portions, slightly overlapping each other, and assigning these zones to his four back-line defenders.

Since attacking players should adhere to the principle of mobility, they will move from one defender's zone to another. Defenders in a zonal defensive structure will thus have to get used to "switching" with

Diagram 3.1 In a zone defense the zones of adjacent defenders overlap.

teammates the responsibility of marking opponents. As with man-to-man marking, there are both advantages and disadvantages to zone defense.

Advantages of zone defense

1. Using a zone defense, it is easier to prevent the opposition from scoring because a team can "stack" players in front of the goal area, thus limiting the opposition's attackers to few if any open shots on goal.

2. Zone defense helps to eliminate the disadvantages of mismatches in ability level that may occur in man-to-man marking. Whenever one man is confronted with marking a superior player, he is also assured of proper cover since his teammates are not preoccupied with marking specific opponents.

3. The defense is easier to regroup in a zonal defensive structure since each player knows into exactly what defensive area of the field he must retreat. As a result, defenders have greater freedom to attack.

4. Since defenders are not constantly watching every move of one opponent as well as the ball, zone defense is not as mentally taxing as man-to-man. Brief mental lapses and breakdowns in concentration will not be as critical as in man-to-man marking since defensive cover and balance will generally be more prevalent.

Disadvantages of zone defense

1. Zone defense will allow opposing attackers greater freedom of movement, especially before the play gets into the defending third of the field.

2. Players may be preoccupied with marking space, instead of the opposition's attackers; such preoccupation can be critical in the danger zone. In general, defending players may play more passively, assuming that others will cover for them.

3. The zone defense structure is built on the assumption that defending players will communicate properly, especially when exchanging the responsibility of marking opponents as they move from one zone to another. Communication may not be adequate in a team that has not played together long.

4. Individual breakdowns in a zone defense are more difficult to pinpoint because zone responsibilities overlap and are not clearly defined. Thus, a player sometimes assumes erroneously that a teammate will perform a task he was leaving.

How to develop a zone defense

The first step in developing a zone defense is to build up proper communication. A coach can stress this in small-sided games, two versus two or three versus three, gradually progressing to five versus five or six versus six. Assign players zones to defend and impress them with the fact that they are to try to eliminate all one-versus-one situations where a defender without proper cover is confronted by an attacking player with the ball. The attacking players must be encouraged to apply the principle of mobility to the fullest in these games.

Once the small-sided games have been built up to five versus five or six versus six, half-field games of attack versus defense can be introduced, stressing the same points as with the small-sided games. Finally the team can play full-sided matches, using zone defenses and stressing all the principles of play.

Combination Defense

Probably the most effective defensive organization would include both man-to-man and zone defense tactics. Defenders would be assigned zones, but they would use tight man-to-man marking in the area of the ball, especially in the defending third of the field. Although a combination of zone and man-to-man defense would assure tight marking near the ball as well as defensive support and depth, it would require players of considerable ability and experience to implement effectively.

DELAY

Whenever a team loses possession of the ball, it needs time to make the necessary transformation from attack to defense. A team can apply the principle of *delay* to obtain the necessary time. This principle is designed to directly counteract the attacking principle of penetration, especially quick penetration.

Once an opposing player gains possession of the ball, the defender nearest him must move to confront and delay him as quickly as possible. The defender must try to position himself in such a way as to eliminate as many forward passing opportunities as possible. By forcing the attacking player to hold the ball, pass it square, or pass it back, the defender manages to delay attacking penetration and acquires precious time for his teammates.

Jockeying

The defender confronting the player with the ball must not commit himself and must jockey his opponent, as shown in Figure 3.1. Repeated

Figure 3.1 Malcolm MacDonald of Newcastle United dribbles while opposing defenders jockey to contain him. (By arrangement with Newcastle Chronicle and Journal Limited, England)

feints will keep the attacking player occupied and wondering if and when the defender will tackle. This pressure will prevent the attacker with the ball from easily locating penetrating passing opportunities and may often make him hold on to the ball longer than he may have wanted.

Proper jockeying can also force an attacker with the ball to move in directions that are advantageous to the defense. The attacker can be forced to move towards another defender who might tackle or towards the touchline or goal line where his playing space is limited. The key to jockeying is to constantly maintain good balance, remain close enough to the man with the ball so that he feels pressured and is wary of a possible tackle, and yet be in a good position to prevent the attacker from getting past with the ball.

While the man nearest the ball gains time for his teammates by jockeying the attacker with the ball, other defenders near the ball must mark opponents in a position to receive penetrating passes. This will further increase the probability that the man with the ball will hold it, pass it square, or pass it back, thus allowing more time for the team on defense to make their transition from attack to defense. The remaining defenders must retreat to set up their defensive structure between the ball and their goal. Throughout this transition all the defenders must be very conscious of the space between them and, most important, of the space *behind* them where the opponents' attack could emerge.

How to Develop Delay

To achieve a rapid, fluid transition from attack to defense each time a team loses possession of the ball requires above all else a great deal of mental discipline and concentration. Players have to be aware of their responsibilities and constant reminders during training sessions can make this almost second nature.

Forwards especially have a tendency to pause a moment after losing the ball before going on defense. This cannot be tolerated if *all* the players are supposed to defend, and if the principle of delay is to be applied. After all, the player who can delay the opponents' attack initially is very often the one who lost possession of the ball.

Remember that players' breakdown in concentration, and thus their hesitation after the ball is lost to the other team, is not necessarily the result of laziness or sloppy playing. Sometimes players hesitate simply because they are disgusted with their own "poor" play when they forfeit the ball to an opponent. Remind them frequently that their role is crucial in the team's effective use of the delay principle to effect transition to defense.

SUPPORT/DEPTH

In defense as in attack, some triangular formation has to be set up to provide adequate support and depth. Support and depth in defense are necessary: (1) to restrict space into which the attackers' passes, and the attackers themselves, can travel, and (2) to provide cover for defenders and for dangerous space, which attacking players could exploit.

Support/Depth for Restricting Space

When a team is on defense, its players must be very conscious of space between defenders and especially space behind defenders because this is precisely the area attacking players will want to move into and into which

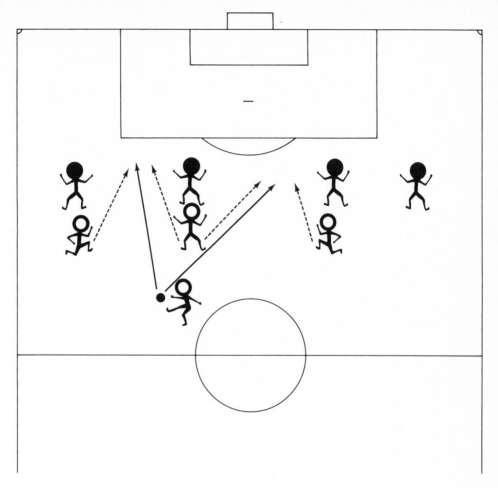

Diagram 3.2 Failure to adhere to the defensive principle of support/depth can allow one pass to beat all four defenders.

they wish to play the ball. A defending player can be effective in preventing goals only if he is between the ball and the goal he is defending. For this reason the space behind him and between him and the goal is what an attacking player wishes to exploit.

By providing each other with support and forming depth, defenders can restrict the space from which attacking players can do damage by scoring goals or initiating scoring plays. Diagram 3.2 shows a group of defenders who have failed to adhere to the principle of support/depth:

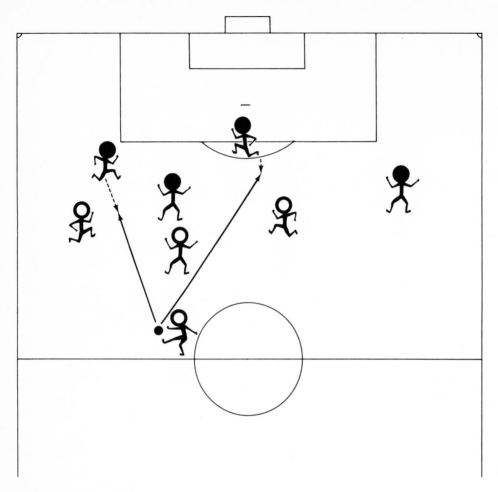

Diagram 3.3 Proper support/depth prevents easy penetration by the attack of the opposition.

One pass from the attacking player with the ball beats all four defenders. This type of flat defensive positioning will also allow attacking players to run into space behind the defenders to meet passes from teammates and possibly score goals.

Diagram 3.3 shows defenders providing proper support and depth; this way no one pass can beat all defenders, nor is space behind defenders left totally open for exploitation by attacking players. As the defenders approach their own goal, they will begin to flatten out to keep attacking players from penetrating too deeply and still remain onside. The goalkeeper provides support for the backs and defensive depth in this situation. For now even if the attackers send a ball behind the defenders, the keeper will in most instances be able to collect it and stave off dangerous scoring chances.

All players must remember to cover space for which the entire defense is responsible. The most important space to defend is in front of the goal where attacking players can score. Thus as defenders apply the principle of support/depth with an interlocking triangular formation, they progressively tighten these triangular formations as they approach their goal.

Support/Depth for Providing Cover

It is essential that defending players use the principle of support/depth to apply pressure on the opponent with the ball. Unless a defender who is pressuring the attacker with the ball is provided with adequate cover, there will usually be nothing and no one to prevent the ball from going through to the goal if he is beaten. This is especially true if the situation occurs in the team's defensive third of the field. Losing support/depth and tackling players without proper cover is a frequent fault of inexperienced players and leads them to concede many goals.

Proper cover permits defenders to impose greater pressure on the attacker with the ball by getting closer to him, which they can do when they know that if they should be beaten, another defender is ready to assist. However, many players are not wholly certain about what constitutes proper defensive cover.

How to Provide Cover

As a general rule, a defender providing cover for a teammate should position himself about 5 yd in back of his teammate and at about a 45° angle to him. This way he is in a position to challenge for the ball right away if his teammate is beaten. However, both the distance from which he gives cover and the angle are dependent on several factors and will vary as the factors vary.

Five primary factors that influence the distance from which one defender gives cover to another are: (1) the *ability* of the attacking player with the ball, (2) the attacker's *speed*, (3) the *position* on the field, (4) the specific *third of the field* that the player is in, and (5) the *location of other defenders*. If the attacker with the ball is very skillful at dribbling, his chances of beating the defender marking him increase, as do the chances that the man providing cover will be called to challenge for the ball. In addition, if the attacker is very fast, he might be able to push the ball forward, outrun both the pressuring defender and the one giving cover, and retrieve the ball if cover is provided from too close.

However, the location of additional defenders may keep the preceding factors from becoming too important. If additional defenders are quite close, they may prevent and discourage such attempts by the attacker with the ball.

Trying to outrun a defender and the man providing cover is more likely to occur near the touchlines than towards the middle of the field, and a forward with the ball will also be more likely to attempt such a maneuver in the central third of the field. Thus the defender providing cover may have to leave more ground between his teammate and himself in the midfield build-up area than in his defensive third of the field.

The angle from which support is given should be dictated by what the man pressuring the ball wishes to accomplish. If he is going to attempt to win the ball through a tackle, a position of cover from an angle of about 45° would be suitable. However, if he is merely jockeying the attacker with the ball, the man providing cover may well be better off to establish a position where he can still provide cover, but also where the player with the ball might be forced. Thus the man providing cover may find himself in a position to win the ball.

One very important thing to remember is that the defender providing cover has more opportunity to continuously analyze the situation than the man pressuring the ball. Therefore it is his responsibility to advise the man for whom he is providing cover of what would be best to do in every situation. He should advise his teammate in which direction to jockey the attacker, and also provide his teammate with constant reminders that cover is available and that he may pressure the ball closely without disaster to the defenders.

All players should also utilize out-of-bounds lines such as the touchline and the goal line to help provide themselves with cover. These lines restrict the space that the attacker with the ball has to work in and limit his effectiveness.

How to Develop Support/Depth

Small-sided games are excellent for teaching and developing defensive support/depth. By having only a few men per side, all the players must remain totally involved at all times. The lack of support at any time by just one player in a game such as four versus four can result in the opponents' scoring a goal.

Another excellent method of demonstrating the importance of support/depth in defense is playing lopsided games of attack versus defense, such as six versus five and six versus four. Since it is impossible for the defenders, who are fewer in number, to mark the attackers man to man, they will be forced to carefully maintain depth and proper support or else give up a lot of goals. Additional games for developing this and the other principles of defense are in Chapter 4.

CONCENTRATION

Since the primary objective of defense is to prevent goals, defenders must restrict the space from which their opponents can score goals. They can do this by retreating the defense and concentrating the defensive players in the "danger area." This area of vulnerability is shown in Diagram 3.4. Two imaginary lines, 30–35 yd in length, joined by an arc and projected outward into the field of play from each goalpost at an angle of 45° to the goal lines, represent the most important defensive area.

Factors Influencing the Danger Area

The threat that any shot poses from within this danger area depends largely on three factors: (1) how far out from goal the shot is taken, (2) by whom it is taken, and (3) the angle from which it is taken. Obviously young schoolboys pose a very slight scoring threat with a shot taken from 20 yd out from the goal. However, a world-class player like Eusebio of Portugal could score from such a distance and from even farther out. Shooting power varies even among world-class players though, and a shot taken from outside the penalty area by one player will not necessarily pose as great a problem as a shot taken by another more powerful player. A respectable goalkeeper should stop most shots taken from more than 30 yd out, regardless of who takes them. The angle of the shot is also of vital importance since the more acute the angle and the farther away from the center of the field the ball is, the less chance there is of a goal.

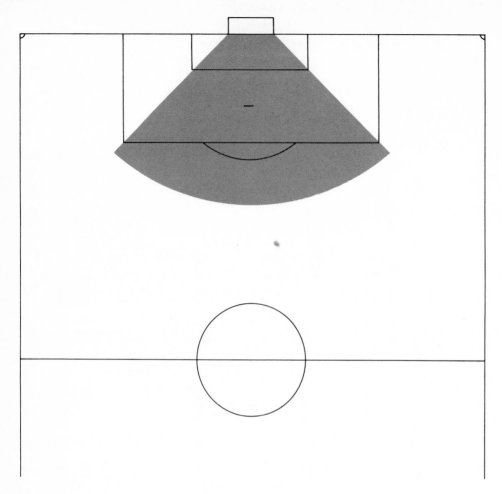

Diagram 3.4 The danger area of a defense.

Funneling

While a team is on attack, the backs will generally be spread across the width of the field, especially if the ball is in the attacking third of the field and the backs are near midfield. Once the players lose the ball to the opposition and begin retreating towards their own goal, they must retreat into more central and concentrated positions as they approach their defensive third of the field, the danger area, and finally their own goal if they still have not won the ball.

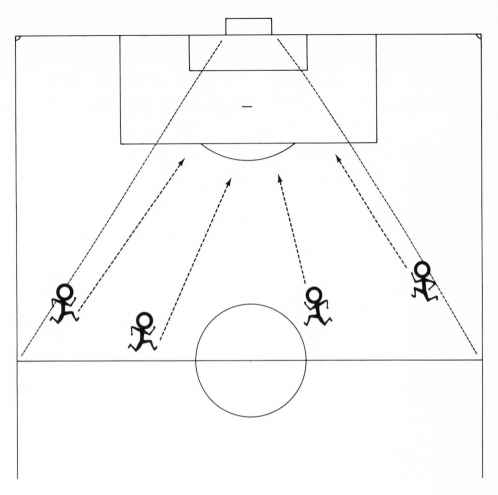

Diagram 3.5 *Funneling* of a defense.

Diagram 3.5 illustrates this form of retreat into defense, often referred to as *funneling*. Funneling is necessary because central space becomes more and more important as the opposition's attack approaches the goal since shots taken from this central space have a better chance of becoming goals than shots taken from outside it.

Individual defending players who are beaten by an attacker with the ball or who find themselves in poor defending positions (any that are not between the ball and the goal being defended) must immediately attempt to get back into good defending positions. To do this they can apply this principle of funneling. This is especially true if a player has any doubts about where to go to establish a positive defending position. Once he retreats into a central position goalside of the ball, he can quickly analyze his personal situation in relation to the total defensive structure and that of the opponent's attack and then react accordingly.

Concentration in Area of Ball

Concentration of defenders in the area where the opponents have the ball is also vital. This is not to say that defenders should all swarm around the ball, as inexperienced youngsters often do. However, attacking players will send several players to support the man who has the ball. Thus defenders must also move to mark these supporting attackers and prevent them from providing passing opportunities to their teammates.

Concentration of defending players in the area of the ball, regardless of what third of the field the ball is in, though important, should not be maintained at the expense of the other defensive principles. By concentrating defenders in the immediate area of the ball, the defense can often greatly limit the attacker's passing opportunities and possibly force the attackers to keep the ball in one relatively small, restricted area of the field. This sort of tactic increases the probability that the defenders will be able to win the ball back from the opposition.

How to Develop Concentration

After explaining the principle of concentration, show players its effect and the dangers of not applying it. In scrimmage situations, stop play at appropriate times to stress these points to the players. As in developing the principle of support/depth, small-sided and lopsided matches with more attackers than defenders are excellent ways of getting players to use defensive concentration.

BALANCE

Defending teams must provide cover for as much space as possible, especially the space that attacking opponents could use effectively in their attempt to penetrate the defense and score goals. To assure the maintenance of proper marking of space at all times, a team must balance their defense and spread out across the field, protecting the most important areas.

Attacking players, using the principle of mobility, constantly attempt to draw defenders out of sound defending positions to create space for other attackers and to help free their teammates of marking defenders. To counteract these tactics, a defense must maintain proper balance.

Unbalancing a Defense

Basically, the balance of a team is disrupted by opponents in one of two ways: Attacking players either (1) use their mobility to draw defenders out of position or (2) quickly play the ball around over sizeable areas of the field and catch the defense unbalanced as they react to the movement of the ball from one area of the field to another.

Teams using strict man-for-man marking are especially subject to having their defensive structures unbalanced. Since defenders are assigned to particular attackers, they follow their men all around the field and thus may leave vital space completely unprotected. Unless free backs are assigned in such defensive structures, proper cover for vital space and defensive balance, are virtually impossible to sustain.

Quickly playing the ball from one side of the field to the other has often been very effective in unbalancing a defense, especially one based on cover provided by diagonal alignments of defenders. As the ball is played around by the attacking players, the defenders may get caught stretched flat across the field as they attempt to re-establish diagonal cover [see Diagram 3.6(a)]. When squarely stretched across the field, they are totally without proper cover and extremely susceptible if a ball is played into space behind them, as shown in Diagram 3.6(b).

How to Maintain Balance

As mentioned before, it is virtually impossible to sustain balance in a team's defensive structure throughout a match if the team uses strict man-to-man marking. It is every bit as important for defenders to mark space as it is for them to mark men when the opponents have the ball.

Outside the danger area it is even more important to mark space than to mark men. Since players will not be scoring goals from here, it is

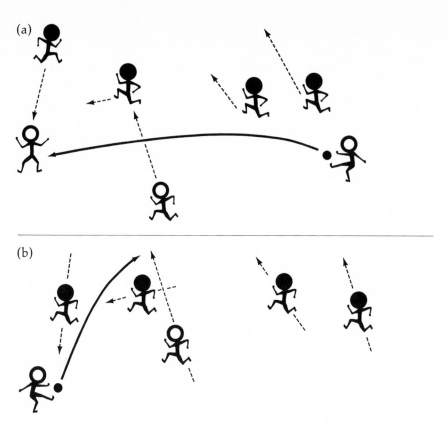

(a)

(b)

Diagram 3.6 Balls played across the field may catch the defense momentarily flat while they attempt to reestablish diagonal cover, and may permit a through pass into space behind the defense.

imperative to prevent them from penetrating into space where they can score goals. However, once the play approaches or is inside the danger area, marking space and marking men become equally important. Now defenders must restrict both space as well as movement of attacking players to prevent their opponents from scoring.

To maintain defensive balance, a team must use a combination of man-to-man and zone marking. Players near the ball should mark opponents, but players away from the ball must put marking vital space ahead of marking men.

Small-sided games and lopsided games of attack versus defense, such as 6 versus 5, are helpful for demonstrating the necessity of defensive balance as well as how and when it can break down. Once players recognize the necessity of maintaining balance in defense, they will be more receptive to constructive criticism during full-field 11 versus 11 training matches. The coach should stop the play during all training matches, especially in initial stages of developing defensive balance, to point out errors and show how to avoid and correct them.

PRESSURING

The primary defensive objective is to deny attacking players space and time so that they cannot score goals. This can be achieved most readily by applying the defensive principle of *pressuring*. Whenever possible, defenders must pressure attacking players, especially the one in possession of the ball, in an attempt to force mistakes. These mistakes, whether mental or technical, are essential for the defending team to gain possession of the ball.

Important factors in pressuring

1. *Remain goalside* Whenever possible the defending player must position himself so that he is on the goal side of the ball and of the man he is marking.

2. *Distance from opponent* To pressure effectively, the defending player must not be more than 1 or 2 yd away from the attacker. The precise distance from which he applies pressure depends on his individual speed and reaction time. This is especially true when he considers the same attributes of the opponent being marked. Slower players must obviously give their opponents more space to play in or else they will be beaten. However, no player can effectively pressure an opponent from a distance more than 2 yd.

When marking an opponent without the ball, a good rule to follow is that the marking should be tightest as play approaches the goal being defended and as the opponent gets within 30 yd of the ball. This way the defender discourages passing attempts to the man he is marking and is in a good position to challenge for the ball if an attacker attempts a pass to his man.

3. *Maintain good balance*   It is imperative that defending players applying pressure maintain good balance. Without proper balance a man cannot react as quickly as he could otherwise and thus can be beaten more readily. A defender also cannot afford to lunge or frequently end up on the ground, for then he puts himself out of play until he is able to recover. This is not to say that there is no room for effective sliding tackles, but as a rule it is unwise for defending players to leave their feet in an attempt to win the ball.

4. *Take an offensive attitude*   Defending players must take an offensive attitude towards their opponents and whenever possible jockey and force them to go where they will cause the fewest problems. To force a player to the outside, a defender must take up a position that cuts off the attacking player's path inside, thus leaving him space only in the area where the defender wants him. Conversely, by cutting off the attacker's path outside, the defender will force him inside. In both cases the defender must still remain goalside of his opponent.

5. *Reduce passing opportunities*   When pressuring a player with the ball, defenders must position themselves in such a manner as to reduce the passing opportunities to a minimum and whenever possible eliminate forward passing opportunities. Two key ingredients to successful attacking play are *improvisation* and *surprise*. If defenders can limit the passing opportunities of attacking players to a predictable few, they can also greatly reduce the effectiveness of their opponent's attacking play by limiting the improvisation possibilities.

Factors Influencing Pressuring

There are two primary factors that influence the ability of defenders to apply pressure: (1) The man applying pressure on the attacker with the ball must have proper support. A defender can pressure an opponent with confidence only if he knows he has support between the goal and himself in the event that the attacking player gets by with the ball. (2) Players must maintain a proper defensive balance. Unbalanced defenses are too easily penetrated and when they are, defenders cannot pressure with confidence. Defending players will know their defense is not secure and will thus have to be more concerned with overall defensive instability rather than with effectiveness of pressure applied to one individual attacker.

Challenging for the Ball

Pressuring attacking players is aimed at forcing them into making mistakes and ultimately giving up possession of the ball. When attackers make errors, defenders often have an opportunity to challenge for possession of the ball. There are only three ways a defender can gain possession of the ball without giving up a goal: (1) He can intercept the opposition's pass; (2) he can challenge for the ball and win it through a successful tackle; or (3) he can pressure the attacker and force him to lose the ball out of bounds.

To intercept a pass, a defender must be mentally and physically quick. He must "read the game" and anticipate the passes the attacker with the ball may make. The more the defensive team pressures the opponent with the ball and limits his passing opportunities, the greater chance the defense has to anticipate and intercept a pass.

Winning possession of the ball through a successful tackle is not an easy task. The ideal time to tackle an opponent is at the moment he receives the ball from a teammate. In such a case the attacking player will not yet have the ball completely under control, and the tackle will stand a good chance of success. Once a player gains control of the ball, a player should make a challenging tackle only if the attacker is pressured into making an error in dribbling such as allowing the ball to stray too far away from his feet. The more the defender marking the attacker with the ball can play aggressively, feint, and apply pressure on his opponent, the more it is likely that his opponent will make a mistake that will allow a successful tackle. Successful defenders are those who master timing, jockey and feint well, and control their opponents rather than fear them.

By forcing attacking players to move where the defenders want them, defending players can sometimes force balls to be misplayed out of bounds. This happens when a pass is technically misplayed and thus passed astray because of defensive pressure. Players who are not pressured and who are afforded the luxury of time to play the ball will usually strike the ball more accurately than those under considerable pressure who are made to hurry their passes for fear of losing possession of the ball.

How to Develop Pressuring

Pressuring is as much an individual defensive principle as a team principle. Therefore players must work on the technical aspects of pressuring such as proper jockeying and marking techniques, without the ball. Defenders must fully understand how to apply pressure before using this principle of defense in match play. Also, since the principles of support and balance influence the effectiveness pressure, these principles must be developed first.

By playing small-sided games such as four versus four or five versus five, players handle the ball frequently, and thus each defender marks a player who has possession of the ball more often. This allows for more frequent practice in pressuring opponents in match play situations. The coach should supervise such games closely to help develop frequent application of proper defensive pressuring.

Other methods of developing defensive pressuring are lopsided half-field games of 6 versus 4 or 6 versus 5 and full-field 11 versus 11 training matches. Close supervision and frequent comments by the coach, both correcting errors and praising proper execution, will speed up the learning process.

CONTROL

Soccer is a game of percentages, and defenders must be especially aware of the risks involved in any situation as well as the possible consequences if they commit errors. Some chances taken in soccer are more costly than others, and one player's foolish defensive gamble may result in his whole team's being punished, possibly by a goal for the opposition. Because the consequences of defensive gambling can be so severe, each defender must know how to control his urges to take chances and must be constantly aware of his role and its importance in the entire defensive structure. Adhering to the defensive principle of control is essential and becomes more important as the play moves from a team's attacking third of the field towards their goal.

Mental Discipline and Control

As players gain experience, they become more disciplined in their play because they learn to concentrate on their roles in the total team structure as well as on their specific responsibilities. This is especially vital in defense, and with experience players become better defenders because they lose their control less frequently and they take fewer foolhardy chances.

Young and inexperienced players often find it difficult to adhere to the defensive principle of control. They have a tendency to grow overexcited while playing and lose sight of defensive priorities. When they first start playing soccer, many youngsters are drawn to the ball like bees to honey and forsake their defensive responsibilities to watch and chase the ball. It is their lack of mental discipline that prevents them from using the principle of control.

When defending players at any level get overengrossed in watching the ball, they become easy prey to attackers who run unnoticed into space behind them and receive the ball. Although defenders must always be aware of where the ball is, they cannot forget about the attacking players without the ball nor the vital defensive space they must protect.

Defenders cannot afford to allow attacking players to roam around unmarked behind them, for an attacker behind a defender is invariably more dangerous than an attacker in front of him. Whenever two un-marked opponents confront a defender, the defender must mark the one closest to his goal, regardless of what third of the field they are in.

Although it is true that less experienced and less skilled players are more prone to lose their defensive control, it is not necessarily true that their opponents will take advantage of their defensive errors. For if their opponents are of comparable age and equally limited in skill, they cannot take advantage of defensive mistakes as would more highly skilled performers. For this reason, even though it is important to stress defensive control, a coach must do so with consideration of the players he works with. It is important to explain why control is necessary in defense, but it is also important not to overexaggerate the possible consequences of defensive errors.

Communication and Control

Proper communication among defenders is a great asset in maintaining defensive control. When a defender is jockeying an opponent with the ball, it is a considerable comfort and very helpful to be advised of what is happening around and behind him by the defender or defenders provid-ing support. Defenders should talk to one another constantly and always alert each other of dangers that may not be obvious.

The goalkeeper, as the last line of defense with the entire playing field in front of him, is especially vital to the communication in a defense. Since all the play is in front of him, it should be his responsibility to constantly alert his teammates of what they may not see and to advise them of the best defensive procedures in all situations. It is far easier for a player to maintain control and be reasonably relaxed if he knows his teammates are always prepared to assist him and alert him of things he may not see.

How to Develop Control

Players develop defensive control primarily through experience in match situations. The more experience a player has, the less likely he is to gamble foolishly and the more likely he is to be aware of the penalty his team may pay for his foolhardy play.

By making players aware of the probabilities of success of various defensive gambles in the various areas of the field and by encouraging and stressing the importance of constructive talking among defenders, a coach can reduce the frequency of players' losing control. He can stress and demonstrate this in small-sided games as well as full-sided matches. Above all else, a coach should stress that mental concentration is imperative in defensive play and in maintaining control.

REFERENCES

Cramer, Dettmar. *United States Soccer Federation "Coaches Manual."* Four Maples Press, Minisink Hills, Pa.

Csanadi, Arpad. *Soccer.* Corvina, Budapest, 1965.

Greaves, Jimmy. *Soccer Techniques and Tactics.* Pelham Books, London, 1966.

Hughes, Charles F.C. *Tactics and Teamwork.* E.P. Publishing, Wakefield, England, 1973.

Jones, Ken, and Pat Welton. *Football Skills and Tactics.* Marshall Cavendish, London, 1973.

Wade, Alan. *The FA Guide to Training and Coaching.* William Heinemann, London, 1967.

Winterbottom, Walter. *Training for Soccer.* William Heinemann, London, 1960.

4

Training Games

COACHING athletic teams is very much like teaching students in a classroom. The two primary differences are that a coach teaches physical things rather than academic, and usually the players a coach works with are more highly motivated and willing to learn than the students in a classroom.

One problem that confronts both the classroom teacher and the athletic coach is how to keep the daily routine of the classroom or training sessions from becoming monotonous. To keep the people you teach constantly interested, you must vary the way you make presentations. You can do this by adding variety to your training sessions with training games. The use of training games permits you to accomplish your objectives while the players perform more enjoyable exercises than the conventional drills.

The training games in this chapter are grouped into four categories depending on their objectives. The warm-up games, the games for ball-handling technique, the games for tactical play, and even the games for physical fitness can all be enjoyed for their own sake by the players. They are fun and yet still perform necessary training functions.

Some games require specific equipment that may not be available to everyone. For example, portable goals, used in many games in this chapter, are a tremendous training aid, but if they are unavailable a coach can substitute such things as traffic cones or corner flag posts to indicate where the goals are. Coaches should modify the games to suit their personal needs and equipment limitations. Also, they can use the basic ideas of many games presented in this chapter to develop additional games for their players.

Normal FIFA rules should be used for all the games unless otherwise stated in the game description. The games are meant to be supplemental to regular training sessions or as substitutes for more conventional exercises and are by no means designed as an entire training session.

The warm-up games are designed as loosening-up exercises and should not involve any excessive exertion for the players. Many games designed primarily for technique development may also be utilized as warm-up games. Juggling games are especially good for warming up since they usually involve the full body but involve no movements that would cause any real muscular strain.

The games for technique development are necessarily repetitious, but disguised in game form, they tend to be far less monotonous. It is important that these games be short enough that they will end before fatigue sets in and technique deteriorates.

The tactical games are useful for developing individual, small-group, and team tactics. It is important that when playing these games players recognize their tactical errors. For this reason it may sometimes be more beneficial to stop play momentarily to make a point regarding an error or a very well-performed tactical maneuver than to let play continue and discuss the situation at the end of the game when it may no longer be fresh in the players' minds.

The fitness games are also enjoyable, but coaches must realize that they are probably better for *maintaining* a level of fitness than for developing it. The games and the competition in themselves tend to distract players from the continuous, all-out effort necessary for fitness development, especially endurance fitness. All kinds of relay races involving fitness exercises, as explained in Chapter 6, can also be used as training games.

To maintain top-level competition and interest, keep score in all games. Designate score keepers, and sometimes have someone who is not playing keep score. Remember also the skill limitations of particular players. Do not start a game limiting each player to one consecutive touch of the ball if most players cannot sustain an enjoyable game at this level. Do not use games that require a high degree of technical ability with beginning players, for they will simply become frustrated because of their inability to perform, and instead of making training more fun, the games will do just the opposite.

WARM-UP GAMES

Team passing (Diagram 4.1)

Objective: Warm-up, passing accuracy, and proper support of the man with the ball.

Equipment: One ball per team.

Description: Two teams of five or six players each are contained in a limited space, such as the penalty area. The members of each team pass the ball only to their teammates. Negative points are awarded to a team when a pass goes astray, out of bounds, or hits a member of the other team or the other team's ball. The length of the game can be set either

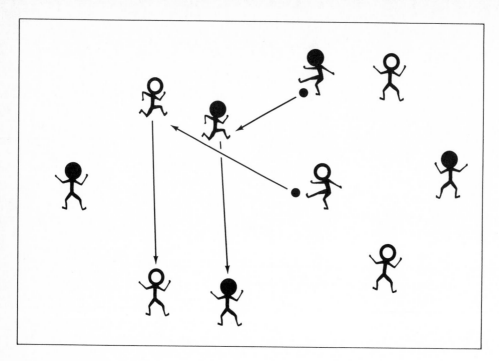

Diagram 4.1 Team Passing.

with a time limit or with a maximum amount of negative points a team can accumulate before losing.

Comments: A coach can make the game more difficult by placing a restriction on the number of consecutive touches of the ball permitted each player and by using a smaller playing area.

Team ball tag (Diagram 4.2)

Objective: Warm-up, dribbling, and passing accuracy.

Equipment: One ball for every player.

Description: Two teams of five or six players are restricted to an area the size of the penalty area. Each player has a ball and tries to tag a member of the other team by passing his ball into an opponent's ball. When a

Diagram 4.2 Team Ball Tag.

man is tagged, he must move to the nearest out-of-bounds line and stand
there with his ball on the line. A tagged player may be set free by having
a teammate's ball hit his own. The game ends when all the members of
one team are tagged without having been set free, or a time limit is set,
and the winner is the team with the most players left on the playing field.

Comments: A variation of the game would allow tagging the opponent
with the hands, and might have the tagged player sit down at the spot
where he was tagged until he is released or the game ends.

Ball tag

Objective: Warm-up and passing accuracy.

Equipment: One ball for every player.

Description: Two players stand next to each other, and the play is started by one of them pushing his ball about 10 yd forward. A point is awarded every time a man can pass his own ball into his opponent's ball. A ball may not be stopped after it is kicked and must come to rest of its own accord. Players take turns kicking, and a player may kick his ball and attempt to score a point as soon as his opponent misses. His opponent's ball can be hit before it comes to a stop. When a man scores a point, his opponent may not take his turn until both balls have come to a stop. The winner is the player who has accumulated the most points within a set time limit.

Comments: To achieve a maximum amount of running from the players, coaches should set no boundaries.

GAMES TO IMPROVE BALL-HANDLING TECHNIQUE

Individual juggling

Objective: Ball-handling techniques and confidence.

Equipment: One ball for every player.

Description: Each man juggles a ball using all parts of his body other than his arms or hands. The player who makes the most consecutive touches of the ball without letting the ball hit the ground is the winner.

Comments: Small groups of players can also perform juggling. A restriction on the number of consecutive touches per player tends to keep one man from dominating a group.

Progressive juggling

Objective: Ball-handling techniques and confidence.

Equipment: One ball for every pair or group of players.

Description: Players are divided into pairs or small groups. Each player must juggle the ball exactly one time more than his partner or the teammate who preceded him. The first man has only one touch, the next has two, the next three, and so forth. The winner is the group that reaches the highest number.

Comments: The groups or pairs could be kept together for more than one training session so that they can better their previous best efforts at progressive juggling.

Keep away juggling

Objective: Technique, confidence, and accuracy in volleying balls as well as proper positioning to support a teammate in possession of the ball.

Equipment One ball for every group.

Description: Three players juggle the ball as in group juggling, but now a fourth player attempts to intercept the passes from one player to another. When a pass is intercepted, the player who touched it last exchanges places with the one who intercepted it.

Comments: The game can be played with three versus one, three versus two, four versus two, and so on. The smaller the ratio between jugglers and players trying to intercept passes, the more difficult the game becomes for the jugglers. Coaches can make the game more difficult by setting a limit on the number of consecutive touches allowed each player and by restricting the players to a designated area such as a 15-yd square.

Soccer volleyball (Diagram 4.3)

Objective: Ball-handling technique, as well as kicking and heading accuracy.

Equipment: One soccer ball or volleyball, a volleyball net, and stanchions placed on a regulation volleyball court.

Description: Volleyball rules are followed, but the players serve the ball by kicking it over the net. Players may not use arms or hands except when holding the ball before serving, and they may allow the ball to hit the floor once before returning it. This one bounce may be taken when the ball first comes over the net or any other time between the allotted three touches.

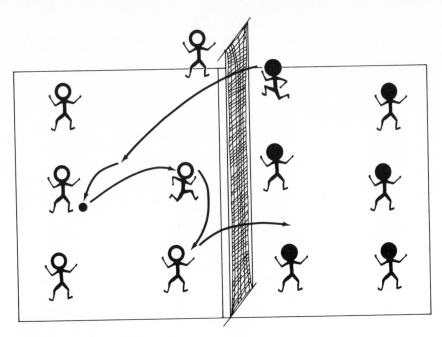

Diagram 4.3 Soccer Volleyball.

Comments: A coach can make the game easier by allowing up to two consecutive touches per person, and more than a maximum of three men playing the ball before returning it. It can be made more difficult by not allowing the ball to bounce at all. A variation of this game that would be a good heading exercise would restrict all touches to the head only.

Soccer tennis (Diagram 4.4)

Objective: Ball-handling techniques, as well as kicking and heading accuracy.

Equipment: One soccer ball and a tennis net set up on a regulation tennis court.

Description: The basic rules of tennis apply except that the game is played using any part of the body except the arms and hands and, of course, no racket.

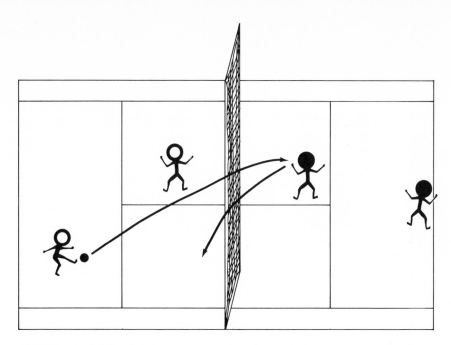

Diagram 4.4 Soccer Tennis.

Comments: Soccer tennis can be played as singles, doubles, or even with teams of three or four players each. When playing with teams, a coach may wish to allow each team to play the ball more than once when it comes into their court.

Four-wall soccer (Diagram 4.5)

Objective: Kicking and heading accuracy as well as fast reactions to balls served quickly or very hard.

Equipment: One soccer ball and a handball court.

Description: The game is played according to regulation four-wall handball rules except that the players use any part of their bodies to hit the ball except their arms or hands. A player serves by bouncing the ball on the floor and then serving it with the foot.

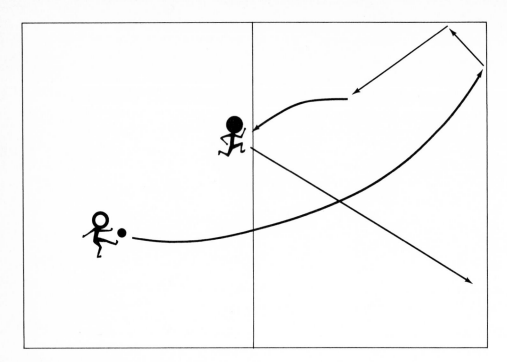

Diagram 4.5 Four-wall Soccer.

Comments: If handball courts are not available, a coach could use a squash court. However, the board at the base of the front wall in the squash court would interfere somewhat with the game. Highly skilled players should try playing this game with a tennis ball instead of a soccer ball.

Through pass (Diagram 4.6)

Objective: Passing accuracy.

Equipment: One ball for every pair of players and traffic cones.

Description: Two players jog around the perimeter of a circle with a 10-yd radius while one of them dribbles the ball. The players should try to remain at opposite sides of the circle at all times. The traffic cones are

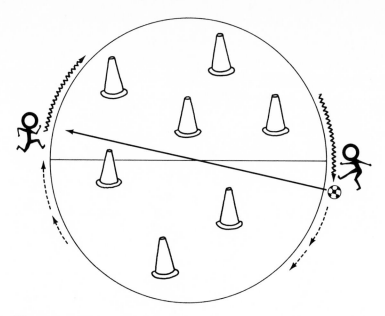

Diagram 4.6 Through Pass.

placed randomly inside the perimeter. The player with the ball must try to pass the ball across the circle to the other man without hitting any of the cones. One point is awarded for each successful pass. The game ends either after one of the players accumulates a set number of points or after a set time limit.

Comments: A coach can make the game more difficult by increasing the number of cones in the circle. More than one pair of players can play at one time using the same circle.

Circle ball (Diagram 4.7)

Objective: Ball-handling techniques and kicking and heading accuracy.

Equipment: One ball per game.

Description: The same basic rules as in soccer volleyball are used. The game is played either in the center circle of a regulation field, or in any circle with a 10-yd radius. There is no net, just a line dividing the circle in

Diagram 4.7 Circle Ball.

half for two teams of five players each. The ball is served by any player and must be lobbed by hand to the other team. Players may not score points directly from the service, and only the serving team may score. The ball remains in play when it hits the circle's perimeter, and it is out of play if it hits the center line dividing the circle. Each player may touch the ball only once in succession. The ball may hit the ground once on each team's side between the time the opponents play it to them and the time they return it. Each side is allowed three touches before the ball must go over the center line to the other side. The ball must be played over the center line and cannot hit the ground on one side and bounce over into the other. The game is scored as soccer volleyball is, and the winner is the first team to get 15 points.

Comments: A coach can make the game easier by allowing more players per team, more than one touch in succession per player, and more than three touches before the ball must be sent over the center line.

Diagram 4.8 Soccer Dodge Ball.

Soccer dodge ball (Diagram 4.8)

Objective: Passing accuracy.

Equipment: One ball per game.

Description: Two teams of five to seven players are confined in a playing field the size of the penalty area. Each team tries to hit the players on the other team with the ball by kicking it into them. A player is out of the game if he is hit by an opponent's ball only if the opponents maintain possession of the ball. Every time a player tries to hit an opponent with the ball and misses or passes the ball out of bounds, his team loses possession of the ball. No dribbling is allowed until a team has only one player left. The game ends either when all the players of a team have been eliminated, or when a predetermined time limit is reached; the team with the most players still in the game is the winner.

Diagram 4.9 Pin Soccer.

Comments: A variation of this game would allow players to stay in the game after they have been successfully hit by an opponent, and then award the teams one point each time they hit an opponent and retain possession of the ball.

Pin soccer (Diagram 4.9)

Objective: Passing accuracy.

Equipment: One ball and six Indian clubs per game.

Description: Two teams of three or four players each use a playing area 40 yd by 20 yd with two 3-yd alleys at either end, as shown in Diagram 4.9. The Indian clubs should be evenly spaced in each alley. Each team defends one end of the field and tries to down all three of their opponent's Indian clubs. Players may not enter the 3-yd alleys, and they must knock down the clubs by kicking the ball into them. Possession of

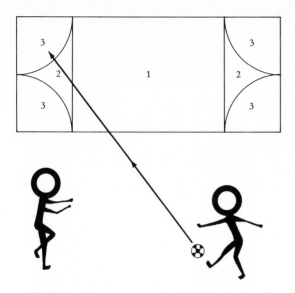

Diagram 4.10 Target Shooting.

the ball changes after a team knocks a club down or kicks the ball out of bounds. The winner is the team that knocks down all the opponent's clubs first.

Comments: Coaches can make the game more difficult by restricting the number of consecutive touches allowed each player. They can substitute traffic cones or additional balls for the clubs and award a point for each hit, even if the targets cannot be knocked down. After a cone or ball is hit, it should be taken out of the alley. This game is especially adaptable for indoor training.

Target shooting (Diagram 4.10)

Objective: Shooting accuracy.

Equipment: One ball per game and one kick board marked as shown in Diagram 4.10.

Description: The game can be played by any number of players, but preferably not more than four so that there are no long waiting periods

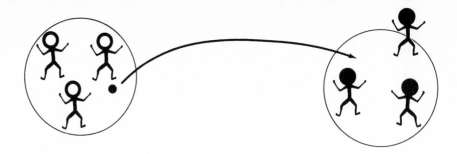

Diagram 4.11 Bulls Eye.

between turns. Each player shoots at the kick board and gets the number of points shown in the area where his ball hits. The game is over when one player accumulates 15 points or more or after a set number of shots per player has been taken; then the one with the most points is declared the winner. The distance from the board to where the shots are taken should depend on the ability of the players.

Comments: This game can also be played by serving balls to the players so that they are not kicking still balls. It can also incorporate heading instead of kicking to provide practice in heading on goal.

Bulls eye (Diagram 4.11)

Objective: Chipping accuracy and trapping technique.

Equipment: One ball per game.

Description: There can be three or four players to a team. Each team defends a circle 10 yd in radius, with the two circles 30 yd apart. Each team in turn places the ball on the ground within its circle and one player tries to chip the ball into the opponent's circle. One player on the receiving team tries to control the ball with a trap and bring it under full control inside his circle. The team that kicks the ball scores a point if it hits the ground in the opponent's circle and was not successfully controlled or if an opponent knocks the ball out of his own circle while trying to trap it. The team receiving the kick can score a point if the ball lands outside its circle without one of the players touching it before it hits

Diagram 4.12 Ring Heading.

the ground. No point is scored if the ball is successfully controlled and brought to rest inside the circle by a man receiving the kick. The player nearest the ball kicks it back to the opposition from the spot where it hit. If the ball lands outside the circle any player can return it from wherever he chooses in his circle. The first team to accumulate 15 points is the winner.

Comments: Coaches can make the game more difficult by increasing the distance between the circles. Also they could require players to control a ball before it hits the ground and juggle it a minimum of three times before bringing it down in their circle.

Ring heading (Diagram 4.12)

Objective: Heading technique and accuracy.

Equipment: One ball and one ring stanchion or suspended ring, about 3 ft in diameter per pair of players.

Description: Two players stand on either side of the ring and head the ball back and forth through it. Each pair tries to get the most consecutive headers through the ring. The winners are the players who reach the highest number.

Comments: A coach can vary the game by having each player head the ball twice in succession (two-touch heading) before the ball goes through the ring to his partner.

Games to Improve Ball-handling Technique   115

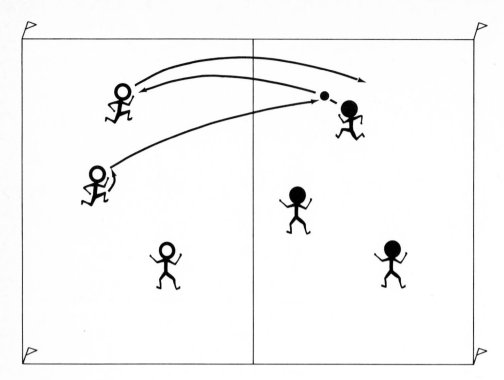

Diagram 4.13 Distance Heading.

Distance heading (Diagram 4.13)

Objective: Develop distance heading with accuracy.

Equipment: One ball per game.

Description: Two teams of three or four players each play in an area 40 by 20 yd. A team scores a goal each time it heads the ball over the opponent's goal line. The game is started by one player, standing 10 yd from midfield in his own half of the field, throwing the ball up and heading it as far as he can into the opponent's half of the field. The same procedure is followed after every goal. The members of the other team try to head the ball back as far as they can. If the ball hits the ground, the closest player from the team that did not head it last picks it up and heads it from that point. Any ball that goes out of bounds is headed from the point where it crossed the touchline. The team with the most goals at the end of a preset time limit is the winner.

Comments: The length of the playing area should be adapted to the skill level of the players. A playing area that is too long for limitedly skilled players will only frustrate them. A reasonable amount of scoring has to be assured to keep the players interested.

Slalom dribbling

Objective: Dribbling technique.

Equipment: One ball and five stakes, prefereably 5-ft corner flag stakes, for every team.

Description: The stakes are placed 2 to 3 yd apart in a straight line. Each team can have an optional number of players, although the more players there are on each team, the longer their waiting periods between turns of dribbling. Each player dribbles the ball between the stakes from the starting line, around the stake farthest away, and back between the stakes to the starting line. The winner is the team whose players all go through the slalom first; or if one player from each team starts simultaneously through the slalom, the player who completes the course first scores a point for his team. After all the players have gone through the slalom a preset number of times, the team with the most points is declared the winner.

Grid dribbling (Diagram 4.14)

Objective: Dribbling and tackling techniques.

Equipment: One ball per group.

Description: Each team is made up of three players. The playing area for each group consists of a grid of four 10-yd squares in a row. One defender is positioned on each line joining two squares; he must stay on his line as long as he remains a defender. The dribblers try to beat each defender to get through to the finish line (see Diagram 4.14). Each time a dribbler beats a defender and moves into the next square he scores a point. If a defender successfully tackles the dribbler, the dribbler still proceeds to the next square but without scoring a point. If a player pushes the ball out of bounds he cannot score a point from that square. After all the players from one team have dribbled the teams exchange places and the game continues. After every player has had a turn at

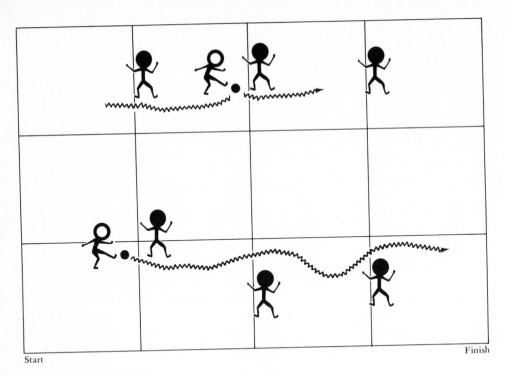

Start

Finish

Diagram 4.14 Grid Dribbling.

dribbling, the team with the most accumulated points is declared the winner.

Comments: To make the game more difficult for the dribblers, coaches can allow the defenders to come off their line to jockey and tackle as soon as the dribbler enters the square in front of them.

GAMES TO IMPROVE TACTICS

One-touch soccer

Objective: A quicker tempo of play by reducing the amount of dribbling and training for supporting the player with the ball.

Equipment: One ball per game.

Description: Players are limited to one consecutive touch throughout the game. If goalkeepers are used, they may play as they do in regular matches. This one-touch restriction forces players to move in support of the player receiving the pass since he must pass it immediately; in addition, the restriction makes the player receiving the pass think ahead about where he can play the ball. Whenever a player does not comply with the restriction, his team loses possession of the ball.

Comments: By placing various restrictions on play during training sessions with matches of 11 versus 11 or small-sided games, coaches can achieve desired objectives, sometimes without the players' ever realizing it. The fewer consecutive touches allowed, the faster the tempo of the game. It is wise to start by introducing this type of game with restrictions of three touches and two touches first.

Low-ball soccer

Objective: Short passing and moving into open space to support teammates with the ball.

Equipment: One ball per game.

Description: Players are restricted to a maximum height that a ball may reach after being passed. By using this restriction, a coach can get more short passes from his players without directly instructing them to pass short. It is virtually impossible to hit a ball any great distance without having it rise over the height of an average man's waist. Therefore, by restricting the passes to a height not to exceed a man's waist, a coach will discourage long passes. Possession of the ball is lost by a team if they break the restriction.

Comments: A restriction of no passes higher than the knees will force players to make even shorter passes. Since the players will be forced to use short passes, they will also be forced to keep moving into open spaces to leave themselves in good supporting positions.

Goals from heads

Objective: More wing play and more balls being crossed to create heading opportunities at the goal.

Equipment: One ball per game.

Description: Players are restricted to scoring goals only from head shots. By using this restriction, a coach can force players to take the play out to the wings so that they can cross the ball in front of the goal. This will create opportunities for them to head on goal.

Comments: This game can be played using full goals and having no goalkeepers.

Goals from back passes

Objective: Support from behind the player with the ball in the attacking half of the field.

Equipment: One ball per game.

Description: Players are restricted to scoring goals only with balls passed back to them by their teammates. This forces attacking players to trail the man with the ball, supporting him and giving him opportunities to pass the ball back.

Comments: A coach may use more than one restriction on the play in any game. For example, he could restrict a game to head goals and two-touch soccer.

Man versus man

Objective: Tight man-to-man marking and heightened awareness of defensive responsibilities.

Equipment: One ball per game.

Description: Every player is paired with one man of the opposing team. When a team is in attack, the player with the ball can be tackled only by his partner on the opposing team.

Comments: This game forces players to be constantly aware of where their opposing partners are. It is also a good fitness game since players often have to sprint considerable distances to mark their opposing partners. It is best to pair players of reasonably equal speeds and abilities so as not to give one a very significant advantage.

No-goal handball

Objective: Movement into proper spaces by players supporting the man with the ball.

Equipment: One soccer ball or one European handball per game.

Description: The team consists of seven players each, and play is in half a regular field. All balls are thrown and caught by hand. No player may take more than three steps while he is in possession of the ball. A team may only gain possession of the ball if they intercept a pass or if the other team throws the ball out of bounds. No player may try to dispossess an opponent of the ball. One point is awarded to a team each time they make 10 successful consecutive passes among themselves.

Comments: This is an excellent game for teaching younger, less skilled players proper movement off the ball and how to make the best use of available space in attack as well as how to create it.

Numbers passing

Objective: Movement into proper space by players supporting the man with the ball and tight man-to-man marking.

Equipment: One ball per game.

Description: Teams of four to six players number their players sequentially. Each player must always pass the ball to the teammate with the next number in the sequence. A team gains possession of the ball when they intercept a pass, when the opponents pass the ball out of bounds, when the opponents pass out of sequence, or when the opponents score a point by completing one full sequence of passes. If a team consists of six players, they will have to make six consecutive passes in numerical order to score a point. If the ball is intercepted by No. 3, that team's full sequence on that turn will end when No. 3 is finally passed the ball by No. 2. The game is started after each point is scored by player No. 1 passing to player No. 2. The playing area should be suited to the number

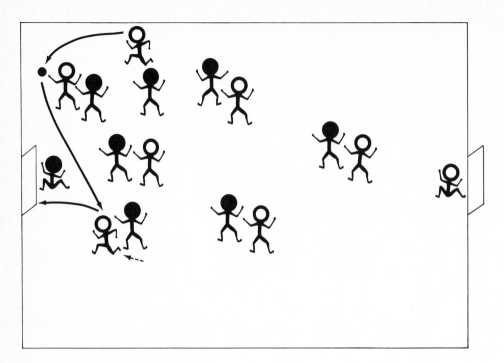

Diagram 4.15 Head-goal Handball.

of players in the game. The less skilled the players, the larger the playing area should be.

Comments: A coach can make the game more difficult by imposing restrictions on the number of consecutive touches allowed each player. The rules of this game can also be applied to No-goal Handball. Coaches may wish to make man-to-man assignments for defensive purposes so that like numbers on the two teams mark each other.

Head-goal handball (Diagram 4.15)

Objective: Good movement off the ball and proper use and creating space in attack.

Equipment: One soccer ball or European handball and two field hockey goals.

Description: The two teams have six to seven players and one goalkeeper each. The playing area is half a regular field, and the rules are the

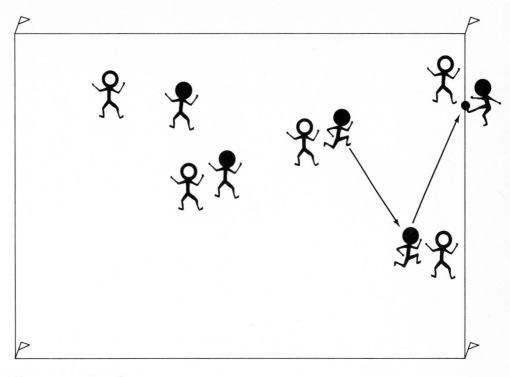

Diagram 4.16 Line Soccer.

same as for No-goal Handball, but now goals are scored by head shots. A player can only head on goal a ball thrown to him by a teammate. He is not allowed to throw a ball up to himself to try a head shot on goal. There is no offside rule in this game.

Comments: Two corner flag stakes may be used to designate each goal if field hockey goals are not available. This game helps players of limited skill to concentrate on the use of space in attack without worrying about their inadequate foot technique. To encourage more passing, a coach could award 2 points for every goal scored and 1 point for every 10 successful consecutive passes a team completes.

Line soccer (Diagram 4.16)

Objective: Proper support of the player with the ball and tight man-to-man marking.

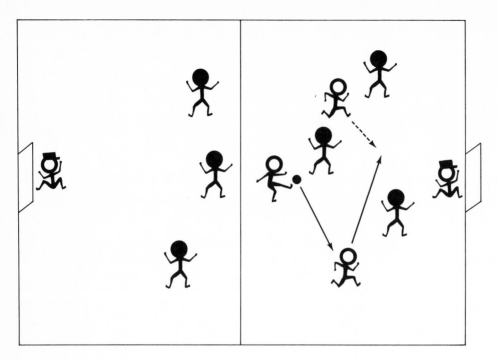

Diagram 4.17 Three-team Soccer.

Equipment: One ball per game.

Description: The teams consist of four to five players. The playing field is the penalty area or an area of 40 by 20 yd. A goal is scored each time a player stops the ball on his opponents' goal line. There are no goalkeepers and no offside rule.

Comments: A coach can make the game easier by allowing the players to score a goal each time they dribble the ball over their opponent's goal line. Various restrictions on the play can be imposed to achieve additional tactical objectives.

Three-team soccer (Diagram 4.17)

Objective: Attacking play.

Equipment: One ball and two portable goals.

Description: The field of play consists of half a regular field with one goal and one goalkeeper on each goal line. There are three teams of three to five players, with one team on attack while the other two each defend one goal. The defending teams must remain in their respective halves of the field. If a defending team gains possession of the ball, they exchange places with the team that was attacking and proceed to attack the goal in the opposite half of the field. Whenever the goalkeeper catches the ball, he gives it to the team that was defending his goal. When a team scores a goal, they are awarded a point, they are allowed to maintain possession of the ball, and they can proceed to attack the other goal. There is no offside rule in this game. The winner is the team with the most goals at the end of a preset time limit.

Comments: A coach can place restrictions on the play to achieve additional tactical objectives.

Zone soccer (Diagram 4.18)

Objective: Specific positional play.

Equipment: One ball and two goals per game.

Description: The two teams consist of 9 to 11 players each and play on a regular field, evenly divided into three sections. The players are restricted to the section of the field that most stresses their individual positions. The defenders remain in the defensive third of the field, the midfielders in the center section, and the attackers in the attacking third of the field. The players work the ball from one section of the field to the other by passing the ball to their teammates in the next section. They can also make passes through or over an entire section. Goals are scored in normal fashion, but there is no offside rule applied in the game.

Comments: To give the attacking players a slight advantage, a coach could assign a section more attackers than defenders. The number of players assigned to each section can be varied to match the number of players a team has in its attack or defense according to its system of play.

Diagram 4.18 Zone Soccer.

Two-way soccer (Diagram 4.19)

Objective: Tight defensive marking and moving in attack to create good scoring opportunities.

Equipment: One ball and two corner flag stakes, each 5 ft high.

Description: The teams consist of five to seven players each and one goalkeeper positioned at the goal. The goal consists of two corner flag stakes placed 8 yd apart. When a team has possession of the ball, it tries to score by shooting the ball between the stakes; the ball cannot exceed the height of the stakes if it is to count as a goal. A goal can be scored from either side of the stakes, and the game continues even after a goal is scored. No boundary lines are needed, although a coach can restrict the players to a given playing area if he wishes. If the goalkeeper saves a shot, he throws the ball back out to an open space in the field of play, and

Diagram 4.19 Two-way Soccer.

any player may try to gain possession of it. The winner of the game is the team with the most goals at the end of a preset time limit.

Comments: This is also a good fitness game since the players are involved in continuous action. It helps to develop shooting accuracy and is very good training for goalkeepers.

Target soccer (Diagram 4.20)

Objective: Tight defensive marking, movement by supporting players in attack, and passing accuracy.

Equipment: One ball and two traffic cones per game.

Description: The teams consist of four to six players and no goalkeepers. Each team attacks one of two traffic cones that are placed inside two circles, each with a 10-yd radius 40 yd apart. The size of the field should be either half a regular field or without outside boundary lines. No player may enter the circles. A goal is scored when a player hits the cone his

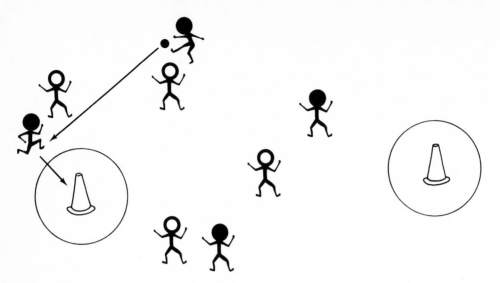

Diagram 4.20 Target Soccer.

team is attacking with the ball. After each goal, possession of the ball changes. The winner is the team to score the most goals within a preset time limit.

Comments: Coaches can also use goalkeepers who are also restricted from entering the circles and can use their hands only within an area 3 yd around the circle they are defending.

Small sides (Diagram 4.21)

Objective: Direct player involvement either in handling the ball or in direct support of the man with the ball. Also puts greater demand on continuous mental concentration.

Equipment: One ball and two portable goals per game.

Description: A regular match is played but with fewer players per team, and the playing area is reduced to suit their numbers. For a game of five versus five, with the addition of a goalkeeper for each team, coaches could use the width of a regular playing field and play with the midfield

Diagram 4.21 Small Sides.

line and the penalty area line extended to the regular touchline to represent the touchlines. There is no offside rule in this game.

Comments: By reducing the number of players on each team, coaches increase the number of times each player is directly involved in the play with the ball. This is an excellent means of tactical training. It is advisable to use full-sized portable goals since they afford the players the opportunity to work on their finishing. However, it is important that restrictions be set down, such as allowing players to take shots only in their attacking half of the field to achieve desired tactical objectives rather than random shooting. Field hockey goals or other substitutes such as corner flag stakes could designate the goals if portable goals are unavailable.

Four-goal soccer (Diagram 4.22)

Objective: Defensive alertness and adjustments to attacking play.

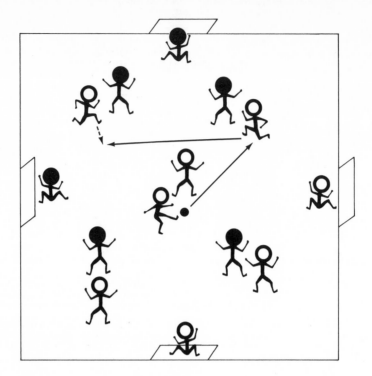

Diagram 4.22 Four-goal Soccer.

Equipment: One ball and four portable goals.

Description: The rules are the same as for small-sided games, but a new dimension is added with the use of two additional goals. One goal is placed on each of the four out-of-bounds lines. Each team attacks two adjacent goals and defends the other two. Half a regular playing field is usually best for a game involving five to six field players and one goalkeeper for each goal. There is no offside rule.

Comments: This game puts great stress on constant defensive adjustments since the opponents can change their attack quickly from one goal to the other. The game also develops constant evaluation by the attacking players of the opponent's defense. It is a useful fitness game since it requires a great deal of running and direction changing.

Diagram 4.23 Half-field Soccer.

Half-field soccer (Diagram 4.23)

Objective: Play in the attacking third of the field.

Equipment: One ball and one goal per game.

Description: The two teams consist of five to six players each, and play in half a regular soccer field with a goalkeeper in the goal. One team

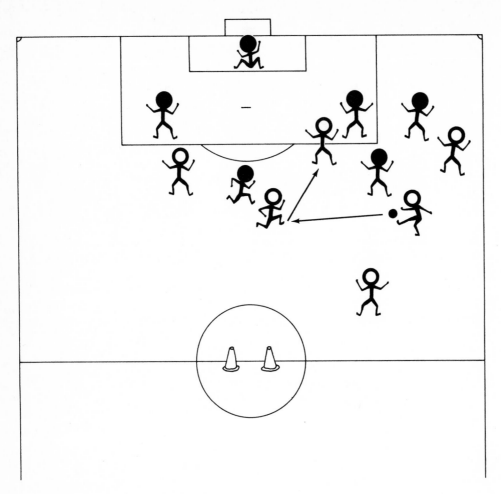

Diagram 4.24 Attack Versus Defense.

attacks the goal and tries to score while the other defends. As soon as the team on defense gain possession of the ball, they go on attack. When the defenders win the ball they must bring it at least 18 yd out from the goal before attempting any shots. The defenders also change places with the attackers after every goal, when the goalkeeper catches the ball, or when the ball last touched by an attacking player goes out of bounds.

Comments: A team could be allowed to keep possession of the ball after scoring a goal. Coaches can impose various other restrictions on the play to achieve other tactical objectives.

Attack versus defense (Diagram 4.24)

Objective: Attacking and defending play near the goal.

Equipment: One ball, one goal, and two traffic cones per game.

Description: The attacking players attack the regular goal with a goal-keeper in half a playing field. The defending players defend the regular goal, and attack a small goal consisting of two traffic cones placed 5 ft apart at midfield. The attacking players have numerical superiority to afford them more opportunities in attack. The attacking players receive 1 point for each goal they score, and the defenders receive 2 points when they gain possession of the ball and pass between the two traffic cones positioned at midfield.

Comments: This is a good method of training to develop a team's attack while giving the defenders a small goal to make their play more realistic. The addition of the small goal forces defenders to think of attack when they win the ball and forces the attackers to remember their defensive responsibilities when their team loses the ball. Coaches could place restrictions on the players to accomplish other tactical objectives. Since the attacking players of a team will generally be more proficient dribblers, one way to take away this advantage in Attack versus Defense is to limit the number of consecutive touches they are allowed.

PHYSICAL FITNESS GAMES

Keep away (Diagram 4.25)

Objective: Endurance and proper support of the player with the ball.

Equipment: One ball per group.

Description: Players are confined to a 10-yd square. The game can be played with two versus one, three versus one, or three versus two. The players with the ball are always given numerical superiority, while the other player or players try to win the ball. To win the ball, a player must touch it or force one of his opponents to pass it out of bounds. Whenever

Diagram 4.25 Keep Away.

a player wins the ball, he exchanges places with the man who last touched it.

Comments: A variation would be to make the player trying to win the ball gain complete control of it before he exchanges places. All the players could rotate and take turns being in possession of the ball and trying to win it.

Piggy-back soccer (Diagram 4.26)

Objective: Strong leg muscles.

Equipment: One ball and four traffic cones per game.

Description: The teams consist of six to eight players each. The players are paired on each team, and half of them carry their teammates on their

Diagram 4.26 Piggy-back Soccer.

backs. The playing area is 40 by 20 yd and has two cones set 5 ft apart at either end marking the goals. A goal is scored when a player pushes the ball between the cones he is attacking. The offside rule is not applied, and the men being carried may not interfere in the play in any way.

Comments: The players should exchange positions with their partners every minute or so to provide all players with a proper rest period.

One versus one (Diagram 4.27)

Objective: Endurance and individual tactical development.

Equipment: Two balls per game.

Description: There are no boundary lines, and one ball is placed on the ground to represent the goal. One player has the other ball and attacks

Diagram 4.27 One versus One.

while the other defends. A goal is scored each time a player passes the ball in play into the stationary ball.

Comments: Players should be paired according to comparable abilities in this game. The players should be given a rest period after each minute of play. The rest need not be totally passive, however, and could consist of some activity such as individual juggling.

Two versus two (Diagram 4.28)

Objective: Endurance and small-group tactical development.

Equipment: Three balls per game.

Description: Eight players are grouped into pairs. Two players position themselves 25 yd apart and stand facing each other with their legs spread about 2 ft apart, representing the two goals. A goal is scored when the ball is passed between the legs of these players. Two more players, each holding a soccer ball, take up a position behind the players representing the goals. To enable continuous play, as soon as a goal is scored or a shot goes wide of the goal, the player standing behind the goal with another ball rolls it into play to the team that was defending. He then retrieves the ball that went astray and takes up his position again. The two remaining pairs of players play a game, each pair attacking one goal and defending the other. There are no offside rules in the games. Each game is 1 minute in duration.

Diagram 4.28 Two versus Two.

Comments: At the end of 1 minute the two pairs that were playing change positions with the other two pairs, and the new field players play for one minute while the other players have a rest. This game should not be continued when the players become fatigued or when their technique begins to deteriorate noticeably.

All attack

Objective: Endurance and small-group tactical development.

Equipment: One ball and two portable goals per game.

Description: The two teams consist of four to six players in the field and one goalkeeper each. The playing field is half a regular field. Whenever a team goes on attack, all its players must be in its attacking half of the field before it can shoot at the goal. There is no offside rule.

Comments: The game is very demanding because it requires constant running from defense into attack and back by all the players on a team. It is important to stop the game if at any point the players begin to show that their technique is deteriorating significantly because of fatigue.

REFERENCES

Allison, Malcolm. *Soccer for Thinkers.* Pelham Books, London, 1967.
Csanadi, Arpad. *Soccer.* Corvina, Budapest, 1965.

Jones, Ken, and Pat Welton. *Football Skills and Tactics.* Marshall Cavendish, London, 1973.

Lammich, Gunter, and Heinz Kadow. *Games for Football Training.* Thomas Nelson and Sons, London, 1974.

Wade, Alan. *The FA Guide to Training and Coaching.* William Heinemann, London, 1967.

Winterbottom, Walter. *Soccer Coaching.* William Heinemann, London, 1952.

———. *Training for Soccer.* William Heinemann, London, 1960.

5

Restarts

SINCE SOCCER involves constant action, players cannot always anticipate where their opponents will be. As a result they cannot use set plays as do American football players. There are, however, many occasions when play is stopped in a soccer game, after which the ball must be put back into play. At these points in a game set plays may be used since defensive players will stay relatively stationary until play resumes. These plays can be collectively termed *restarts* since they are used to recommence action.

As modern teams are learning to play better defensive soccer, often stacking their defenses against stronger teams, attacking teams are finding themselves relying more and more heavily on restart plays. As many as 40 percent of the goals scored in today's soccer come directly from restart situations. Many crucial matches during which a team had very few good scoring opportunities have nevertheless been won as a result of a corner kick, a throw-in, or a free kick. In top-class, international matches the percentage of goals coming from restarts is often even higher than 40 percent.

The reason restart situations produce so many goals is simple. There is no other time in a soccer match when an attacking player can serve the ball to a teammate without feeling a great deal of pressure. Except during a throw-in restart, no defender will be closer than 10 yd to the player serving the ball. Obviously, the lack of pressure increases the accuracy of the attacker's service and results in better scoring opportunities. In addition, during the restart plays attackers can place as many men as they wish in preplanned attacking positions. These players can create many problems for the defense since some will go on runs to receive the ball and others on dummy runs to create space for teammates and distract defenders. Therefore the probability of scoring a goal increases in such situations.

By making it extremely difficult for opposing players to anticipate the attackers' actions, players gain a tremendous advantage in attack. A defender who can anticipate his opponents' moves has only to worry about where the ball is. He is not upset by an attacker's move if he was expecting it. The more relaxed a player is, the less prone he is to make mistakes, and every attacking team wants to force the defense to make as many mistakes as possible. If a defender is confused by the movements of the attackers, he now has to worry not only about the ball but also about the movement of the players without it. The defender is never quite sure whether the player without the ball is moving to draw him away from a position where some other attacker can receive a pass or if the player himself is moving somewhere to receive a pass.

When developing and teaching restarts, a coach should keep several factors in mind. After a set play has been established, the team must practice it often so that everyone knows exactly what to do and when to do it. Every run and pass must be executed properly for the play to work. Each pass must be exact; otherwise the team will not be able to carry out the next part of the play. The runs must be made at precise times, for a premature run can give the play away, and a tardy run will make the pass go astray.

Too many coaches overlook the importance of restarts and do not devote enough time to practicing them during training sessions. If a coach expects 40 percent of his goals from restart situations, then the training sessions should reflect this and an appropriate amount of time should be devoted to restarts.

The most important thing to remember when working on restarts is not to develop a team of automatons without initiative. In all set plays the players must learn to adapt and improvise in case the play breaks down. Every play should have variations based on expected defense reactions. However, players cannot memorize all playing situations, and they must be able to adapt themselves to every situation.

Do not use over-complex restart plays. These plays will confuse not only the defenders but also the players attempting to execute them. Also recognize the skill limitations of your team and select only those restart plays that your players can execute well.

Finally, accept the fact that your play may not work right away in a game situation even though it goes smoothly in practice. Do not discard it! Find out what caused it to collapse, correct that problem, and you will probably succeed.

KICK-OFF

The first restart situation comes with the opening kick-off. During a kick-off the positioning of defensive players is generally more predictable than at any other time during the game. Most teams generally position their players the same way for all kick-offs.

Attacking from the Kick-off

Because players can anticipate where all their opponents will probably be, a set play is generally easy to devise. However, since all 11 opposing players are situated between the ball and the goal, the probability that a

Diagram 5.1 Kick-off restart.

set play will culminate in a goal is relatively low. Nevertheless, a set play at kick-off that produces deep penetration into the defensive area of the opposition can be an important attacking tool.

A very popular method of kicking off is to pass the ball back after the initial kick-off to give the forwards time to advance into open spaces in the other team's defense. As the forwards move into their attacking end of the field, some of them will go on dummy runs to draw defenders away from the intended area of attack and generally to try to confuse the opposition. If the dummy runs are successful and the rest of the play is properly executed, a chance may very well develop for an immediate attack on goal.

In Diagram 5.1 No. 9 kicks off to No. 10 who passes the ball back to No. 6. On the kick-off No. 11 and No. 7 sprint down the touchline and then cut diagonally towards open space in the middle of the field. No. 9 and No. 8 sprint diagonally towards the touchline and then head for the corners. No. 10 moves into open space just beyond the center circle to provide depth. After receiving the ball, No. 6 waits a second to give the forwards a little more time to get down field and then makes a long pass to whichever one of them is open. He may predetermine where the pass is to go, but he must be able to improvise if the man he chose to receive the pass is covered.

This play may be initiated from the right side by using No. 4, as well as from the left. Regardless of which side is used to start the play, usually the man ending up as the winger on the far side from the ball (in Diagram 5.1 it is No. 8), is going strictly on a dummy run. His job is to draw the fullback on his side towards the touchline, creating more space for the wing moving away from it.

No matter what defensive alignment the opposition uses, all your forwards must end up breaking for open space between the defenders. Once one of the forwards gets the pass from the halfback, the others break directly for open space near the goal, and the man with the ball should send a through pass to one of his teammates. If this play is executed properly, a team could be making a shot on goal within seconds of the start of play.

In Diagram 5.2 No. 9 kicks off to No. 8 or No. 10. No. 7 and No. 11 sprint down the touchline. The second pass goes to either wing, depending on which one is in the clear. No. 9 and the inside without the ball criss-cross and break towards the goal to supporting positions. Whichever wing gets the ball should control it and send a long pass over the last defender towards the far goal post or a short through pass to the supporting striker so that a shot on goal can be taken right away. The pass to the wing is naturally a long lob pass, and the pass from the wing is either a brisk pass on the ground or another long lob pass, this time over the last line of defense.

In the plays illustrated in Diagrams 5.1, 5.2, and 5.3, speed and pass accuracy are essential. Players must diligently practice timing the passes so that they can make immediate attacks on goal. Also, the forwards without the ball must time their runs so that they do not end up in an offside position, which would ruin the play.

Diagram 5.2 Kick-off restart.

In the play illustrated in Diagram 5.3 the half-back again starts the action. No. 9 passes to No. 8 or No. 10 who then passes back to No. 5. This play can use any of the halfbacks, preferably the one with the best long-passing accuracy. Once the ball is in play, both wingers, No. 9, and the inside without the ball sprint towards the penalty area, as indicated in the diagram. The halfback makes a long pass to the player in the least congested area. After the long pass from the halfback a shot on goal is taken either at once or after one or two short passes among the forwards.

Diagram 5.3 Kick-off restart.

Diagram 5.4 illustrates a kick-off play with shorter passes. No. 4 starts to sprint forward, and as he gets to midfield, the ball is kicked off to No. 10. The second pass goes to No. 4 who should take the ball in stride and continue towards goal. On the kick-off No. 7 runs toward the corner, No. 11 goes diagonally towards the goal, No. 8 and No. 9 break straight ahead, and No. 10, after making his pass, moves to provide depth.

No. 4 has several options on where to send the third pass, depending on how the defenders have reacted so far. If the ball goes to No. 7, the next pass could be a brisk pass across the front of the goal. If the ball goes

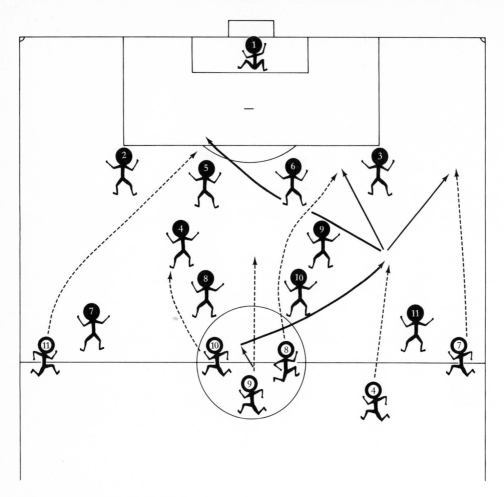

Diagram 5.4 Kick-off restart.

either to No. 8 or to No. 11, a shot on goal could be taken right away.

A team may also attack on the kick-off if the attacking forwards use a series of short passes to get past the defensive forwards. The attack then continues according to the game plan, that is, by capitalizing on the defensive team's weakest area.

Long pass kick-offs like those illustrated in Diagrams 5.1 through 5.4 will generally be more effective than short passes mainly because the long pass immediately achieves deep penetration into the defense. It also carries with it greater surprise than the short pass kick-off since usually after three or four passes a team can take a shot on goal.

Defending at the Kick-off

The defending team on a kick-off has a great numerical advantage in having all 11 players between the ball and the goal. Thus they should not have too great a problem preventing a goal immediately after the kick-off. The defenders must simply remember to adhere to the principles of defense. In addition, it would be wise for them to try to arrange themselves so that they can eliminate the most dangerous attacking space. They should mark opposing forwards tightly as they go on their runs and put immediate pressure on the men playing the ball after the kick-off.

GOAL KICK

Goal kicks are restarts that can also utilize set plays. Usually goalkeepers take goal kicks, so they should practice various types, and take pride in kicking them as well as the field players. However, if a team's goalkeeper is unable to take goal kicks, then a fullback should be used for them.

Initiating Attack from Goal Kicks

Assume that the goalkeeper is the one to take the goal kicks. There are basically two types of goal kicks: the *short*, shown in Diagram 5.5, and the *long*. When the goalkeeper takes the short goal kick, he may throw the ball, punt it, or drop-kick it. When he takes a long goal kick, he does so from inside the 6-yd box, and the ball does not return to him.

Diagram 5.5 illustrates the way in which the goalkeeper takes the short goal kick in order to get the ball back. Remember that the ball must go outside the penalty area before the kick is deemed to have been taken properly.

If the fullbacks line up for every goal kick, as shown in Diagram 5.5, then the goalkeeper has as many as four options for a short goal kick and takes whichever one seems most suitable at the time. The easiest is from the goalkeeper to the near fullback, in this case No. 2, because the ball has to cover a minimum distance. The second choice is to No. 4, or whichever back is unmarked with no opposing player near him. These plays are made possible by the law of soccer that states: "Players of the

Diagram 5.5 Short goal kick restart.

team opposing that of the player taking the goal kick shall remain outside the penalty area until the ball goes over the penalty area line after the kick is taken." If it were not for this rule, an opposing player could rush in to cover the goalkeeper as soon as he took the goal kick, thus preventing a return pass.

Even though this law prohibits attackers from entering the penalty area too early, the goalkeeper should always come to meet the return pass made to him. This will further diminish the chances of its being intercepted.

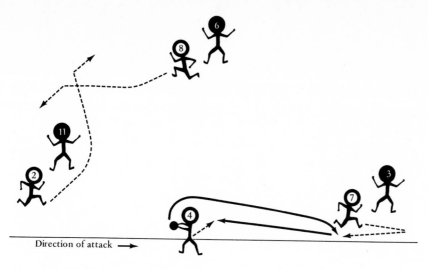

Direction of attack ➝

Diagram 5.6 Throw-in restart.

Most goalkeepers will prefer a short goal kick to a long one. The main reason for this is that a goalkeeper has greater accuracy in passing the ball up the field when the ball does not have to remain stationary in the 6-yd box. Once the goalkeeper receives the ball again after passing it to one of his fullbacks, he may initiate the attack, as shown in Diagram 5.5.

Kicking or throwing the ball out to either wing is usually the best play since the wing's position is usually in the least congested area. Although a winger will be marked closely by opposing players, he can start on a run in almost any direction and then quickly cut back to the touchline to gain a few steps on the man marking him. If the goalkeeper and the wings practice synchronizing their timing, one of the wings should usually be in the clear to receive the goalkeeper's pass.

The goalkeeper may also pass the ball to either of the inside forwards, although the center of the field is usually so congested on the goal kick that they would not have much time to control the ball before a defender challenged them. Also any ball thrown by the goalkeeper into a congested area must be extremely accurate.

In the event that both wings are for some reason unable to receive a pass, then instead of placing the ball in the middle of the field, the goalkeeper should simply give it to one of his backs who can initiate the attack himself. The first back to pass to would be the nearest center fullback, as shown in Diagram 5.6, since he will be the farthest upfield.

When deciding which player should receive the pass, remember that the most important objective is to get the deepest penetration into the opposition's defense with a minimum number of passes.

Even though defenders are not permitted in the penalty area during a goal kick, sometimes they can position themselves so that they can easily intercept the return pass from the fullback to the goalkeeper. In this case, when the back sees the defender move into the penalty area, he should simply avoid the return pass and either proceed with the ball up the field or pass it to a teammate other than the goalkeeper. Again, this simply points out the need for every player to be able to improvise at any given moment in the match.

When all the fullbacks utilized in the short goal kick are marked by defenders, the goalkeeper should then simply make a long goal kick from inside the 6-yd box. Here again the best pass will be to either wing, with a pass to any other forward being the second choice. Once again the objective is to make the deepest possible penetration into the defense on the first pass and to minimize the probability of losing possession of the ball.

When a goalkeeper cannot take the long goal kicks, a fullback will usually take his place. The goalkeeper should in this event place the ball down inside the 6-yd box. The backs not taking the kick should position themselves as they normally do for a short goal kick.

If a short goal kick is possible, the goalkeeper makes it immediately after placing the ball down. If the short one cannot be used, then the fullback takes the long goal kick.

Defending at Goal-kicks

When defending against the goal kick, the immediate objective is to intercept the initial pass. Therefore the defending forwards should mark closely the backs of the team taking the goal kick. This will eliminate the possibility of a short goal kick and thus increase the chances of intercepting the ball. Long goal kicks are, of course, less accurate passes and thus the defending team has increased the chances of gaining possession of the ball.

THROW-IN

Every throw-in provides an opportunity to start a direct attack on goal. In the offensive end of the field, a well-planned throw-in will often result in an immediate shot on goal. There are times when a quick throw-in, even without a set play, may catch the defenders so unprepared that the attacking team can immediately shoot on goal. However, all teams should establish set throw-in plays, for they cannot hope to catch the opposition unprepared very often.

Attacking from Throw-in

One very effective and frequently used play on a throw-in is to return the ball immediately to the thrower. For the most part the man taking the throw is left unmarked by the opposing team so that he is free to receive a return pass. As a rule, his teammates should be no closer to him than about 15 yd. As shown in Diagram 5.6, this will leave him sufficient space to work the ball when it is returned to him.

To provide the man receiving the throw with time to control the ball or make an unharassed pass, he and his teammates should use a variety of individual feints and interchange positions frequently. These movements will help confuse the defenders and allow the attackers, if only briefly, to free themselves of the men marking them.

If the attackers are not to return the ball to the man taking the throw-in, then he should throw it forward whenever possible. Every time the ball passes a defender towards his goal, he is put out of the game for all practical purposes until he can again position himself between the ball and the goal. For this reason attackers should try to put the ball forward whenever possible. By playing the ball back towards his own goal, a player is generally putting some defender back into the game and thus helping the other side.

As in all restart plays, the use of dummy runs on throw-ins should increase the probability of a set play's success. These runs will create more open spaces where the thrower can place the ball. Dummy runs are used in all of the illustrated throw-in plays that follow. Both No. 8 and No. 2 in Diagram 5.6 go on dummy runs, starting out towards No. 4 and then moving away from him. If a throw cannot be made to No. 7, No. 4 may throw the ball to either No. 8 or No. 2 since one or both of them should lose the men marking them. No. 7 starts a run away from No. 4, then quickly reverses direction to receive the ball. Upon receiving the ball, No. 7 first-times it back to No. 4. With all the players at least 10 or 15 yd away from him, No. 4 should have time to control the ball and make a good pass to start the attack downfield.

The dummy runs in this play are designed to make the defenders think that the men are moving to receive the throw. One or both of them could

Diagram 5.7 Throw-in restart.

even call for the ball as they approach No. 4. As they turn away from the thrower, they draw their markers with them and then attempt to lose them by interchanging positions.

One of the easiest and most successful ways for a player to clear himself for a pass, as shown by the movements of No. 7, is to move away from the ball and then quickly return towards it. Since the defender tries to position himself between the attacker and the goal, when the attacker moves back towards the ball he catches the defender unprepared, and usually finds himself free long enough to play the ball without a great deal of pressure.

An effective variation of the play illustrated in Diagram 5.6 is to have player No. 7 reverse his run. Instead of drawing the defender away from the ball and then returning himself to receive it, No. 7 will make a run towards the ball, calling for it to draw his defender with him. Then after a quick feint, No. 7 would reverse direction and sprint down the touchline away from the man with the ball. No. 4 would then lead No. 7 with the throw if the defender was beaten. Again, either No. 2 or No. 8 can receive the ball if No. 7's defender was not taken out of the play.

In Diagram 5.7, No. 8 and No. 7 go on dummy runs to create ample space for No. 4 to receive the return pass. No. 2 makes a quick feint in

152   *Restarts*

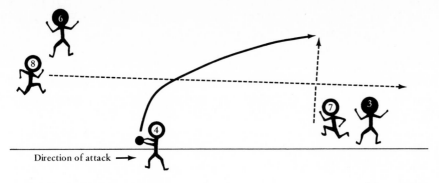

Diagram 5.8 Throw-in restart.

any direction to clear himself briefly for the throw. Upon receiving the throw, he immediately returns the ball to No. 4. The second pass is a lead pass, and No. 4 takes the ball in stride, thus proceeding with the attack.

The play in Diagram 5.8 does not involve a return pass to the thrower. Here No. 8 calls for the ball and runs almost parallel to the touchline, taking his marker with him. At the same time No. 7 runs towards the center of the field and receives the throw. The interchanging of positions between No. 8 and No. 7 will enable No. 7 to lose the man marking him long enough to play the ball without harassment.

Perfect timing is required here as always when players attempt to interchange positions effectively. Proper timing and frequent practice are necessary for the play to succeed.

Any variety of feints and dummy runs may be used in throw-in plays. The ones shown in the previous plays are merely suggestions. As long as the feint or dummy run is effective, it does not matter whether it was very simple or very complex. The simpler a play is, however, the more frequently it will succeed, for there is less chance that a simple play will be poorly executed.

One often very effective throw-in play is to have one player pick up the ball as if to throw it in. Another player will come up to him and ask to throw the ball instead. As the first player walks out onto the field of play, the second player throws the ball against his back. The ball returns to the thrower off his teammate's back and play proceeds from there.

This type of play is very simple, needs no practice to speak of, and yet can be very effective. The defenders are not usually prepared for play to resume in this way, since they are waiting for the first attacker to get out of the way of the new thrower. This example emphasizes a major element of restarts, surprise. Any time a team can initiate play unexpectedly, it will gain some advantage.

In all throw-in plays, coaches must stress accuracy of the throw. When the man receiving the throw has to make a first-time pass, the ball should be thrown either directly to his feet or to his head if he is to make a head pass. A poor throw jeopardizes the play's success.

If the throw-in occurs deep in a player's own defensive area, many times the wisest throw will be to the goalkeeper. The goalkeeper simply moves towards the thrower, calls for the ball, and the throw is made so that he can catch it. He is now in a position to get deep penetration with a long throw, punt, or drop-kick, very much as he would on a short goal kick or any save.

When the throw-in takes place near the opponent's goal, the play should always produce an immediate attack on goal. Well-rehearsed throw-in plays in this area of the field will result in shots on goal that ordinarily may not have come about.

Since the laws of soccer permit players to be in an offside position and still receive the ball on a throw-in, a team may use the play illustrated in Diagram 5.9 when a throw-in occurs near the opponent's goal.

No. 7 makes a feinting move towards the goal and then returns to receive the throw-in from No. 4. The throw, regardless of whether it is to the head or the feet, is first-timed to No. 8 who is running in from outside the penalty area. The ball is shot by No. 8 in stride, and the result could very well be a needed goal.

Before the shot, No. 8 and No. 9 interchange positions in an attempt to free themselves of the defenders marking them. No. 9, while on a dummy run, should call for the ball as he approaches No. 4, adding to the defenders' confusion. Again, in this play as in all restarts, timing and good passes are essential for success.

The right fullback could be used instead of No. 8 to take the shot in this play. Most teams do not pay a great deal of attention to attacking teams' backs. As a result an unmarked fullback could come through from behind.

Some teams have players who can throw the ball great distances. If so, the man throwing the ball has the strength and technique to turn a throw-in, deep in the attacking area, into a play similar to a corner kick. These players who can throw a ball literally into the goal mouth from the touchline add an entirely new dimension to a team's attack. In this case a team can effectively use special throw-in plays similar to corner kicks.

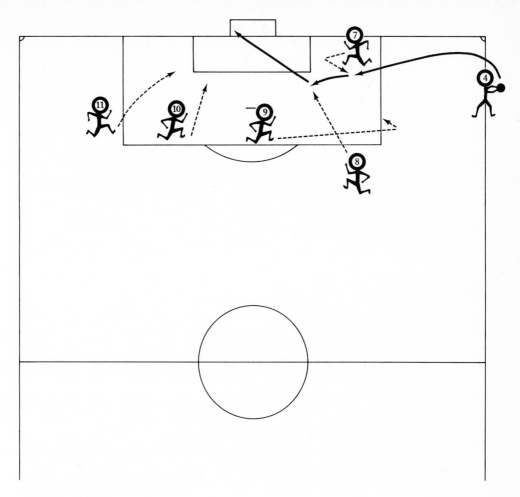

Diagram 5.9 Throw-in restart.

Another very good way to produce a scoring opportunity from a throw-in near the opponent's goal is to use a play involving a head flick. The play in Diagram 5.10 illustrates such a play. No. 4 throws the ball hard and head high to No. 7 who runs to meet it. No. 7 simply flicks the ball back over his head, preferably towards the far post of the goal. No. 11 and No. 10 time their runs so that they will be able to head on goal the flick from No. 7. No. 11 will make his run towards the far post, where we hope the ball will end up, and No. 10 runs towards the center of the goal in case the flick-header ends up short of the preferred spot.

Diagram 5.10 Throw-in restart.

The play illustrated in Diagram 5.10 is very effective because as No. 7 makes his run towards the ball, he draws at least one defender with him out of the area where we hope the ball will go. Also the flow of the defense on a throw-in in this area will be towards the ball, leaving some space by the far post of the goal.

Defending During Throw-ins

The most important thing to remember when defending against a throw-in is to tightly mark the attacking team's players. By also marking the man throwing the ball, a team can readily eliminate any return passes and thus make restarting play more difficult for the opposition.

When defending against a throw-in near the goal, it is even more vital to mark the opponents tightly and track down attacking players coming into the penalty area. The defenders' mental concentration is vital; there must be no break in concentration between the time the ball goes out of bounds and the time it is thrown in by the opponents. Many teams have been punished by having goals scored against them for being unprepared for a restart due to a breakdown caused by a lack of concentration.

CORNER KICK

The corner kick is a tremendous scoring opportunity for the attacking team and a very dangerous situation for the defenders. Many goals have been scored from corner kick situations. As a result, attacking teams should utilize well-rehearsed set plays to reap the maximum benefits of this restart situation, and all teams must diligently practice defending against corner kicks to minimize the chance of the opposition's scoring.

Defending Against Corner Kicks

When defending against a corner kick, teams will generally either adhere to strict man-to-man marking or maintain a zone defense where each defender is responsible for a given space near the goal and in the other parts of the penalty area. Diagram 5.11 illustrates the positioning of defenders when they are utilizing a zone defense during a corner kick.

Positioning players in a zone defense is very important during a corner kick. One player, No. 11 in Diagram 5.11 should be about 10 yd from the ball. His responsibility is twofold. First of all, he is there to distract the player taking the corner kick and perhaps even block the kick as it is taken. His other responsibility is to discourage the opposition from attempting a short corner kick. His presence alone may accomplish this since he can quickly mark any opponent who runs to the corner to receive a short pass.

In the event that the opponents do try a short corner kick, another defender must come to the area to help. A team must always try to maintain a numerical balance of defenders and attackers, preferably with one more defender than there are attackers.

No. 11's position for a long corner will depend on whether it is to be an outswinger or an inswinger. For an inswinger No. 11 will position

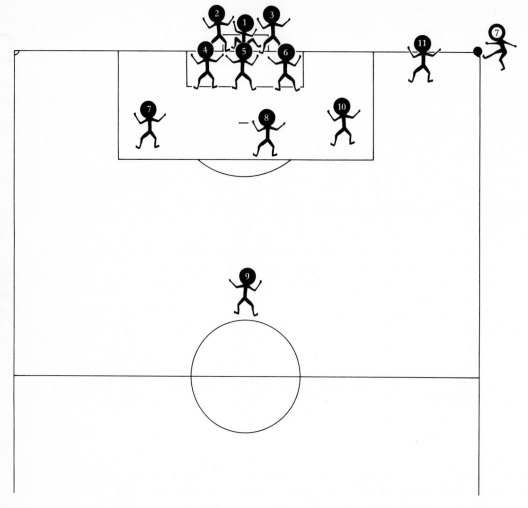

Diagram 5.11 Positioning of defenders utilizing a zone defense for a corner kick.

himself about 3 or 4 yd into the field of play from the goal line. For an outswinger he will place himself right on the goal line. The purpose of this is to attempt to stand in the path of the kicked ball. The approach that the kicker takes will cue the defender as to whether the kick will be an inswinger or an outswinger.

The goalkeeper should position himself somewhere around the center of the goal. Many goalkeepers align themselves at the far post from where the corner kick is being taken. However, the area directly in front

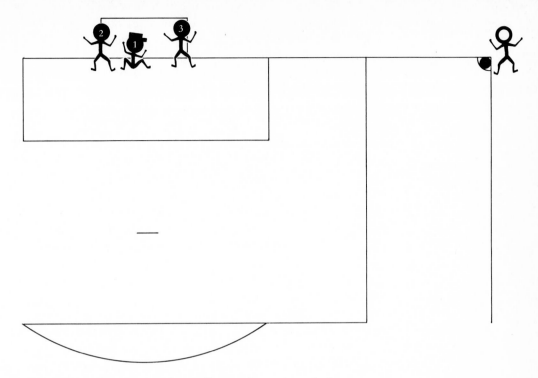

Diagram 5.12 Positioning of a goalkeeper for a corner kick.

of the goal will get very crowded, and if the goalkeeper is at the far post, he may have a difficult time getting through traffic to collect a ball hit to the near post. By being in the middle of the goal, the goalkeeper will generally be in a better position to come out and collect balls in the air. He should face more towards the field of play than the corner. The reason for this is the same as during regular play. A player will rarely attempt a shot from near the goal line and to the side of the goal where his angle is very poor and his chances of scoring are practically nonexistent. The ball will generally be brought back out in front of the goal, and there a shot will develop. Therefore the goalkeeper should face more in the direction from which the shot will be coming or at least where the ball is more likely to be played. The proper position of the goalkeeper is shown in Diagram 5.12.

One player should position himself near the goal post closest to the corner where the kick will be taken, and another player should be near the far goal post. The player by the near post should be closer to the goal post than his teammate at the other end of the goal since he will have less time to react to a hard-driven inswinger to the near post. Both of these players must step in front of the goal to defend against any shots in the event that the goalkeeper must leave the goal while trying to collect a cross from the corner. Many goals have been saved by backs clearing the ball from in front of their own goals while their goalkeepers were out of the net.

At least three other defenders must position themselves within the 6-yd box near the 6-yd line, as shown in Diagram 5.11. They should be good headers and must be capable of challenging for the ball in the air and winning it.

Three more defenders should position themselves about 12 yd out from goal to protect the remainder of the penalty area and pick up any attackers who come into it on a run during the corner kick. All of the players must of course be aware of the area that they are in and also mark attackers who come into their assigned area as the ball is put into play.

Diagram 5.13 illustrates a corner where the defenders have decided on strict man-to-man marking. Here it is imperative that each player mark his man tightly and position himself on the goal side of the attacker. Two defenders must still be assigned the area near the two goal posts to protect the goal in the same manner as when a team uses a zone defense. It is also still wise to position one player 10 yd in front of the ball.

Attack Alignment for Corner Kicks

Attacking players usually use one of two methods of aligning themselves for a corner kick: Either they position their players inside and around the penalty area, as in Diagram 5.13, or they use an echelon formation, as in Diagram 5.14.

When players position themselves in a nonechelon formation for a corner kick, they must take up positions depending on the type of kick to be used and must also plan for the possibility of the ball going somewhat astray. Dummy runs are usually effective, especially if the defense is marking man-to-man. Players will clear out the area where they hope the kicker will place the ball, and other attackers will go on a run to meet it and finish with a shot on goal. In Diagram 5.13 attacker No. 8 runs away from the goal just before the kick to create space for his teammates in the area where the ball will be served.

The echelon formation of attackers during corner kicks is especially effective if the defenders are marking man-to-man. By lining up just

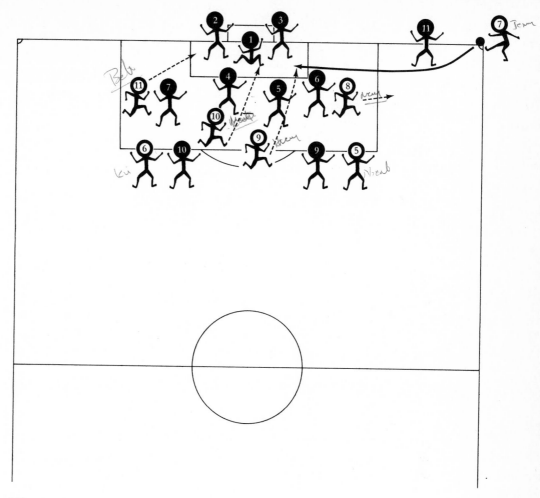

Diagram 5.13 Positioning of attacking players for a corner kick.

inside the penalty area, as in Diagram 5.14, the defenders will be drawn out from the area directly in front of the goal. As the kick is taken, the attackers go on designated runs to free themselves briefly of the men marking them and arrive near the ball in time to shoot on goal. The runs must be designed so that there are players running to the near post, far post, and other spaces near the goal where the ball may be hit. The players obviously cannot expect the ball to be served perfectly to where they want it, and thus they must take this into consideration when running.

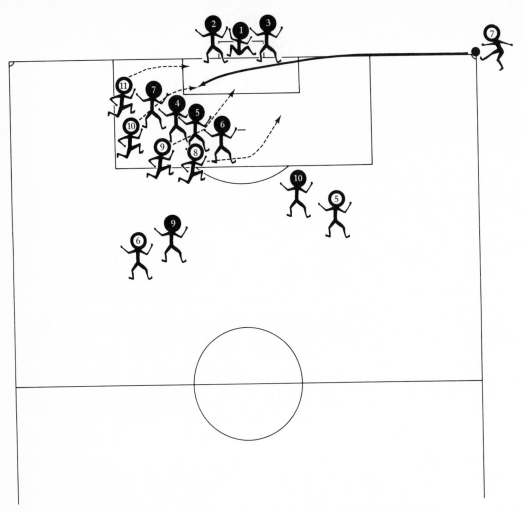

Diagram 5.14 Positioning of attacking players in echelon formation for a corner kick.

Some teams use an attacking forward to obstruct the view of the goalkeeper and impede his progress in getting to the ball on a corner kick. For example, if a team is using the echelon attack on a corner, only three forwards would align themselves in echelon formation; the fourth would stand in front of the goalkeeper. This impedes somewhat the goalkeeper's ability to see the ball, and creates another obstacle for him when he tries to come out of the goal to make a save.

The forward who positions himself in front of the goalkeeper must be careful and aware of two important factors. First of all, he cannot simply obstruct the goalkeeper once the ball has been kicked since that is deemed illegal obstruction. However, he may move away slowly enough to make it difficult for the goalkeeper to get around him. Second, he must make sure that he is not in an offside position when one of his teammates takes a shot on goal: A goal scored may be taken away if the referee makes an offside call.

If a team wants to place a forward in front of the goalkeeper, it should use one of the taller men, so that the goalkeeper will have a more difficult time seeing over him. An experienced goalkeeper will not be bothered to any great extent by this tactic, but it can be used successfully if he is relatively inexperienced or a weak netminder.

Diagram 5.15 illustrates another means of blocking the goalkeeper on a corner kick. The ball is crossed head high from the corner, No. 8, No. 9, and No. 10 rush in to head the ball while No. 11 goes on a run to block the goalkeeper from coming out of the net to make a save. In this play it is important that No. 11 be moving while he attempts to block the goalkeeper, otherwise he may be called for illegal obstruction.

Long Corner Kicks

The man taking the corner kick may choose to serve a long or short corner. Both types of corners can be very effective and can create tremendous scoring possibilities.

If a player decides on serving a long corner kick, he has three additional options. He may hit an inswinger, an outswinger, or a hard-driven straight ball across the front of the goal.

The inswinger, as shown in Diagrams 5.13 and 5.15, bends towards the goal because the ball was kicked so that it will spin in that direction. This type of serve will converge players in front of the goal, and even if the attackers do not take a good shot right away, it is very difficult for the defenders to clear the ball from among the congested players.

The inswinger should be served to the near post, about 4 to 6 yd out. This will be an area from which a goal could be scored, but still a little far out for the goalkeeper to easily make a save. If the attacker who gets to the ball finds that it is head high and his chances of scoring seem poor, he should simply flick the ball on with his head towards the far post. On the kick most of the players will have converged near the front of the

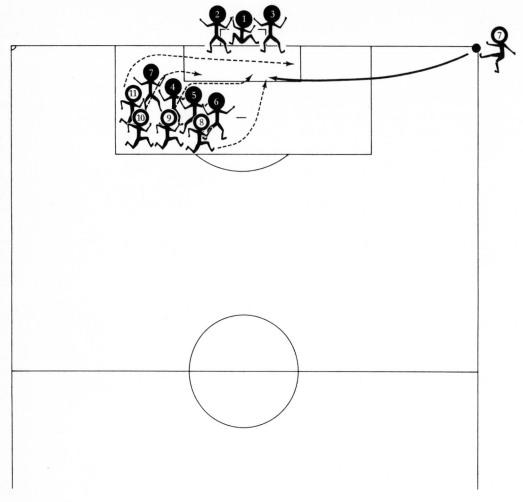

Diagram 5.15 Attacking run to block out the goalkeeper during a corner kick.

goal, and a flick-header to the far post could find an attacker with a reasonably easy chance for a goal.

Another major advantage for an inswinger from a corner kick is that the players shooting the ball on goal would be hitting it with the spin. An inswinging ball spins towards the goal, and it is far easier to keep a ball down when hitting it with the spin. Low shots on goal have a better chance of going into it because they are harder for the goalkeeper to save.

The outswinger, as shown in Diagram 5.14, drifts away from the goal mouth because the ball is kicked with a spin away from the goal. This type of ball is easier for the attacking players to shoot hard since it is served towards rather than away from them. However, it is more difficult to keep a ball low when hitting it against the spin so that the attacker must take more care when attempting a shot.

Since an outswinger drifts away from goal, it is possible that it may catch a less experienced goalkeeper out of position. He might come out to attempt a save and if the ball curves sharply away from goal, he may find himself out of the net as his opponents take a shot. Another advantage of the outswinger corner kick is that it is harder for defenders to clear out of the penalty area. Since the ball's flight is away from the goal, it will be harder for a defender to head it any considerable distance away from goal. Therefore a defender's head clearance of such a corner kick could still drop in the penalty area and allow the attackers a shot on goal.

Another very effective way for the player taking the corner kick to serve the ball is to drive it hard across the goal mouth. The ball should be served head high or lower and not more than about 6 yd out from the goal line. The advantage of such a kick is that it can be easily deflected into the goal by a forward, and because of its velocity, it does not have to be shot with any power. It is also a very difficult ball for defenders to clear since it is moving very quickly and can be easily misplayed. Therefore even if an attacker does not get to the ball first, it is probable that the ball will not be cleared out of danger right away by the defenders, and an attacker may still get a shot on goal.

A hard-driven ball head high can also be very effective from a corner if it is flick-headed to the far post of the goal. If an attacking player goes on a run to meet the ball in front of the near post, he will usually draw defenders with him, leaving space near the far post. A flick-header could well become an assist for a teammate's goal.

Short Corner Kicks

Many times a short corner kick will be more effective in breaking down a defense than the long corner kick just discussed. It may be used regardless of how the attackers align themselves for the corner kick, and it is most effective if the attackers use it quickly and catch the defense unprepared.

One of the primary objectives of a short corner kick is to gain numerical advantage in attack. That is, the attackers want to establish a

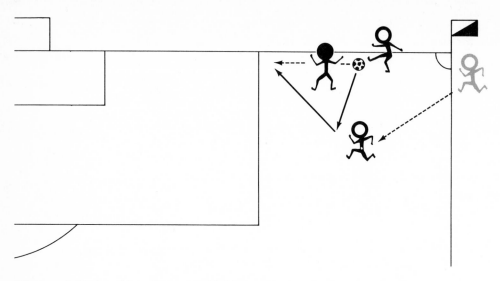

Diagram 5.16 Attacking players establishing a two-versus-one situation after a short corner kick.

two-against-one or three-against-two situation in the corner area, as shown in Diagram 5.16. This will enable them to get the ball more easily into a very dangerous position nearer the goal from which they can shoot and score.

Diagram 5.17 shows one way attackers can get effective penetration after gaining a numerical advantage from a short corner kick. No. 7 passes short to No. 4. If the defensive team has only one man defending in the corner, in this case No. 6 who ran there when he saw that the short corner kick was on, then they have achieved a numerical advantage. At this point No. 7 immediately comes onto the field of play to support No. 4. Number 4 can either feint a pass to No. 7 and then dribble down the goal line or interpass with No. 7 to get past the defender and then penetrate down the goal line. Once the defender No. 6 is beaten, the other defenders will often be drawn towards the ball and may expose space in front of the goal. No. 4 would hit a crisp pass into this open space for one of his teammates to run into and finish with a shot on goal.

If the defensive team is not very alert, an attacking team may initiate a short corner kick without harassment. As a team gets set for a corner kick, one of the fullbacks can run up from behind to receive the ball. It is usually easier to initiate a short corner kick with a player from the

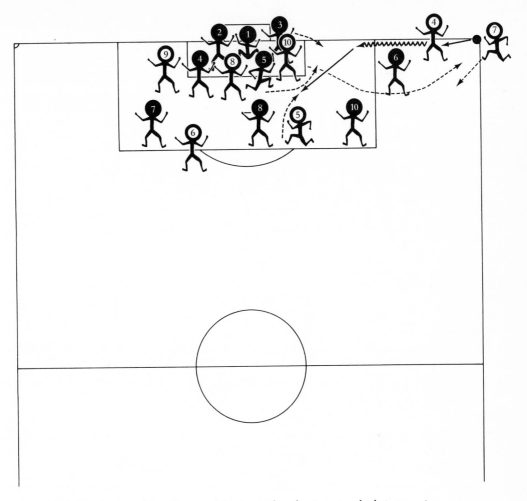

Diagram 5.17 One of the primary objectives of a short corner kick is to gain numerical advantage in attack.

defensive area, running up to receive the ball, for the forwards will generally be marked tightly and the backs will not. However, several set plays can be devised for short corner kicks with front-running players.

A short corner play in which a midfield player receives the initial pass is illustrated in Diagram 5.18. No. 11 starts on a run towards No. 7, and as he approaches the corner, he calls for the ball. As No. 11 calls for the ball, No. 4 starts on a run, feints to free himself of the man marking him,

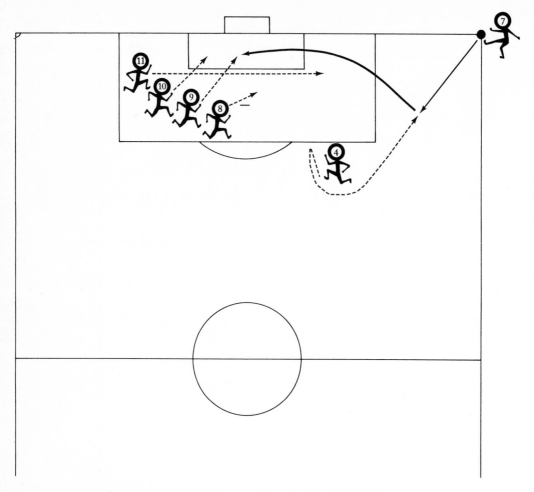

Diagram 5.18 A short corner kick utilizing a quick cross after the initial pass can find the defenders out of position and can be very effective.

and receives the ball from No. 7. As No. 7 passes the ball to No. 4, the other attacking forwards start their runs towards the goal. No. 4 hits the ball first-time and crosses it for his teammates to shoot on goal.

A variation of this play is shown in Diagram 5.19. This time No. 11 and No. 4 start their runs simultaneously. No. 4 runs towards the goal, doubles back, and then runs towards the goal again looking for a pass from No. 11. No. 11 runs across the penalty area, receives the ball from

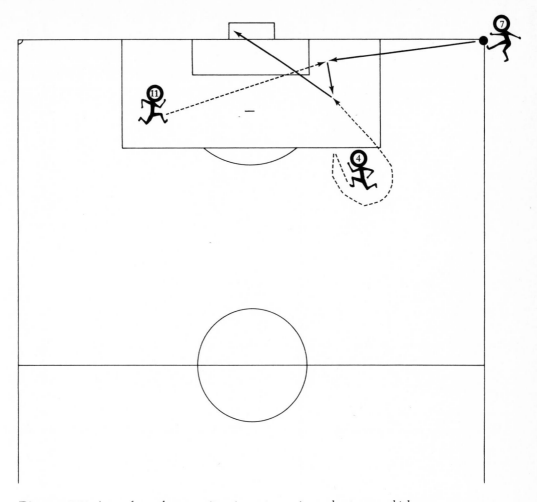

Diagram 5.19 A run from the opposite winger to receive a short corner kick can produce a quick shot on goal.

No. 7, and makes a quick pass to No. 4 who shoots on goal as soon as he gets the ball.

This play may be further altered if No. 4 receives a pass directly from No. 7. A team might do this if No. 11 were too closely marked and not really in a position to receive a short corner kick.

Diagram 5.20 shows yet another way to utilize the opposite wing on the short corner kick. The attacking No. 8, No. 9, and No. 10 align

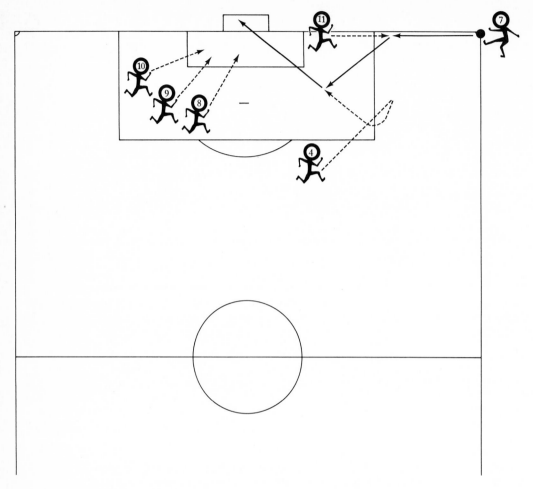

Diagram 5.20 The short corner kick can produce shots on goal from a close range.

themselves in echelon formation. No. 11 comes across to the side of the goal where the corner is being taken and positions himself on the goal line just in front of the near goal post. As No. 7 prepares to take the kick, No. 4 runs towards the corner and calls for the ball. No. 7 plays the ball along the goal line to No. 11. No. 11 passes the ball to No. 4 who has freed himself of his marker by suddenly doubling back and then breaking for the goal.

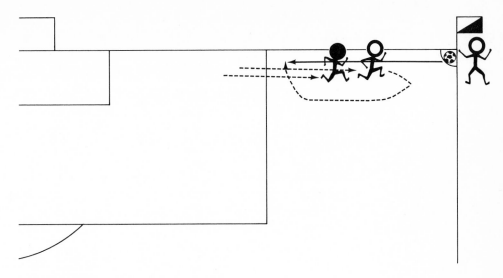

Diagram 5.21 Short corner kick restart.

Generally, No. 4 should shoot the ball immediately after getting the pass from No. 11. The other attacking forwards close in on the goal after the shot, hoping to pick up a rebounding ball.

A variation of the play shown in Diagram 5.20 is for the player who receives the initial pass from the corner kick, No. 11 in Diagram 5.20, to turn with the ball on the goal line instead of passing it. He would then dribble it towards the goal, attempting to draw defenders in his direction, and then pass it to a teammate for a shot. If the man receiving the initial pass is closely marked, he could let the ball go past him as he turns into the field of play. The defender will usually react to this by staying with the attacker, and the attacker could quickly turn around the man marking him to play the ball, as shown in Diagram 5.21.

In the preceeding short corner plays, the opposite wing and the near halfback receive the initial pass, but they need not be the only attackers in the play. The plays illustrated in Diagrams 5.18 through 5.20 could just as easily have used an inside forward in place of the wing and midfielder. A team might even have a fullback receive the initial pass from the corner. This could be even more unexpected by the opposing players, and the attacking back can probably initiate his runs without an opponent marking him.

All the corner kicks, especially the short ones, require a great deal of practice of the set plays. Timing and accurate passes are a must for the plays to work well. Also, a coach can make simplifications and other adjustments to the plays to suit the skill level of a particular group of players.

FREE KICK

Whenever a free kick is awarded a team they should take it as quickly as possible to catch the defensive team lagging and unprepared. A team will generally benefit most from this tactic when the free kick is awarded the team at a spot from which a shot on goal is not likely to be taken. Whenever the kick is awarded close to the goal so that a shot could beat the goalkeeper, the defense is usually alert enough to set up a defensive wall. The formation of this wall, probably more than any other thing, dictates to the attacking side to have well-rehearsed set plays, to get the ball past the defensive wall and into the goal.

Defending Against the Free Kick

From the defensive standpoint, when the opposition is awarded a free kick outside the penalty area, and a shot on goal is not likely, one defender should always align himself 10 yd from the ball and in a direct line between it and his own goal. Even though the opponent taking the kick will not be shooting on goal, the defender can harass the kicker simply by being near the ball. If the ball is played short, the defender is in position to pressure it quickly, and if the attackers wish to play the ball long, they must pass to one side of the defender or play over him with a chip pass. All of this simply puts more pressure on the man taking the free kick and can cause his service to be poorer than if he were completely relaxed.

Whenever the attacking side is in a position to score a goal directly from the free kick, the defenders must form a defensive wall, lining up next to each other and 10 yd from the ball. Diagram 5.22 shows the proper positioning of a defensive wall. It should be aligned so that one player, No. 2 in the diagram, is directly between the ball and the goal post nearest it. The rest of the players in the wall line up next to this man, sealing off part of the goal.

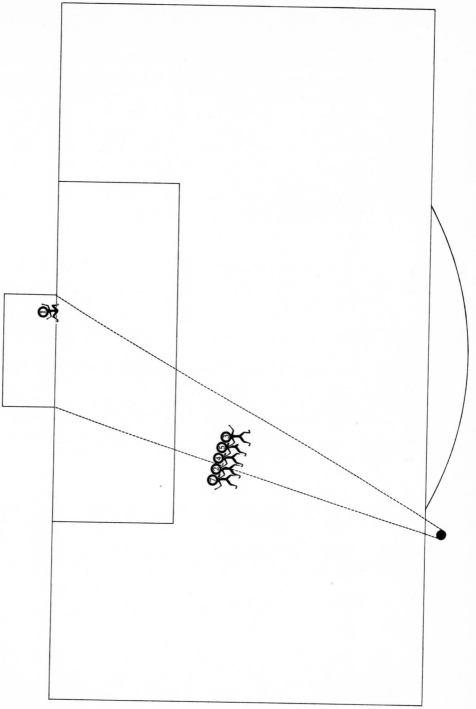

Diagram 5.22 Free kicks near the goal generally require the formation of a defensive wall.

If the opponents have a player who is especially adept at bending a still ball, it may be wise for the defenders to place one more player to the side of the wall so that he can seal off additional space and overlap the wall past the near goal post. This would most probably prevent the attacker from bending a ball around the wall and into the goal at the near post.

The proper number of players for the defensive wall depends on the position of the ball and its relationship to the goal. As the ball moves towards the touchlines and the shooting angle becomes more acute, fewer players will be needed in the wall. If the ball is to the side of the penalty area, then the number of players needed in the wall becomes even less since the angle of a shot on goal is even worse.

Generally, five men would be the maximum for a defensive wall. The only exception to this would be if an indirect kick were awarded 10 yd or less in front of the goal mouth. In such a case it is best to bring all players onto the goal line and form a wall of 11 players directly in the goal mouth. They will attempt to block off as much of the goal area as possible.

By putting more than five men in the defensive wall, the defensive team leaves itself with very few, and usually not enough, field players to mark all of the attacking players who come to support the kick. Even when only five players are in the wall, the team is left with only five more field players to mark the attackers. This may be very risky since some attackers could now position themselves in support of the kick and be left unmarked. After all, the defenders have only five field players outside the wall, while the attackers could bring as many as nine players up the field to support the man taking the kick. These would certainly be unfavorable odds for the defense. Also, the best defenders should stay out of the wall. Anyone can act as part of a wall, so why waste a team's best headers or tacklers in it?

The goalkeeper should always stay to the side of the wall, as shown in Diagram 5.22. He should not be behind it, where he cannot see the ball. He does have to be careful, however, not to move too far to the side or he will leave himself too vulnerable for a chip shot over the wall to the corner farthest from him.

Attacking from Free Kicks

Whenever a free kick is awarded to a team from a position on the field where an attacker could shoot on goal and score, we must assume that the defenders will establish a wall to prevent a clear shot at the goal. If the attackers notice that the defensive wall is improperly set up for some reason, it may very well be best to shoot directly at the goal. Also, if a player feels that he could score with a chip shot over the wall into the side of the goal farthest from the goalkeeper or a bending ball around the outside of the wall, then it is a chance worth taking.

Any time the defense of the opposition has made a mistake, the attackers should try to capitalize on it. However, a team must assume that the defenders will perform their duties properly, and devise methods of beating the wall and the goalkeeper to score goals.

When establishing set plays for free kicks, it is a good policy to include one or more feints before actually embarking on the play. The defense will usually tense up just before a free kick. This is the time to feint, while the defenders are keyed up and expecting the kick. Using feints in free kick plays will keep the defense guessing as to when the attackers will really shoot or pass, and thus may make them unprepared when the play does begin.

The play illustrated in Diagram 5.23 is one way an attacking team may circumvent a defensive wall. No. 8 approaches the ball as if he is going to shoot at the goal, but instead of shooting he steps over the ball. As the defense relaxes momentarily, realizing that the ball was not kicked, No. 4 makes a brisk pass to No. 10 who comes to meet the ball. No. 10 first-times the ball behind the defensive wall to No. 7, who immediately shoots it. No. 9, for the attacking side, is positioned at the side of the wall to prevent the defenders from intercepting his teammates' passes. This is a relatively simple play, yet if executed properly, it can be most effective. It is important to note again that very often the simplest restart plays are the most effective.

The play in Diagram 5.24 begins in the same way as that in Diagram 5.23 in that No. 8 fakes a shot before No. 4 makes his pass to the side of the defensive wall. In this case, however, the pass from No. 4 goes to No. 7. When the pass is made to No. 7, No. 11 and No. 10 move towards No. 4 in an effort to draw their markers with them and create more space for No. 6 to run through. No. 7, as soon as he receives the initial pass, crosses the ball to No. 6, who takes it in stride and immediately shoots at the goal. If No. 6 is closely marked, he will have to do a little preliminary feinting to clear himself of his defender so that he may go on his run unharassed. Also, an attacking fullback from the left side could be used in place of No. 6. The pass from No. 7 should be shot immediately at the goal or if it is high enough, headed.

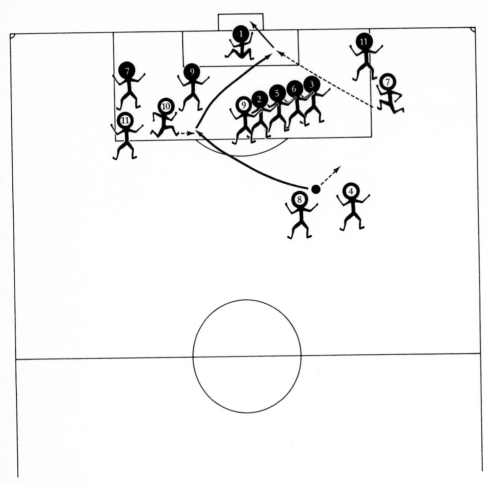

Diagram 5.23 The defensive wall may be beaten by passing the ball around it.

In diagram 5.25 No. 8 uses a false kick and No. 4 starts the play. No. 6, after giving his marker a good feint, runs towards the ball as No. 10 runs out of the penalty area. The runs are timed so that the paths of the two men cross and No. 6 can clear himself if his initial feint is not completely effective. No. 9 lines up at the end of the defensive wall to prevent the last defender in the wall from intercepting the pass to No. 4. The moment No. 10 and No. 6 cross paths, No. 4 makes a crisp lead pass to No. 6 who shoots the ball as soon as he reaches it.

A chip pass to No. 10's head is used to beat the defensive wall in the play illustrated in Diagram 5.26. The feinting before the kick is the same

Diagram 5.24 Quickly changing the flow of the play from one side to the other on a free kick can often get the attackers a clear shot at the goal.

as in the previous few plays, but the play is equally effective without it if the offensive team feels that the defenders are expecting No. 8 to fake a kick. None of the free kick plays need to use an initial feint if the defense seems to be expecting it. Also, more than one player could fake a kick. Sometimes it might prove profitable to use two fake kicks before making the initial pass.

In this play, No. 10 must clear himself of his marker first, then turn quickly and run towards the goal. The chip pass from No. 4 should then be headed to the far corner of the goal, away from the goalkeeper. No. 9

Diagram 5.25 Attackers can sometimes free themselves of the men marking them by going on criss-crossing runs.

and No. 7 run towards the goal in case the play breaks down, and a loose ball in front of the net can be converted into a goal. Supporting attacking players should always use this type of follow-up. Many players score goals by picking up these loose balls in front of the net.

In Diagram 5.26, as in any restart play with a run involving possible offside positioning, it is of utmost importance that the kick be taken before the man who has started on his run crosses the imaginary offside line made by the last defensive field player. Again, timing and frequent practice of restarts for game play is important.

Diagram 5.26 Chipping the ball over the wall can sometimes get the attackers a clear shot at the goal.

An attacking team gains a great advantage if it can initiate a restart with unprepared defenders. In direct and indirect kick restarts, this can sometimes be done by distracting the defenders just before taking the kick.

Several fake kicks are used in the previous plays. Another way to distract the defenders is for the man who is to initiate the play to stand by or over the ball and direct his teammates into their preplanned positions. Then, without stepping back, he can merely make a crisp pass, or he could have a teammate pass the ball from between his legs as shown in

Diagram 5.27 Free kick restart.

Diagram 5.27. Since this may be done while the man over the ball is still shouting instructions to his teammates, the defenders may be relaxed and not ready for the play.

Another method that has sometimes been successful, even in world-class competition, is for the player who is about to kick the ball to bend over the ball and turn it with his hands as if he is dissatisfied with its position. As he is doing this, and while most of the defenders are watching him, a player from the back starts on a run. While still in a bent position, the man over the ball passes it to the teammate making the run, who shoots it immediately, as in Diagram 5.28.

Diagram 5.28 A player running in from behind the ball may often find it easier to receive a ball during a free kick than a front-running player.

It is much easier for a player such as a fullback coming from the back to take advantage of open space in the other team's defense than it is for one of the attacking forwards. The forwards are always closely marked while the player from the back may be able to come through completely unmarked.

When an indirect free kick is awarded to a team in the opponent's penalty area, all the preceeding free kick plays are applicable. However, when the kick is 10 yd or closer to the goal line, the defense, instead of forming a wall of four men, will probably form a line of as many defenders as possible in the goal mouth, on the goal line. In a situation like this attackers may use a set play, but most of the time it would be wiser for one man just to softly push the ball to a teammate who will then shoot directly on goal in the hope that he can get it past one of the defenders. Even if the ball does not go into the goal on the shot, it will be very difficult for the defenders to clear and will probably rebound off one of them so that the attacking side can shoot again.

It cannot be stressed enough that all restarts must be practiced diligently and often before being put to use in a game. All the runs and passes must be timed as close to perfection as possible. And perhaps most important, the players must be able to improvise and adapt if the play breaks down!

REFERENCES

Allison, Malcolm. *Soccer for Thinkers.* Pelham Books, London, 1967.

Csanadi, Arpad. *Soccer.* Corvina, Budapest, 1965.

Hughes, Charles F.C. *Tactics and Teamwork.* E.P. Publishing, Wakefield, England, 1973.

Joy, Bernard. *Soccer Tactics.* Phoenix House, London, 1962.
Wade, Alan. *The FA Guide to Training and Coaching.* William Heinemann, London, 1967.

Winterbottom, Walter. *Soccer Coaching.* William Heinemann, London, 1952.

————. *Training for Soccer.* William Heinemann, London, 1960.

6

Fitness

During a 90-min professional match players may need to cover a distance of as much as 6 to 8 miles. They will cover about 25 percent of this distance at a run, and the rest at a slower pace, a jog or a walk. The distance a particular player covers during a match is influenced greatly by his specific function on a particular team, for some positions require more running than others. However, regardless of differences in position or function, there is no question that fitness is vital for all soccer players.

To play to his fullest ability, a player must be prepared both mentally and physically to give his best effort throughout the match. This is as true of the professionals, playing for 90 min, as it is of the schoolboy playing shorter matches. To be able to perform like this, a player must develop his fitness through intensive training.

A fit player can delay the onset of fatigue during a match and will therefore perform better. The more tired a player is, the more prone he is to making errors, and a player who makes a lot of errors will often shake his confidence, which all players need to perform well. Fitness will aid them in the proper execution of various techniques as well as in running.

Physical fitness for soccer can be divided into three areas: *endurance, speed,* and *strength*. In this chapter we will discuss these three areas, how they affect a player's performance, and how a coach can develop them in his players. We will generally be referring to male adult players, but the principles discussed can be applied to all levels by coaches after making adaptations to suit their own particular situations.

It is important to adhere to certain overall conditioning principles, but whenever possible coaches should utilize exercises designed specifically for soccer. The conditioning exercises for a soccer player should not be the same as those for a basketball player or boxer. All sports make unique physical demands on their participants and the players' conditioning programs should reflect these differences.

In many cases, coaches can do little about circumstances that affect a team's training program. This is true especially at the nonprofessional level. The number of players a coach has to deal with, the amount of time available for training, and the equipment and facilities he has to work with are factors influencing all forms of training. A coach must adapt principles and methods to fit his situation, unfavorable as it may be.

One other important fact that coaches must consider when they approach training is that a team is composed of unique individuals, and each player has his own desires, needs, and psychological make-up. Therefore even though there are some things that *all* players must do in training, coaches must make every effort to gear their training to individuals rather than to an anonymous group. Some players will need more fitness training than others since age, size, and general physiological make-up differ from one player to another. In addition, the mental attitude of all players is not the same, and if a coach wishes to obtain the maximum effort from every player, he cannot overlook an individual's personality.

Contrary to some peoples' belief, soccer teams are not armies and cannot be treated the way a drill sergeant handles his platoon. Of course, a coach will have to remember that some players are lazier than others; a player may say he does not need any more work which is not always necessarily true. A good coach will know all his players as individuals and set up training programs that will give each player the maximum benefit.

WARM-UPS

Before going into the specific methods a coach can use to develop fitness in his team, it is necessary to mention the role of warming up before such exercises. Muscles require oxygen for contraction, and they need increased amounts of it as activity becomes more vigorous. More economical and faster respiration as well as increased circulation will move more oxygen to the muscles.

Warming up before strenuous activity is beneficial because the warm-up exercises will increase circulation and the metabolic process. They will gradually ease the body into strenuous activity, and by providing increased amounts of oxygen and blood to the muscles, they will reduce injuries like muscle sprains and ruptures that come from sudden and unexpected movements.

Young schoolboys, and even some advanced players who are very eager to play, often go out on the field and start shooting at the goal right away or attempt to kick with power without any warm-up. This is very foolhardy and can often result in muscle injury.

Types of Warm-ups

There are two types of warm-up exercises. The general warm-up exercises simply loosen and prepare the entire body for activity. The more specific exercises ease certain muscles into exact types of movement they will make. For example, both distance runners and soccer players will do general body warm-ups, but their specific warm-ups will differ greatly since soccer players need to make quick direction changes and the distance runner works with a steady rhythmic running style.

Specific warm-ups are geared to individual players as well as to specific sports. After players go through some general warm-up exercises, they should work individually or in pairs for their specific warm-ups. The goalkeepers, being real specialists, will obviously require different exercises than the rest of the field players. In addition, individuals on the team lead different lives away from the practice or game field. Some are physically very active while others are involved in more sedentary activities during the day. The player who has been active all day long will therefore not need the same amount of warming up as the player whose muscles have not been under stress. Age is also a factor. A coach must familiarize himself with every member of the team and then treat each one individually when it comes to specific warm-ups.

Conditions that Influence Warm-ups

The conditions that influence warm-ups may often change. *Weather, time of day,* and *travel* are three very important factors to consider when planning warm-up exercises. Muscles will warm up much more quickly in warm weather than in cold, damp weather. Players tend to feel much stiffer in the morning than in the afternoon and evening, and will take a longer time to limber their muscles. Finally, when players have to travel by bus or plane to a game, they tire enroute and may need a longer warm-up period than they do when playing at home.

The warm-up exercises should not fatigue a player. Generally the warm-ups should not last longer than 10 or 15 min, although specific conditions may require them to be a bit more lengthy. They should be used to prepare a player's body for his job, and should not precede activity by more than a few minutes. Warm-ups followed by a lengthy interval before the action serve no purpose and are wasted.

Rubdowns

Players may often start general warm-up exercises in the dressing rooms before a match, which will cut down on the time they need to prepare once they take the field. In addition, massages and chemical rubdowns can be given to players before they go out on the playing field. Massage makes the muscles relax and the blood vessels expand, allowing a greater blood supply to the muscles. The chemicals used in the rubdowns warm the body and are especially helpful on cold days. However, massages and rubdowns do not replace warming up with body movements and physical exercises.

Soccer players should warm up and develop their fitness through many exercises. In addition, a coach can use various types of warm-up training games, as described in Chapter 4, to make training sessions more enjoyable.

GENERAL WARM-UP EXERCISES

The team can perform the general warm-up exercises collectively. For stationary exercises it is best to arrange the players in a semicircle or in several lines so that the coach can observe them easily and make his instructions clearly heard. For exercises that require walking or running, it is best to divide the team into pairs or groups of three and form two or three columns. Pairing players is especially useful since in pairs they can encourage each other to perform well.

The warm-up exercises should be the first part of a training session and should usually last no more than about 5 min. Also they should be progressively more demanding, starting out with light activity that will ease the players' bodies gradually into the more strenuous exercises.

The following is a list of some exercises a coach can use for general warm-up purposes:

Stationary exercises

1. Push-ups.

2. Sit-ups.

3. Trunk twisting.

4. Alternate toe touching.

5. With legs spread wide apart, lean sideways in one direction as far as possible and then in the other, especially stretching the groin muscles.

6. Jump in place, lifting the knees as high as possible.

7. Lying on the back lift the legs, fully extended, 6 in. off the ground and hold them in that position.

Exercises with a soccer ball

1. With feet together, jump forward and backward over the ball.

2. Same as exercise 1, but jump from side to side over the ball.

3. With feet together, jump up and down while bouncing the ball with both hands.

4. Same as exercise 3, but after three bounces bounce the ball between the legs, make a 180° turn, and continue the exercise.

5. Lift the right and left feet alternately over the ball while bouncing it.

6. Stand with legs spread, throw the ball up behind the back from between the legs, turn and catch or trap it before it hits the ground.

7. While sitting on the ground with the legs extended, roll the ball behind the back and around the legs.

8. Lying on the ground with the arms and legs extended, hold the ball between the feet, lift the ball with the feet and place it into the hands, then return the ball to the feet after placing the feet back on the ground.

9. While standing, throw the ball into the air, then sit down, get back up, and catch the ball or trap it before it hits the ground.

10. Same as exercise 9, but do a forward roll instead of sitting down.

11. Holding the ball between the heels, jump up and throw it over the shoulder.

Walking exercises

1. Walk on the toes.

2. Walk on the heels.

3. Walk while holding the ankles with the hands.

4. Walk with the arms extended to the side and do arm circles.

5. Walk on all fours.

6. Do scissor kicks while walking.

7. Kick the left hand with the right foot and the right hand with the left foot alternately while walking. Hold hands shoulder high.

8. Walk and lift the knees as high as possible.

9. Walk while lifting the knees high and do cross-over steps.

10. Same as exercise 9, but instead of cross-over steps, step to the side.

Jogging exercises

1. Hold the hands waist high in front and lift the thighs to the hands while jogging.

2. Hold the hands down by the sides and lift the heels to the hands while jogging.

3. Same as exercise 2 but hold the hands in back.

4. Jump up and head while jogging.

5. Turn sideways and proceed in a shuffle step.

6. Jump up while jogging, make a 180° turn in the air, and after landing continue to jog in the opposite direction.

7. Jump up while jogging, make a 360° turn.

8. Hop on one leg.

9. Hop with legs together.

10. While jogging jump up and do a split in the air.

11. While jogging in columns of two or three, the last men in the lines sprint to the front.

12. Same as exercise 11 but weave between the players to get to the front.

13. While jogging, turn 180° and sprint in the opposite direction.

Partner exercises

1. Partners face each other and shadow box.

2. Standing back-to-back with arms locked, one partner bends forward and lifts the other on his back.

3. One man holds the ball in his hands while the other tries to pull it away from him.

4. With two balls placed on the ground next to each other, the partners get into push-up positions with their hands on the ball and face each other. Each man tries to knock away his partner's ball without falling off his own.

5. Both men hop on one foot and charge each other with legal shoulder charges in an attempt to knock each other off balance.

6. One man is the attacker and the other is the defender. The defender jockeys the attacker and tries to prevent him from getting by as they run from the goal line to midfield.

SPECIAL SOCCER WARM-UP EXERCISES

Special warm-up exercises for soccer involve performing the techniques necessary to master the game. These exercises should precede the actual training session since they will enable the muscles to ease gradually into the exact type of action they will perform vigorously later. In addition, these exercises give individual players the opportunity to practice technique and concentrate on their weakest areas.

It should be noted that players must never perform any technique exercises in a lackadaisical manner. Since they will be using the same techniques in a match, they should take pride in executing them to the best of their ability whenever possible. If a player cannot perform technical exercises to the best of his ability, he is usually better off not doing them at all. Sloppy practice can lead to sloppy technique during match play.

Goalkeepers, the greatest specialists in soccer, should do completely different warm-ups from the field players. Many of the goalkeepers' special warm-up exercises in this chapter can also be used as exercises to practice goalkeeping techniques. It is especially important to take each player's individuality into account when performing special warm-ups.

Warm-ups for field players

1. At a leisure pace, dribble a ball the width of the field and back.

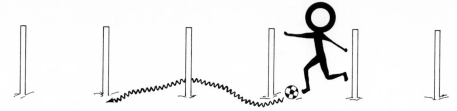

Diagram 6.1 Slalom dribbling exercise.

2. Same as exercise 1, but add occasional bursts of speed and push the ball ahead about 5 yd, sprinting to catch it.

3. Ball juggling.

    a. Simply juggle the ball with the feet, thighs, body, and head.

    b. Juggle while moving the width of the field.

    c. Juggle with a limit on touches. (*Example:* three with feet, four with the head, three with the thighs, and back to the feet.)

    d. Juggle a specific number of times, send the ball up into the air, control it before it hits the ground, and continue to juggle.

    e. Juggle in pairs or small groups with a limit on the touches.

    f. Same as exercise (e) but restrict it to all heads. The players may add additional restrictions such as being seated on the ground or standing but joining hands.

    g. Three players stand in a straight line about 5 yd apart. No. 1 heads to No. 2, No. 2 flick heads the ball to No. 3, and No. 3 heads it over No. 2 back to No. 1.

4. Two or three players interpass the ball. Use two-touch passing at first and then go to one-touch passing.

5. Same as exercise 4 but players move about as they pass the ball.

6. One player runs around the other, remaining about 5 yd away, while the two pass the ball back and forth.

7. Slalom dribble as illustrated in Diagram 6.1.

8. Dribble in a confined area. (*Example:* Fifteen players dribble around

in the center circle of the field, constantly maintaining possession of the ball while looking for space and avoiding the other players.)

9. One man jogs while the other man follows, dribbling a ball. The leader should change directions frequently and abruptly.

10. Have players pair up and practice the techniques they are weakest at.

Warm-ups for goalkeepers

1. Throw the ball against a wall to practice catching. Vary the throws so that some will come off the wall high, some low, and some to the side.

2. Same as exercise 1 but have a partner throw the ball at the wall from behind the goalkeeper who will catch it so that the one catching will not know when or how the ball will come at him.

3. Have two goalkeepers throwing the ball at each other, varying the type of throw.

4. With the goalkeeper on the goal line, another player kicks balls at him from 6 to 10 yd out. The kicks should vary and make the goalkeeper reach down for some and up for others. He should not dive in the very beginning, and the speed of the ball should progress with the exercise.

5. Same as exercise 4 but the goalkeeper kneels on the goal line.

6. Same as exercise 4 but the goalkeeper sits on the goal line.

7. The goalkeeper places a ball to his side, just barely close enough to reach by diving. He then practices diving for the ball.

8. The goalkeeper lies face down on the goal line with his arms fully extended, touching the inside of one of the goalposts. On a command the goalkeeper gets up while another player serves a ball to the other goal post, and the keeper dives to make the save.

9. The goalkeeper positions himself in the middle of the goal. Two additional players alternate serving balls high and low to the sides of the keeper. As soon as the goalkeeper catches one service and throws the ball back, the other player serves the ball. The players should serve the balls so that the goalkeeper will have to keep moving from one side of the goal to the other.

10. The goalkeeper positions himself in the middle of the goal but facing

Diagram 6.2 Pendulum heading.

the back. On the command *"turn"* he turns to face the field while another player serves high and low balls to either side of him and the keeper dives to make the saves.

11. The goalkeeper positions himself 12 yd out from the goal line. Another player serves high lobbing balls over his head, which he tries to catch, punch clear, or tip over the bar.

12. Two goalkeepers practice long and short throws to each other.

13. Two goalkeepers practice kicking dead balls, half-volleys, and punts to each other.

USING THE PENDULUM BALL FOR WARM-UPS

The pendulum ball is one of the most useful pieces of equipment a team can possess. Players can practice many necessary soccer techniques with it and can also use it for special warm-up exercises that incorporate game techniques. The pendulum ball is especially helpful in developing heading techniques and timing. (See Diagram 6.2.)

Individuals can use the pendulum ball to do repetitions of various techniques to perfect them for match play as well as use them for warm-up exercises. A coach can devise many exercises for the pendulum ball involving more than one player such as the following exercises.

Pendulum ball exercises with partners

1. One man stands still while the other jumps over him to do repetitive heading.

2. One man moves in a circle around the pendulum ball while the other keeps heading the ball towards his partner.

3. Same as exercise 2 but volley the ball instead of heading.

4. One man heads the ball and the other stops it with his head when it returns.

5. Same as exercise 4 but volley the ball instead of heading.

6. Two players try simultaneously to see who can get the most jump-headers. This is a good way to develop timing and learn to get up for head balls in a crowd.

7. Similar to exercise 6 but a goalkeeper substitutes for a field player and tries to punch the pendulum ball while the field player tries to jump up and head it.

8. Goalkeepers can practice punching the ball using most of the same exercises that the field players use for heading.

Remember to vary the warm-up exercises, whether they are general, special, or pendulum exercises, to provide variety. Training is difficult enough without the coach's making it boring and monotonous because of his lack of effort and imagination.

ENDURANCE

A player who has trained and developed the quality of physical endurance can delay the onset of fatigue, sustain intense activity for a prolonged period of time, and recover rapidly. In soccer it is vital that the players have endurance, for it is useless to dominate a match in the beginning because of superior skill only to lose it eventually because the players become exhausted and can no longer perform well.

It was the tremendous endurance of players like Mario Zagalo of Brazil and Alfredo Di Stefano of Real Madrid that allowed them to offer so much to their teams. Zagalo's amazing stamina allowed him to play nearly as much in attack as in midfield. He performed almost a dual role during the 1962 World Cup when he was the left midfielder in Brazil's 4–3–3 system. It was not unusual to see Di Stefano playing a defensive role in his own penalty area one moment and scoring a goal for Real at the other end of the field the next.

A lack of endurance results in fatigue, which diminishes several elements of good performance such as timing, coordination, reaction time, general alertness, and concentration. Since increased endurance delays the onset of fatigue, it therefore must improve overall performance during the match.

When training soccer teams, coaches should concentrate on two types of endurance. The first is general, or *cardiovascular*, endurance, which enables a player to sustain activity in many of his large muscles, and thus withstand the intensity of a full match. The second is *local* endurance, necessary for a single muscle or localized group of muscles to repeat or sustain contraction. A lack of this type of endurance is noticeable in players who do not yet appear fatigued but begin to suffer from cramps.

General Endurance

The movement of the large muscles of the body is extremely important, for these muscles receive the greatest demands during the game. For the muscles to function, they must receive fuel, that is, the oxygen brought to them through the circulatory system.

Before going any further on the topic of endurance, it is necessary to understand a little about muscles and how they function. Also since muscles need a constant supply of oxygen, coaches have to have some understanding of the respiratory and circulatory systems.

The body has three types of muscle tissue. The one that concerns soccer players most is the *skeletal*, or *voluntary*, muscle. This muscle is responsible for limb movements and body support. It is called "voluntary" because a person's will can directly control it. Another name for this muscle is *striated* which derives from the fact that when viewed under a microscope it has a striped appearance.

The other two types of muscle tissue are the *cardiac* muscle in the heart and the *smooth* muscle in the blood vessels, the digestive tract, and certain other organs. Under normal circumstances a person's will does not control these two kinds of muscle fiber.

Muscle fibers have nerves that control their action. Muscular contraction occurs when nerve impulses originating in the central nervous

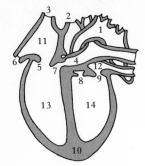

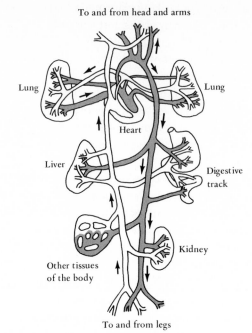

1. Aorta
2. Pulmonary vein
3. Superior vena cava
4. Pulmonary artery
5. Tricuspid valve
6. Inferior vena cava
7. Pulmonary valve
8. Aorta valve
9. Mitral valve
10. Apex
11. Right atrium
12. Left atrium
13. Right ventricle
14. Left ventricle

Diagram 6.3 The heart and circulatory system.

system, reach the nerves in the muscle fibers. When the impulses cease, the muscle fibers relax.

A muscle can contract because it is supplied with oxygen for the process of oxidation. Oxidation in turn produces energy, as well as such waste products as carbon dioxide. As long as enough oxygen is available, muscular work can go on. The relative ability to supply oxygen while a muscle contracts is called *aerobic capacity*. It refers to the maximum oxygen consumption and is considered the most reliable measurement of endurance a person possesses.

Oxygen is transported to the muscles by the blood. The heart serves as the pump that circulates the blood throughout the vascular system. It is composed of cardiac muscles that contract and relax rhythmically, and has four chambers, the right and left *atrium* above and the right and left *ventricle* below (see Diagram 6.3).

The left atrium receives freshly oxygenated blood from the lungs. The blood is then transferred to the left ventricle and pumped through the body. The blood supplies the cells with fresh oxygen and takes away waste products such as carbon dioxide. The deoxygenated blood returns to the heart by way of the right atrium and is then pumped back to the lungs by the right ventricle. The oxygen and carbon dioxide are then exchanged between the lungs and minute blood vessels, and the process repeats itself.

When muscles contract more frequently than usual due to vigorous activity, the demand for oxygen increases. Therefore during vigorous activity the heart must pump faster to supply more blood with more oxygen; consequently, a person's breathing becomes more rapid.

The cardiac *output,* or volume of blood pumped by the heart in one minute, is approximately 5000 milliliters (ml) when a person is at rest. Vigorous activity can cause this volume to become five times greater than it is at the resting level. The heart rate can increase from about 70 beats/min to around 180 beats/min, and the amount of blood pumped by the heart with every beat can increase from approximately 70 ml to around 140 ml.

The aerobic capacity of a player, or the maximum amount of oxygen he can take in every minute and use for oxidation, can be increased through fitness training. Since aerobic capacity is a measurement of a person's endurance, it is obviously vitally important to a soccer player.

Note that an individual's genetic make-up plays an important role in his performance capacity. Some people are born with the ability to run faster or jump higher. However, a player can make a definite improvement in his physical performance through proper training.

Local Endurance

When a single muscle or a localized group of muscles need to repeat or sustain contraction, they may require a greater source of energy than can be supplied through the aerobic process. The breakdown of glycogen to lactic acid can make this energy available. This is called the *anaerobic process*, and is sometimes referred to as *working under oxygen debt*.

The lactic acid produced during the anaerobic process is a fatigue toxin. Therefore, once the muscle can no longer tolerate the level of lactic acid present, it will slow down or stop working. It may then be unable to respond properly to the stimulus of the nerve, meaning that the muscle will contract insufficiently for the task at hand, or go into a spasm and produce cramps.

Once the work has stopped, the oxygen consumption that was increased during the muscle contractions will remain high to change the lactic acid back to glycogen. This is the period when the oxygen debt is repaid.

During segments of a soccer game, players may often be called on to work extremely hard. These will be the times that they will incur an oxygen debt. However, when they have performed the task, the oxygen debt will be repaid; this is the player's *recovery* period. The less fit a player is, the sooner he will find himself working under oxygen debt. In addition, his recovery period will be longer than a fit player's because the more fit a player is, the greater his ability to dispose of the lactic acid and the higher his lactic acid tolerance level.

METHODS OF IMPROVING ENDURANCE

For players to develop and improve their endurance for full-match competition, they must have a well-planned training program. They must do exercises to increase local and general endurance, and their training must reflect the type of running required in matches.

In a match, a player does most of his running without the ball at his feet. Therefore, although usually a coach should adhere to the principle of training with the use of a ball, he should not carry it to extremes and interfere with the primary objectives of an exercise. Endurance training should usually be done without the use of a ball because when a player has a ball at his feet, he will undoubtedly concentrate somewhat on his technique, which will prevent him from putting all his effort into running.

The most important aspects of endurance are speed, time, and strength: A player must maintain his speed for a long period of time while performing a strenuous activity. Endurance is also greatly influenced by the efficiency of a player's respiratory and circulatory systems and by the ability of his nervous system to provide sufficiently strong stimulation.

Endurance fitness is basically of a specific nature. Thus the exercises to improve endurance must be oriented to the precise type of activity to be performed. Marathon runners, for example, need endurance to run extremely long distances. Through their training, they develop hearts with relatively thin walls and large chambers that hold greater amounts of blood than normal, giving them extremely low pulse rates. Some have pulse rates below 40/min when at rest. Sprinters, on the other hand, develop hearts with smaller chambers but with relatively thick walls, which enable them to work extremely hard and fast for short spans of time.

A soccer player must try to develop endurance that is a cross between that of a marathon runner and that of a sprinter. Even simple repetitions of specific activities can develop some endurance in players, but to achieve the endurance fitness necessary for match play, a coach must incorporate the "overload" principle into the endurance training.

The overload principle means making the player perform beyond his previous level of endurance. If a player stops when he is tired, he is only training within his capacity; to build up endurance, he must train *beyond* that point. For this reason it is wisest for players to work in pairs or groups when involved in endurance training so that they can help each other through example and encouragement to continue working after they begin to tire.

Local Muscle Endurance

Obviously, local and general endurance are very closely related, and many exercises used for endurance training are effective in developing both. When selecting exercises for endurance training, remember that lactic acid is produced during anaerobic activity. After about 45 seconds of total effort by a player involved in anaerobic activity, there will be so much lactic acid present that his muscles will cease to function properly and he will collapse. Therefore if a coach demands total effort from his players while they are performing exercises for local muscle endurance, each exercise should last not longer than 40 seconds. Longer exercises may exhaust players, and the purpose of the exercise is to develop endurance, not to see how soon a player will collapse.

A widely used and popular exercise to develop local muscle endurance is shuttle running. An area of 25 yd in length is marked off in 5-yd segments, as in Diagram 6.4. The players sprint from the start to the 5-yd mark and back, then to the 10-yd mark and back, to the 15-yd mark and back, the 20-yd mark and back, and finally to the 25-yd mark and back, covering a total of 150 yd in one run. Players should cover the total 150 yd in between 30 and 35 seconds, take a rest, and repeat the run.

An effective way to organize shuttle running is to divide the players into groups of three and have one player from each group run while the other two are resting. Eventually, during a two-hour training session, the players should do three or four sets of shuttle runs, each involving three or four runs per player. This way the players can cover as much as 2400

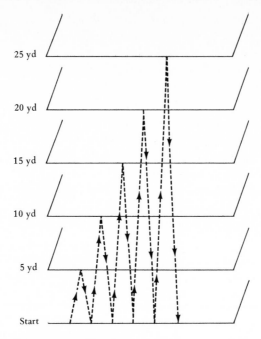

Diagram 6.4 Shuttle run.

yd in sprints during one training session, which is close to the distance they may have to sprint during a match.

Shuttle runs also duplicate the type of running done in match play. In a match, players often have to run 5 or 10 yd and then quickly turn and run another 10 or 15 yd in a different direction. A coach can also place some additional stress on the players during shuttle runs by having them bend down and touch the ground, sit down, or even fall down and get back up quickly before they make their turns.

General Endurance

Players can develop general endurance through distance running, perhaps 6 or 7 miles at a fairly constant speed. However, by running distances it is possible for a player to develop a rhythm in his running that would not be much help for playing soccer. Some people can run great distances, but when they are called on to produce frequent bursts of speed and quick changes of direction, as often happens in a soccer match, they become fatigued fairly rapidly.

The main limiting factor in general endurance is the oxygen supply to the working tissues, and the most effective way to increase the efficiency of the circulo-respiratory system and improve general endurance is through "interval training." In interval training players perform short spans of vigorous exercise with brief recovery periods following each one. The primary objective is to perform a maximum amount of work before fatigue sets in.

According to Herbert De Vries, research has found that an individual under interval training can withstand for an hour the same work level that would have exhausted him in 9 min if performed continuously.[1] The stress period in interval training should be ideally about 30 seconds long and raise the individual's pulse rate to between 150/min and 180/min. The rate at which a person's pulse rate rises depends on his fitness, and the more fit he is, the slower the rise of his pulse rate as a result of exercise. The interval of rest or light exercise that follows the stress period should be 1 to 2 min long, and the pulse rate during this time should drop down to about 120/min. The amount of work players can do can be three times greater with interval training than with continuous training. Interval training is the most efficient means of endurance training

Coaches can increase the work load in interval training to adhere to the overload principle by increasing the amount of work, the speed with which it is performed, the number of times it is done in a training session, and by shortening the rest interval. However, remember again not to exhaust players when training them for endurance.

Endurance Exercises

It is important to time endurance exercises whenever possible since to adhere to the overload principle, players must work at increasingly faster rates. The running exercises should resemble match play as much as possible, including quick changes of direction and the physical contact that increases stress. Also, the rest periods should not be passive but should involve some activity, even if it is simply mental concentration, since in a match a player should always be active and involved in the game.

Endurance training is very demanding physically and therefore not

[1] Herbert A. De Vries, *Physiology of Exercise for Physical Education and Athletics*, William C. Brown, Dubuque, Iowa, 1966.

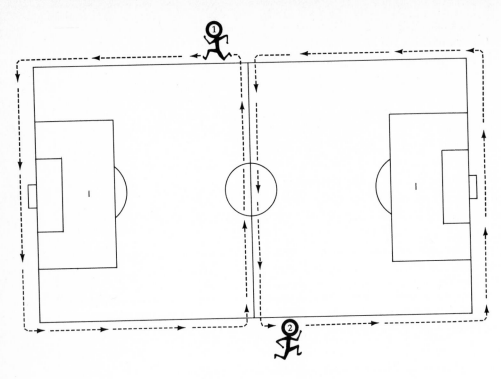

Diagram 6.5 Interval training exercise.

something that players enjoy or look forward to. As a result it is the responsibility of the coach to try to make endurance training as varied and interesting as possible.

Interval training

1. Players sprint the length of the soccer field (120 yd) within 16 seconds. In their rest interval they jog back to the starting line within 1 min. The players' fitness should dictate the number of repetitions, which need never exceed 10.

2. The players are paired, and one player positions himself on the touchline at midfield while his partner is on the touchline on the other side, also at midfield, as shown in Diagram 6.5. Player No. 1 in the diagram runs halfway around the perimeter of the field until he reaches his partner. When No. 1 reaches No. 2, No. 2 runs around the perimeter of the remaining half of the field, while player No. 1 takes his rest

Diagram 6.6 Pressure training exercise.

interval by jogging across the field to get back to his starting point. The exercise repeats when player No. 2 reaches No. 1. The fitness of the players involved must determine the number of repetitions and the speed of the exercise.

Pressure training

Pressure training involves the use of the ball and thus is a more entertaining form of endurance training. It is usually more helpful for developing local muscle endurance than it is for general endurance.

In pressure training one player is served balls continuously during the exercise; he must return them, using some soccer technique such as heading or passing as quickly as they are served. Coaches should emphasize that the aim of the exercises is to develop endurance and not to perfect their technique. However, a player should not continue performing when his technique deteriorates, for by so doing he would only reinforce the use of poor technique.

The duration of pressure training exercises should be limited by setting a time limit on each individual's performance, preferably 35 or 40 seconds. To increase the pressure a coach need only increase the frequency of the ball services.

The following pressure training exercises require three players standing in a straight line, about 5 yd apart, as in Diagram 6.6. The two players on the ends serve the balls to the one in the middle. The services should keep the man in the middle turning quickly and under constant pressure. If one of the balls should go astray, the man in the middle should continue to work, receiving services from just the one player until the third man has retrieved the other ball.

1. Balls are served on the ground and returned as push passes.

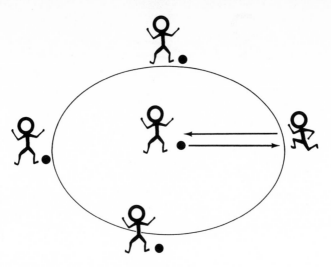

Diagram 6.7 Pressure training exercise.

2. Balls are served head high and are headed back.

3. Same as exercise 2, but the services are higher to make the middle man jump to head the balls.

4. Balls are served knee high and volleyed back.

5. The services are varied and the man in the middle must return the balls any way he can with one touch.

In a variation of the preceding exercises, one player jogs backward and his partners facing him serve the balls.

Pressure training can also be done with one man standing in the middle of a circle of players as in Diagram 6.7, turning around in a circle to receive the ball. It should be noted, however, that the greater the number of players in a group for pressure training, the longer will be their rest periods between strenuous activities.

Another form of pressure training is shown in Diagram 6.8. Four players are positioned at the corners of the penalty area. They are responsible for serving the balls to the 12-yd spot, where the man performing under pressure will shoot at the goal. The shooter starts from behind a marker placed at the top of the arc of the penalty area, 10 yd away from the penalty spot. After each shot he must sprint back around

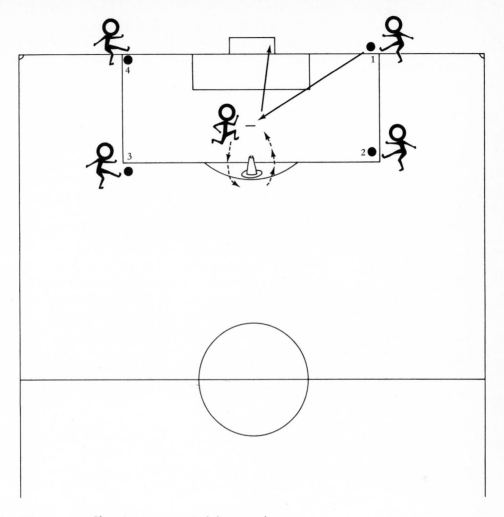

Diagram 6.8 Shooting pressure training exercise.

the marker and return to take his next shot. The services should be in numerical order so that the shooter knows where the next ball is coming from, as shown in the diagram where corners are numbered from 1 to 4.

Circuit training

Circuit training can be used in developing all forms of fitness, indoors or out, by one individual or by a group, and in an area to match the available space. It is actually a form of interval training, but the rest intervals of circuit training consist of resting one major group of muscles from a specific activity while performing another exercise.

The circuit consists of performing a sequential number of exercises, usually somewhere between 8 and 12, each requiring a predetermined number of repetitions, depending on the individual's level of fitness. The players move from one exercise station to another and go through the circuit a designated number of times.

This method lends itself very well to out-of-season training. Many athletes use circuit training when working with weights, and have found this a most efficient method of getting continuous activity. Fatigue does not set in early since the emphasis is on each individual's level of fitness and a different muscle group at each station of the circuit, so that those muscles worked last can rest while another muscle group is exercised.

The circuit shown in Diagram 6.9 and the description that follows were developed by Professor Julio Mazzei, the Brazilian physical preparation expert who worked closely with Pelé for many years.[2] The circuit was originally designed to meet the requirements of the players of Santos FC of Brazil, professionals who play about 85 games a year; with modifications it is equally suitable for young players. The figures given for the number of times each exercise should be performed and for the dimensions of the apparatus are intended for boys between 11 and 14 years old.

Station 1

Equipment: Eight sticks, 5 to 6 ft high, arranged in a straight line about 5 ft apart.

Exercise: The player zigzags through the sticks. He should perform the exercise as fast as possible and keep as close to the sticks as he can without touching them. Ideally he should maintain a sort of 1–2–3 waltz rhythm, with each third step marking a change of direction as he pushes off from his right, then his left foot. He should also be told to use his arms freely to maintain his balance during these rapid direction changes.

With the ball: The player starts with the ball at his feet, some 30 ft back from the first stick. He dribbles the ball at increasing speed until, just as he approaches the first stick, he passes it to a player stationed off to the side. He makes his run through the sticks without the ball. The player

[2]Paul Gardner, *Pelé: The Master and His Method*, Pepsico, Purchase, New York. 1973.

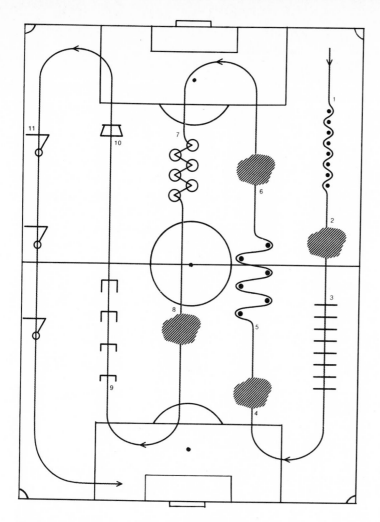

Diagram 6.9 Circuit developed by Professor Julio Mazzei for PC Santos. (Reproduced with permission of the Pepsi-Cola Youth Sports Program from their book *Pelé: The Master and his Method* by Paul Gardner.)

receiving the ball should pass it immediately back to the next player waiting in line; he then runs to the rear of the line, his place being taken by the player who has just completed the circuit.

Duration: At the beginning of training, this station should be performed three times. As the players' physical condition improves, the number of times the exercise is performed can be gradually increased over a period of several weeks up to a maximum of six times.

Station 2

Equipment: None.

Exercise: This is the first of four exercises designed to strengthen mainly the abdominal muscles. Players work in pairs. Player *A* lies flat on his back with his hands touching behind his neck, elbows spread. Player *B* kneels at his feet, with his hands on *A*'s ankles, leaning forward so that he is pushing them down. Player *A* must sit up—keeping his legs as straight as he can and pushing his head down between his knees—then return to his starting position. He does this for a specified number of times after which the players exchange positions and repeat the exercise. All the pairs should keep to the same rhythm during the exercise, with the kneeling players calling out *"up . . . down"* or *"one . . . two."* Working together in this way helps to foster the feeling that players are functioning as a team.

Station 3

Equipment: Eight sticks, 4 ft long, placed flat on the ground, parallel to each other and about 5 to 6 ft apart.

Exercise: Station 3 is designed to develop a correct running position. The player must run rapidly over the sticks, landing each time between them, never on them. The sticks are placed so that the player must exaggerate his normal stride. The increased length of the stride means that he has to lean his upper body forward and swing his arms fully to maintain his balance. The exercise also requires the player to land on the ball of his foot, and not heavily on his heel.

Note: This exercise should be performed only on a soft surface such as grass or sand, never on concrete or wooden floors.

With the ball: The player can make a preliminary 30-ft run with the ball, as described for station 1, before passing it off and running over the sticks without the ball.

Duration: Three times, working gradually up to six times.

Station 4

Equipment: None.

Exercise: Station 4 is the second of the abdominal muscle exercises. Players work in pairs. Player *A* lies flat on his back with his arms stretched out above his head, where he grasps the ankles of Player B, who is standing with his legs about 24 in. apart. Player *A* lifts his legs, keeping them together and his knees straight, until they are vertical. At this point Player *B* reaches forward with his hands and pushes *A*'s feet away from him. Player *A* must then lower his legs in a controlled descent; he must not just let them fall to the ground. The players exchange roles after the exercise has been performed a specified number of times.

With the ball: Player *A* performs the exercise holding the ball firmly between his feet.

Duration: Six times each player, working gradually up to 16 times each.

Station 5

Equipment: Six sticks, each 3 ft high, arranged in two staggered rows of three. The two rows are 10 to 15 ft apart, with 6 ft between the sticks in each row.

Exercise: The player must shuffle sideways between the two rows, changing his direction sharply each time he passes a stick. As he changes direction, the player should spread his legs wide and bend his knees considerably so that his body is in a semisitting position. In this way he lowers his center of gravity, giving himself greater control over his balance. He performs the shuffling movement by bringing his feet together, then moving off with one leg to the left or right, bringing his feet together again, and so on. The player should not cross one leg in front of the other.

Duration: Three times, working gradually up to six times.

Station 6

Equipment: None.

Exercise: The third of the abdominal muscle exercises. Player *A* lies on his back, his hands stretched out above his head. He raises his legs so that the standing Player *B* can grasp his ankles. Player *A* must sit up, keeping his knees straight as he stretches up to touch his own feet, then returning to his starting position with his hands touching the ground behind his head. The exercise is designed to strengthen both the upper and lower sections of the main abdominal muscle; it also stretches the muscles at the back of the thigh and the calf and increases the flexibility of the lumbar region of the spine. As in all the other abdominal muscle exercises, the partners should work in rhythmic unison.

With the ball: Player *A* performs the exercise holding the ball in his hands.

Duration: Six times each player, working gradually up to 16 times each.

Station 7

Equipment: Six hoops, each about 2 ft in diameter, placed on the ground in a zigzag pattern with a distance of 12 in. between each hoop.

Exercise: Station 7 is another exercise designed to teach a player to maintain his balance while moving quickly and changing direction. The player must run quickly along the line of hoops, placing each foot alternately into a hoop as he jumps from side to side. Players should also perform with their feet held together as they make two-footed jumps from hoop to hoop.

With the ball: The player makes a preliminary 30-ft run with the ball, as described for Station 1, before passing it off and running over the hoops without the ball.

Duration: Three times (including one two-footed version) working gradually up to six times.

Station 8

Equipment: None.

Exercise: The final abdominal muscle exercise Station 8 is designed to strengthen the main abdominal muscle and the lateral muscles as well. It also increases the flexibility of the spine, as do all the abdominal muscle exercises. The players work in pairs. Player *A* lies on his back with his knees spread apart. Player *B* kneels so that his knees touch the inside of *A*'s ankles, which he holds with his hands. Player *A* bends his arms so that he holds his hands on a level with his face, palms facing upwards. He then swings his shoulders to one side, twisting his body so that he faces the ground, touching it with his hands, then pressing his forehead to the ground between them. Most of the twisting movement is made from the waist upward, but there will also be some movement of the pelvic region. The exercise is then immediately repeated as Player *A* swings his body in the reverse direction. The exercise should be performed to a rhythm of *"left . . . press . . . right . . . press . . .* and so on. Player *B* must press down on *A*'s ankles, to make sure that *A* does not bend his knees during the exercise.

Duration: Six times, working gradually up to 16 times.

Station 9

Equipment: Four hurdles of different heights—12 in., 20 in., 24 in., and 30 in. (If hurdles are not available, ropes stretched between sticks can be used—but the sticks should be secured lightly in the ground so that if a player hits the rope, he will pull the stick out and not trip.) Place the hurdles in a straight line, approximately 25 ft apart, progressing from the lowest hurdle to the highest.

Exercise: The aim of the exercise is twofold: to provide the player with jumping practice and to teach him not to overexert himself unnecessarily. He must learn to use the spacing of the hurdles, which can then be altered so that he has to make some left-foot and some right-foot take-offs. Include two-footed take-offs occasionally for the lower hurdles. The sequence of the hurdles can be varied so that the highest hurdle comes second or third. From time to time the player should duck underneath the highest hurdle, sometimes leading with his left foot, sometimes with his right. Players should perform this exercise only on soft surfaces like grass or sand, not on wood or concrete floors.

With the ball: Increase the distance between the hurdles to approximately 35 ft, and station players off to the side between the hurdles. The player making the run receives a ball on the ground as he lands after his first jump; he dribbles it forward, passing it to the side just before he makes his second jump. As he lands from that jump, he again receives a ball from one of the players off to the side, and again dribbles it forward, passing it just before his next jump, and so on. When the player has completed his run, he should replace one of the players at the side who then joins the line waiting to make the hurdle run. To keep the exercise flowing quickly, it is probably better for the players feeding the ball to use their hands to roll it along the ground.

Duration: Three times, working gradually up to six times.

Station 10

Equipment: Vaulting horse about 2 ft high, two sticks about 5 ft high, stuck into the ground 5 ft apart and 10 yd from the vaulting horse.

Exercise: The player should take a short run and jump up to land on the horse with one foot; he then swings the other foot quickly forward to the front edge of the horse and pushes off from this foot as he jumps to the ground. As he hits the ground, he must immediately start a hard 10 yd sprint, running through the gate formed by the two sticks. In performing the exercise, the player must use first one foot, then the other, to make his take-offs. It is particularly important to use the arms to gain elevation for the jump and maintain balance as the player lands and begins to sprint.

Duration: Three times, working gradually up to six times.

Station 11

Equipment: Three soccer balls with loop and cord attached, which can be suspended from horizontal bars. The ball should be at a height of about 12 to 18 in. above the head of a player of average size. If horizontal bars—or perhaps the branches of a tree—are not available, the coach can stand on a chair dangling the ball at arm's length. (If a ball with attached cord is not available, he can hold a ball with both hands as a target for the players, drawing it away as they make their jump.) If three balls are used, there should be a space of about 15 yd between each of them.

Exercise: The players run along the line of the balls, jumping up to head each one in turn. They should use in sequence a left-footed, a right-footed, and a two-footed take-off. They should hit the ball as hard as possible, using the jackknife technique.

Duration: Three times, working gradually up to six times.

The layout of the circuit designed by Professor Mazzei uses an entire soccer field, but the same circuit can be set up over a much smaller area. A coach can also modify this circuit to his personal needs. Entire stations can be completely altered to include different exercises. However, one important thing to bear in mind when developing circuits for soccer is that circuit stations must allow the major groups of muscles used in the preceding station an interval of rest.

Obstacle maze running

Obstacle maze running exercises can be used to develop endurance as well as agility. These exercises are geared to duplicate the type of running and body movements a player uses during an actual match.

A coach must first allow the players to run through all the exercises so that they can familiarize themselves with them, and to make certain that this particular maze run is appropriate for his players. The players should be able to complete the maze run in between 30 and 40 seconds. If players can complete the maze run in less than 30 seconds, then it is probably too easy for them, and if they are unable to complete it within 40 seconds, then it is probably too difficult. In either case the coach should make necessary adjustments in the maze.

Players will work in groups, and while one runs the maze, the other players of the group rest. This type of training lends itself very well to relay races. Also coaches can and should keep time to see how long it takes an individual or group to complete the exercise so that he can note progress. They can use these records as incentive for the players to better their previous performance.

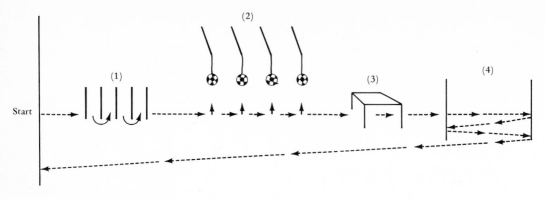

Diagram 6.10 Obstacle maze run exercise.

The total distance players cover and the number of repetitions performed must be dictated by the players' fitness. Initially, if their fitness level is low, a total distance of 800 yd covered during maze running may be sufficient. Ultimately the distance should be increased to about 2000 yd to match the distance a player may have to run during a match. The number of repetitions necessary to meet the desired total distance required of each player will obviously depend on the length of the course being used. Ideally the course should not be shorter than 50 yd and not longer than 100 yd.

Groups of three or four players are preferred for maze running, but in the very beginning a coach might want to use slightly larger groups to allow the players slightly longer rest intervals. Once the groups are set at the desired numbers, the work load can be steadily increased by increasing the repetitions each player performs until each man is covering the ideal distance during every training session. How quickly a coach should increase the number of repetitions depends primarily on the fitness of his players and their ability to adjust to increased work loads. Usually, if the team runs mazes a couple of times a week, increasing the total distance a player covers by 200 to 300 yd a week will enable the players to adjust without too much difficulty.

A sample maze is shown in Diagram 6.10. The player starts with a sprint to the first obstacle where he weaves between stakes placed 1 yd apart. Next he comes to a set of four pendulum balls 3 yd apart, adjusted so that he will have to jump up to head them. The third obstacle is a table of average height that the player has to crawl under. In the fourth

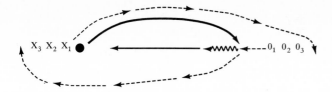

Diagram 6.11 Skill and endurance exercise.

position each player must do three shuttle runs before he turns and sprints back to the starting line. The shuttle runs are each 10 yd long and the coach can place additional requirements on the players such as touching the line at either end of the run. As with most fitness training exercises, the coach should select or devise obstacles that he feels will be most beneficial to his particular players.

Skill exercises

Players can also develop endurance while performing exercises designed for skill practice. However, they should only use those skill exercises that incorporate a substantial amount of sprinting without the ball. Exercises that are overcomplicated or require considerable technique prevent players from putting maximum effort into their running. The following skill exercises represent the many that can be used not only to practice specific skills but also to develop endurance.

1. Two groups of players, with three in each group, position themselves in two columns facing each other and 50 yd apart, as shown in Diagram 6.11. X_1 has the ball and starts the exercise by serving it in front of 0_1. After passing the ball X_1 sprints to the end of the line behind 0_1. 0_1 runs to meet the pass, controls it, and then makes a pass to X_2. The exercise continues as each player receives a pass, controls it on the move, and sends a pass to the man in front of the line opposite him before he sprints to the end of the line of the man he passes to. Two players from each line have their rest periods while one man in each line performs the exercise.
2. The players are divided into groups of three and line up next to each other about 5 yd apart, as in Diagram 6.12. No. 2 has the ball and starts the exercise by passing the ball in front of No. 1. As soon as a man passes

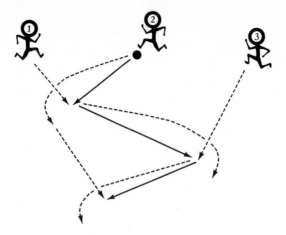

Diagram 6.12 Skill and endurance exercise.

the ball, he must sprint behind the man he passes to. No. 1 then passes the ball to No. 3 and runs behind him. No. 3 passes the ball back to No. 2, and the exercise continues over a predetermined distance. They must perform the exercise quickly, and coaches must stress sprinting at full speed after the pass. Players take their rest periods while one or two other groups perform the same exercise.

3. Four benches are evenly spaced over half the length of the playing field and are laid on their sides to provide a flat surface for rebound passes, as shown in Diagram 6.13. Each player starts on the goal line. He begins the exercise by passing the ball into the first bench and then sprinting to receive the rebound. He continues by passing the ball into each successive bench and sprinting to receive each rebound until he crosses the finish line at midfield. Each man takes his rest period while he dribbles the ball and jogs back to the starting line as shown in the diagram. To add competition and a little more interest, the coach could set up teams and run this exercise as a relay game.

To increase the stress during all skill exercises, the coach can increase the distance to be covered, or shorten the rest intervals by reducing the number of players involved in each group. Remember, however, that whenever players are performing with the ball, the exercise should not continue after significant technique deterioration sets in as a result of fatigue.

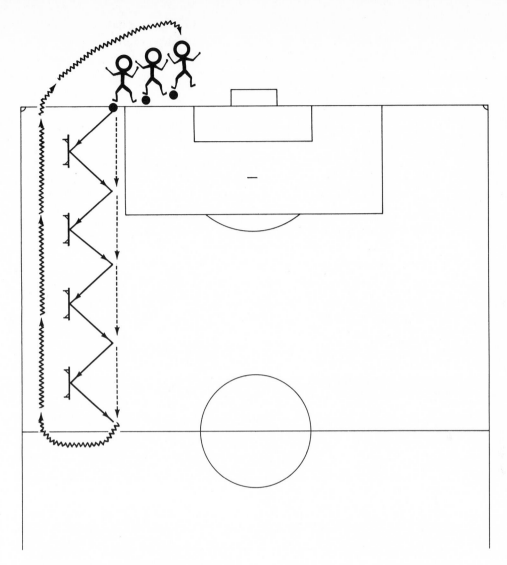

Diagram 6.13 Skill and endurance exercise.

Speed includes more than just how fast a player can run. A soccer player who is not an extremely fast *runner* can still be a very fast *player*. How quickly he reacts and anticipates situations in a match can often make up for a deficiency in his running speed. In addition, to be a fast soccer player, he needs to have the ability both to control a ball and to pass it quickly, thus increasing the tempo of the match. Many internationally renowned players such as Didi, the great midfielder of the Brazilian National team, have been very fast players as a result of their skill and knowledge, but not extremely fast runners. All this is not to say that sheer speed is not helpful to a player, for certainly if all other things are equal, a coach would much prefer a player who can run with great speed than one who cannot. Also some positions such as wing forward generally require a player with better-than-average physical speed. Francisco Gento, the great outside left who played for Real Madrid for many years, added a new dimension to Real's attack as a result of his blinding speed.

The physical speed required in soccer is different from that needed to run track. What really counts in soccer is the ability to accelerate quickly from a standing position or while jogging, to be agile enough to change directions quickly, and to be fast for stretches of 5 to 50 yd with or without the ball. Therefore specific training simulating match conditions is necessary for improving speed.

METHODS OF INCREASING SPEED

Quick Acceleration

Many exercises for developing endurance incorporate quick starts, which makes them most helpful in practicing and improving acceleration. The mere physical ability to accelerate is useless, however, if a player does not know when he should use it.

Every player learns to "read the game" through the experience he acquires while playing: A player will learn many things simply through the process of trial and error. However, he must also be well coached in tactics so that he will understand the game better and as a result be able to anticipate the opposition's play more often. Thus he must know when to accelerate and also how to position himself to make up for a lack of speed.

Speed Resulting from Skill

The tempo of a soccer game is set not by how fast individual players run but by how quickly they move the ball around to one another as well as up and down the field. To play the ball quickly and well, a player needs to have very good technique and be able to use it under match conditions. The ability to apply technique effectively in match play is called *skill*.

The more skillful a player is, the less time he wastes trying to control balls that come to him and distributing them to his teammates. Thus all the technique and skill training an individual does can benefit his speed. Games with restrictions like one-touch passing are especially helpful in developing the speed with which individuals and teams play. Dribbling exercises such as dribbling through a slalom course are also very useful since they improve ball control and enable players to run faster with a ball at their feet.

Agility

Agility is the ability to make quick direction changes. It depends on an individual's coordination, strength, and reactions to overcome the momentum of body weight. A player can increase his agility most effectively by practicing specific movements. Through this practice he can improve his coordination. Strength development is covered in a separate section of this chapter, but there is little a player can do specifically to improve his reactions other than compensate for slow reactions by anticipating the opponents' play. Obstacle maze running is one of the most effective ways for soccer players to improve their agility.

Speed Exercises

Most of the exercises for endurance fitness are also helpful for improving speed. The following are some additional speed training exercises. They should be performed adhering to the interval training method, with proper amounts of stress exercise followed by rest intervals.

1. Two players stand next to each other at midfield facing the goal. A server stands behind them and rolls the ball out towards the goal. As soon as they see the ball, the players must sprint after it. The first one to reach the ball becomes the attacker and tries to get a shot off on goal while the other is the defender and attempts to dispossess the attacker of the ball.

2. Every player has a ball and dribbles at a moderate pace. The ball is pushed 10 yd forward on command from the coach; and the players must sprint to catch it.

3. Two players, one of whom has the ball at his feet, stand on the starting line. The man with the ball pushes it forward and the other man must sprint and stop it before it crosses a line 15 yd away.

4. One player stands with his legs apart, facing the goal and 25 yd out. A second player pushes a ball between his legs towards the goal. As soon as the first player sees the ball, he sprints after it and takes a shot at the goal.

5. Same as exercise 4, but the player who will take the shot on goal faces the man serving the ball. As soon as the ball goes through his legs, he must turn and chase it.

STRENGTH

Strength is the ability of the body or its parts to apply force. Since the application of force at a rapid rate results in power, strength is possibly the single most important factor in athletic performance. Most athletic performances require an individual to apply considerable force against resistance, and with greater strength an athlete can move the resistance faster, resulting in better performance.

Several factors influence strength: (1) the coordination of the muscles involved in the desired movement, (2) the actual contraction of the muscles that results in the application of force, and (3) the position of the bones involved in the movement that determines the mechanical ratios of the levers in the movement of the resistance. Coaches must remember these factors when devising exercises to improve strength.

Muscle coordination can be improved through simple repetition. For example, to improve the coordination of the muscles involved in shooting, a player must simply practice that technique. The force resulting from the muscular contraction can be improved through resistance training while adhering to the "overload" principle. Players can do this most easily through exercises with weights. They can alter the mechanical ratio of the levers to their benefit through the most efficient positioning of the parts of the body involved in an application of force, producing the greatest amount of power. For example, the positioning of the feet and legs greatly influences the power with which a player kicks a ball.

Strength deserves considerable attention from soccer players. Players need to produce power when kicking a ball long distance or shooting at the goal, when changing directions against their own momentum or that of an opponent, when accelerating quickly or jumping, and when facing geographic or climatic resistance such as the physical characteristics of the playing field or inclement weather.

Unfortunately, many people associate strength development and weight training with musclebound individuals who are slow and have very limited flexibility. Research in the area of muscular development has shown this to be a misconception. Soccer players can and must work at improving their strength and power to play more effectively.

Remember that although muscles will increase in strength when subjected regularly to contraction against a greater than normal resistance, all muscles do not respond in the same way. The response of muscles to training will vary from one person to another and even from one muscle to another within an individual. The general increase in muscle strength after initiating an exercise program will vary from 5 percent to 1 percent per week. One reason for this difference is that some muscles are in poorer condition to start with than others and will show greater percentages of strength gain, especially during the initial weeks of the training.

METHODS OF INCREASING STRENGTH

Technique Repetition

Through the simple repetition of those soccer techniques that require strength such as heading, shooting, and kicking, a player can develop greater strength and power. The repetition improves the muscular coordination involved and helps to increase strength since it involves repeated muscular contraction and application of force to a resistance.

Most of the great forwards who have powerful shots developed strong legs through hours of training. The cannonlike shots that came off the feet of Puskas of Hungary, Charlton of England, and Eusebio of Portugal represented hard work; they were not merely a result of good fortune. Eusebio, for example, practiced shooting on goal for hours each week, often after all the other players had left the practice field. His reward for this training was the powerful shooting ability that came from the strength in his legs. As a result, every goalkeeper who played

Figure 6.1 Eusebio's powerful shooting ability comes from the great strength of his legs. (Courtesy Keystone Press Agency)

against him feared his shots on goal, knowing that he could score from as far as 40 yd away. (Note the size of the leg muscles of Eusebio in Figure 6.1.)

Sandor Kocsis, who was one of the "Magic Magyars" of the 1950s, was a tremendous header. This too was a result of hard and repetitive technique work. It was not uncommon for him to practice heading several hundred balls each week. This refined his technique by perfecting his timing and muscular coordination, as well as providing him with great heading power that came from the strong neck muscles he developed.

There is no question that repetitive technique practice can be boring. However, there is no other answer if a player wants the necessary power and coordination in his technique. Heading, shooting, and powerful kicking must be practiced through lengthy periods of repetition if this form of training is to be truly beneficial.

Players can increase muscle strength through exercises where they contract muscles regularly against greater than normal resistance. The resistance must be increased as the muscle strength increases to apply the "overload" principle.

Players can perform resistance training with either isometric or isotonic exercises. The *isometric*, or *static*, exercises involve little or no movement, and the muscles apply tension but the fibers do not shorten. *Isotonic*, or *dynamic*, exercises involve movement of parts of the body and shortening of the muscle fibers during contraction.

Doctors dealing with patient rehabilitation have applied the principles of isometric exercises for quite some time. They are especially useful to maintain tone in muscles restricted by a cast on a particular part of the body. However, it was not until after 1953, when German physiologists T. Hettinger and E. A. Muller published their work on static exercises that much thought was given to the use of isometric training for strength development in athletics. Today many athletes use isometric exercises especially during their respective seasons, to maintain muscular strength and to replace isotonic training whenever they lack time or equipment.

The primary advantages of isometric exercises is that they require little or no special equipment, can be performed in limited space, and can be completed in a short time. To achieve maximum strength development, the exercises should be performed daily. The performance should be at maximum or near maximum effort, and the static contraction should be held for 6 to 8 seconds each time, with 5 to 10 repetitions of each exercise. Beginners should work at lower than maximum effort when they first start their isometric training.

Several muscles are usually involved in a particular body movement, but not all of them are involved in putting a joint through an entire motion. Because of this, strength development exercises have to cover the full range of motion. Isometric exercises develop strength only in the position where the effort is made in a given exercise. Thus for static exercises to involve all the muscles in any one movement and develop maximum strength throughout, they must be performed at various points (beginning, middle, and end) of the motion.

These exercises are most useful in maintaining strength during the season. Although significant strength gains have been achieved through isometric training, it has not always produced better performance and has resulted in few endurance benefits with limited hypertrophy.

Some comparisons of isometric and isotonic exercises seemed to indicate that both methods produced similar results after six weeks of training. However, the initial increases in strength after the first few weeks of training could often be attributed more to improved neuromuscular functions than to actual muscular change. Comparisons over periods longer than six weeks would indicate that strength and muscle size are developed better through the use of isotonic, or dynamic, weight training.

Isotonic exercise programs are currently the most popular method of developing strength and power in athletic performance. However, such training did not become popular until after World War II. Dr. Thomas De Lorme used heavy resistance exercises with great success for patient rehabilitation during the war. It was because of his work that more researchers began to examine the effectiveness of resistance training in athletics.

Initially De Lorme recommended that dynamic weight training use as many as 70 to 100 repetitions, but later he modified this to 20 to 30 repetitions for each exercise. In 1948 De Lorme and A. L. Watkins proposed that an individual can increase strength most rapidly through heavy resistance exercises by doing 10 repetitions per set and 3 sets of each exercise. Using this method, an individual is required to determine the maximum amount of weight he can lift 10 times in succession. This weight is the individual's 10 repetition maximum or 10 RM. He can then proceed with the exercises. He must do the first set of 10 repetitions with half the 10 RM, the second set with three-quarters the 10 RM and the third set with 10 RM. Although most of the current isotonic strength development programs use the recommendations of De Lorme and Watkins, there is no real consensus among the experts as to the best program.

Coaches should note that there is a distinct difference between weight *training* and weight *lifting*. Weight training is the application of progressive resistance training for the development of strength, power, and muscular size through the use of weights. Weight lifting requires special technique and strength in lifting the maximum amount of weight at one time and is a sport in its own right.

As a rule, weight training is most beneficial during a player's off season. Once a player has been conditioned for the soccer season, it is more difficult to increase muscular strength and size with weight training. It will generally take an individual about 12 weeks in a regular program of progressive resistance exercises to derive full benefit from it.

Ideally players should follow an isotonic weight program to develop strength and power out of season and then have a program for maintaining their improved strength during the season.

Remember the following points when preparing and using isotonic progressive resistance training programs:

1. The program must include exercises that will place stress on the muscles to be developed.

2. Initially coaches must select a weight for each exercise that players can lift 8 to 10 times without placing great strain on their muscles.

3. Players should perform the exercises either every other day or three days per week. (*Example*: Monday, Wednesday, and Friday.)

4. The increase in the number of sets performed in each exercise and how close to maximum effort they should be performed depend on the individual's initial fitness and on his progress. After about six weeks in the program, an individual should be doing three sets of 6 to 10 repetitions of each exercise with the third set being done at near maximum effort and the first two sets easing the muscles progressively into the third set.

5. Maximum effort while using light weights develops local muscle endurance while the development of strength and power requires near maximum effort with the use of heavy resistance.

6. Increase weight progressively at an average rate of 5 percent each week, to provide continuous overload to the muscles. This is the progression of the resistance.

7. The full range of motion should be performed during each exercise.

8. Include momentary rest intervals between repetitions and full rest intervals of a couple of minutes between sets.

9. Players should maintain proper breathing during weight training exercises, inhaling before exertion and exhaling during exertion.

10. All participants must adhere to proper safety precautions.

Although the legs are of prime consideration in soccer, players must develop strength in all major muscle groups. The following is a list of the most important areas of the body in which strength should be developed

Diagram 6.14 Heel raises.

Diagram 6.15 Half-squats.

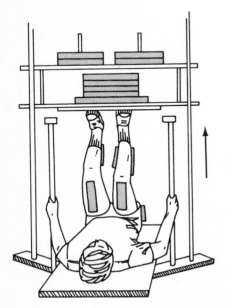

Diagram 6.16 Leg press.

Diagram 6.17 Leg extension.

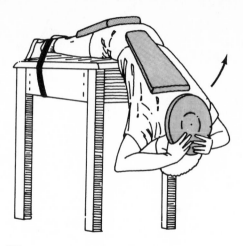
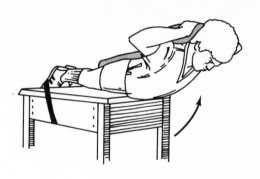

Diagram 6.18 Back arching.

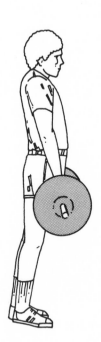

Diagram 6.19 Stiff-legged dead lift.

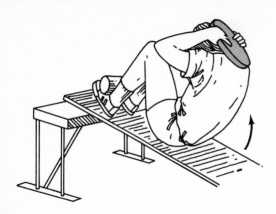

Diagram 6.20 Sit-ups.

Diagram 6.21 Bench press.

for soccer. The exercises listed are just a few of many that are applicable for the different muscles.

1. Feet and calves.

　　a. Heel raises—Start standing with a barbell placed across the shoulders behind the neck and the ʋalls of the feet on a board about 2 or 3 in. thick. The exercise consists of raising and lowering the heels. See Diagram 6.14.

2. Ankles and anterior thighs.

　　a. Half-squats—Start standing with the barbell across the shoulders behind the neck and proceed into a half squat and return to standing position. See Diagram 6.15.

　　b. Leg press—Lying on the back, press the barbell with the bottom of the feet until the legs are extended. See Diagram 6.16.

　　c. Leg extension—From a sitting position, extend the leg with a weight attached to the foot. See Diagram 6.17.

3. Posterior thighs and trunk.

　　a. Back arching—Lying face down on the table with the upper body

Diagram 6.22 Head harness weight.

off the table's end, place a weight on the upper back and arch the back. See Diagram 6.18.

b. Stiff-legged dead lift—Bend at the waist with the legs stiff at the knees and lift a barbell from the floor until reaching an upright position. See Diagram 6.19.

4. Abdomen.

a. Sit-ups—Perform sit-ups with the knees bent and a weight on the upper back. See Diagram 6.20.

5. Arms and chest.

a. Bench presses—While lying on a bench on your back, have a partner hand the barbell into your arms, extended over your chest. Lower the bar to your chest and then press it back to arms length. See Diagram 6.21.

6. Neck.

a. Head harness weight—Using a weight on the end of a head

harness, move the head up and down while maintaining a position as in Diagram 6.22.

Circuit Training

Strength development through the use of isotonic weight exercises is very well suited for circuit training, especially since both strength development and circuit training are geared towards individuality. As mentioned earlier in this chapter, circuits are used for endurance development, and the introduction of weights at the stations would provide good methods of working on both strength and endurance.

A circuit of weight training with 6 to 10 exercise stations will generally be adequate. A player should initially perform a trial run of each station to see what his maximum number of repetitions is for each exercise. In the trial run the weights should be heavy enough so that no one does more than 30 repetitions and yet light enough so that anyone could do at least 10. Once an individual determines his trial number of repetitions, the number is then reduced by one third to establish the number of repetitions he must perform of each exercise per set. The number of repetitions and the amount of weight resistance will be progressively increased, probably every couple of weeks, as players increase the speed at which they complete the circuit.

The exercises in a circuit should include all the major muscle groups with emphasis on the particular areas important to soccer. Take care to see that the same muscle group is not exposed to stress at two consecutive stations which would eliminate the rest interval and possibly bringing on premature fatigue.

Each individual must complete three sets of each exercise in the circuit. He can perform these sets one after the other with adequate rest intervals, or repeat the entire circuit three times doing only one set at each station per round. Every individual's completion time must be recorded, and each player should constantly try to better his times.

The coach must devise the best weight training circuits for his particular players, taking into consideration their ages, fitness levels, and other individual characteristics. Also all participants must go through some warm-up exercises before working in the circuit to avoid unnecessary muscle sprains and ruptures.

Extensive coverage of the circuit training method can be found in *Circuit Training* by R. E. Morgan and G. T. Adamson (G. Bell and Sons,

London, England, 1962). These authors introduced this training procedure, and their work prompted other experts to do research in this area.

MENTAL FITNESS

Mental fitness can be divided into the three areas: *attitude, concentration,* and *confidence.* It is essential to all soccer players and must be a prime area of concern of every coach. A player who is not in the proper frame of mind to play may prove worthless to a team regardless of his individual ability.

Attitude

The attitude with which an individual approaches the game is immensely important. All of us work harder and perform better when we enjoy what we are doing. Regardless of his skill level, if a player does not enjoy playing, he will never put forth 100 percent effort. Rarely if ever has there been a world class player who did not play soccer primarily because he loved the game.

It is very difficult to instill the proper attitude in all the players of a team, but it is certainly not impossible to derive one aspect of attitude, enthusiasm, from many of them. Perhaps above all, their enthusiasm is influenced directly by the coach's example. If the coach is enthusiastic and makes every effort to have enjoyable training sessions, it is likely that the attitude of the players will be a reflection of his own. His enthusiasm for the game itself and the training sessions is contagious, and by affecting some players either in a positive or negative way, the coach may affect the attitude of the entire team.

Another important aspect of a player's attitude is the degree of his competitiveness. This manifests itself in his willingness to work hard, withstand pain during matches and training, and in the degree of aggressiveness in his play.

The work rate of a player is partially affected by whether or not he enjoys the game itself. Running is a vital part of soccer so that a player must be willing to run if he wants to play effectively. However, the willingness to continue playing when the accompanying pains of fatigue set in is something a coach cannot really influence to any great extent.

Unlike some individual sports such as swimming or track and field where a participant can finish second or third, soccer is a game of winning or losing. The results of each match are greatly influenced by just how much the players really want to win. Those individuals with very strong competitive drives will usually be willing to endure more physical and mental anguish than others if it can affect the result of a match. They will be most aggressive in their battles for the ball, trying to run faster and jump higher to win every ball possible.

An excellent example of this is Alan Ball when he played for England in the 1966 World Cup Final against West Germany. His constant hard work and running with seeming disregard of physical and mental anguish in extra time, after the initial 90 min ended in a draw, played a major role in England's winning the Cup.

Aggressiveness can be influenced somewhat by a player's level of skill since less skilled players are sometimes intimidated by those who are more proficient and may hesitate to take necessary chances to win balls or score goals. However, for the most part a player's competitive drives are not something a coach can alter significantly.

Concentration

To be mentally alert and concentrating on the play for an entire match is vital to every soccer player. However, it is difficult and tiring since mental tension can also bring on fatigue. Each man must constantly assess the immediate situation in a match, anticipate what can happen next, and be planning his reactions in advance. Many errors result directly from lapses in concentration. It is safe to say that at the top professional level, most of the mistakes are mental ones and do not result from a lack of technique.

Every time a player goes on a run, he may be triggering a sequence that will lead to a goal. A player never knows which pass will be the one that eventually results in the winning goal. Thus every moment of play during a match could be the most crucial one, and every player must be alert and concentrating if he is to involve himself directly in the play when he is needed.

One of a coach's most difficult responsibilities is to analyze a situation and determine the cause of its success or failure. Too often coaches, especially those with limited experience, will find an effect but not the real cause of the problem. This is especially true when the cause is a breakdown in an individual's concentration.

When a defender near his own goal allows his opponents to go on a dangerous run, is it because he does not know enough to mark tightly in such situations, or is it because he lost his concentration momentarily? Certainly for any player who has had even a minimal amount of coaching the lapse indicates loss of concentration. Yet some coaches would remind the player to mark tightly and say nothing at all of the breakdown in concentration that actually caused the problem.

Lapses in concentration will most frequently occur as a player begins to tire and also in certain match situations. The two situations where it is most often apt to occur is immediately after possession of the ball changes from one team to another and when play is stopped for a restart.

All the players on the field should be totally involved in what is happening throughout the match. Yet it is not unusual to see forwards stop playing momentarily after their team loses possession of the ball, or to see defenders stop playing momentarily after their team gains possession. When this happens, their team is really playing with fewer than 11 men.

Have you ever seen a defender leaning against a goal post just before a corner kick or turn his back, even if only momentarily, to the spot where his opponents are about to take a free kick or throw-in? If so, you have seen a man who could not possibly be prepared to play and who is definitely not concentrating on the situation at hand. It is really not an uncommon occurrence to see players lose their concentration before a restart, yet it is vitally important that they all concentrate on the match the entire time they are on the playing field.

Players' mental concentration can be improved through experience playing in regular matches and through participation in small-sided games, especially after the players have been made aware of the importance of concentration. The small-sided games require even more intense concentration since by limiting the number of players, the coach increases the frequency of any one individual's being directly involved in the play. Lapses in concentration during matches are not intentional, and they can be minimized by alerting the players when they are most likely to occur.

Confidence

Confidence is an essential quality for all athletes. It is the assurance that a player has that he can accomplish the tasks he must perform. Having confidence allows him to play in a composed manner, eliminates anxiety and fear of failure, and enables him to perform to the best of his ability even under match pressures.

Total confidence for a soccer player is composed of several variables. He must be confident of his technique and his ability to apply it under match conditions, which is developed through training and match experience. He must know that he can play for the duration of the match without total exhaustion, which he can attain through proper fitness training. In addition, a player has to be aware of the fact that soccer is a contact sport. He must be willing and able to endure a certain amount of physical punishment during a match. Thus, it is essential that a player's training reflects the physical contact he will experience in match play.

The primary difference between professional players and high-level amateurs is their ability to perform well under considerable physical abuse from their opponents. Granted there are some differences in the levels of skill, but these are not as great as some lead us to believe. One of the biggest problems that young players who sign with a professional club for the first time have is the adjustment to the physical play they encounter. This is not to say that the play necessarily involves a great deal of illegal charging. It is simply play of a much more physical nature. Highly skilled young players have been so intimidated by such contact that they become totally ineffective during a match.

Every player must have a sound working knowledge of the game so that he has the ability to correctly assess each situation while he is playing and plan his moves in advance with confidence. This is an aspect that coaches must not overlook in preparing their teams, and all the players should be properly schooled in tactics.

The players must also understand how their team is to approach every given match and have confidence that it is the best way for them. A coach must explain to his players not only how he wants them to play but also why he feels it is the best method for them. If the players do not believe that the approach of their team to a match is correct and affords them the best chances of winning, they will play less confidently and with far less enthusiasm, making their efforts less effective.

To instill total confidence in his players, a coach also has to make use of what each individual does best. The players have to play in positions that will make them useful to their teams and at the same time make them feel comfortable. Many players do not know what their best positions are, but they invariably know where they do not like to play and have played poorly. It is up to the coach to place his players in positions where they can do the best jobs and still feel comfortable and happy.

Ideally coaches want to prepare a team so that they will be fit and capable of playing up to their potential. To do this coaches must plan training sessions carefully and give physical and mental fitness proper consideration.

REFERENCES

Allison, Malcolm. *Soccer for Thinkers.* Pelham Books, London, 1967.

Astrand, Per-Olof, and Kaare Rodahl. *Textbook of Work Physiology.* McGraw-Hill, New York, 1970.

Cramer, Dettmar. *United States Soccer Federation "Coaches Manual."* Four Maples Press, Minisink Hills, Pa., 1973.

Csanadi, Arpad. *Soccer.* Corvina, Budapest, 1965.

DeVries, Herbert A. *Physiology of Exercise for Physical Education and Athletics.* William C. Brown, Dubuque, Iowa, 1966.

Falls, H.B., E.L. Wallis, and G.A. Logan. *Foundation of Conditioning.* Academic Press, New York, 1970.

Gardner, Paul. *Pelé: The Master and His Method.* Pepsi Co., Purchase, N.Y., 1973.

Homola, Samuel. *Muscle Training for Athletes.* Parker Publishing, West Nyack, N.Y., 1968.

Hughes, Charles F.C. *Tactics and Teamwork.* E.P. Publishing, Wakefield, England, 1973.

Jensen, C.R., and G.W. Schultz. *Applied Kinesiology.* McGraw-Hill, New York, 1970.

Karpovich, Peter. *Physiology of Muscular Activity.* W.B. Saunders, Philadelphia, 1959.

Rasch, P.J., and R.K. Burke. *Kinesiology and Applied Anatomy.* Lea and Febiger, Philadelphia, 1967.

Wade, Alan. *The FA Guide to Training and Coaching.* William Heinemann, London, 1967.

Wilson, Bob. *Goalkeeping.* Pelham Books, London, 1970.

Winterbottom, Walter. *Soccer Coaching.* William Heinemann, London, 1952.

———. *Training for Soccer.* William Heinemann, London, 1960.

7

General Principles
of Coaching

A COACH's task is to teach players how to play soccer properly as individuals, and then mold them into a collective unit that will ultimately function effectively. Unfortunately, there is no magic formula to accomplish this task. To be successful, a coach must (1) have a sound working knowledge of soccer, (2) be able to analyze both individual and team performance to determine what is being done well and how to improve those things that are being done poorly, (3) understand the learning process so that he can teach properly, (4) prepare his training sessions carefully in advance so that they are well organized, and (5) learn how to motivate the players so that they will put maximum effort into training and matches.

Besides being a soccer expert, teacher, and psychologist, a coach who wishes to win consistently must also be lucky! For regardless of how well prepared the players are, many games between evenly matched teams are won or lost as a result of a little luck.

KNOWLEDGE OF SOCCER

One major drawback to soccer progress in areas where the sport is in its infancy is the lack of competent people to coach the game. The saying, "a little knowledge can be a dangerous thing," is most applicable in this situation, for unfortunately many times people who are asked to coach a team have never studied the game and bring with them limited experience as players or spectators. Thus they are really not prepared to handle a coaching assignment competently.

Like any good teacher, a coach must thoroughly study his subject, in this case soccer, to gain a solid working knowledge of all its aspects. Participation in coaching clinics and courses and exposure to various philosophies through literature and films are essential for coaches at every level. Above all else, no coach should ever stop listening to what others in the game have to say! After all, his knowledge is basically the assimilation of all that others have directly or indirectly taught him.

Performance Experience

Although having played soccer and having the ability to perform with a ball are not mandatory for coaching it, it is unquestionably a tremendous asset. First of all, it is easier for a former player to understand the difficulties that players confront during match play since he himself has experienced the same things. This understanding facilitates comprehending tactical schemes and the difficulties involved in applying them. The more extensive an individual's playing background, the greater will be the reservoir of experience he can draw on while coaching others.

It is extremely beneficial if while training players, a coach can use himself as a visual aid by demonstrating what he wants his players to accomplish. This is helpful not only in illustrating technique to players but also in winning their confidence.

It is important to note that good players do not necessarily make good coaches. The lack of personal practical experience can be a severe handicap for a coach, but it is one that he can overcome. All things need not be demonstrated for the players, and often it is even more helpful for a coach to utilize one of the players to demonstrate instead of himself. Using a player to demonstrate gives that player a certain amount of self-satisfaction for being singled out in the group and also makes the other players realize that they too should be able to master whatever is being demonstrated to them since one of their peers is doing it.

Regardless of the coach's ability level, he should take an active part in every training session. This is especially true when working with young players and will serve to create a friendlier relationship between them and the coach.

Coaching Methods

Through the years coaching methods vary and change, but basic principles of coaching remain the same. Perhaps the most important thing to remember is that the needs of different groups of youngsters vary tremendously and are influenced by circumstances around them. Thus the coaching methods used in England may not be proper for coaching youngsters in the United States. The general schemes of coaching may well be quite similar, but there are specific problems confronting coaches in the United States that do not confront coaches in England and vice versa. Coaching methods must be adapted to suit the needs of the players.

One primary difference between soccer-playing youngsters in the United States and in Europe is the frequency of exposure to top-level play. All good players learn from watching world class players perform. It does not matter whether they see them on television or in person, as long as they are exposed to top-level soccer. In the past this has not been available to North American youngsters, and as a result coaches have had to show these players a great many more basic techniques of ball handling. Where a boy in Europe could see Cruyff or Beckenbauer perform and then go into his back yard and try to imitate some of their techniques, the average young player in North America may not even have heard of these world-class players, much less see them frequently. With the growth of the professional game in North America, however, and the arrival of players like Pelé and Eusebio in the North American Soccer League, youngsters here may not have long to wait before they are exposed as frequently to top-level play as youngsters in Europe and South America.

Another major difference between North American and European youngsters learning the game is that in Europe, or for that matter almost anywhere else in the world, a youngster's parents and siblings also have an interest in soccer and many times can teach him at least some basic techniques. In the United States quite the opposite has been the rule. Thus American coaches have had to do far more coaching of pure technique than coaches in the rest of the world.

ANALYZING PLAY

The ability to analyze the play of individuals and of entire teams is essential to successful coaching. The match tells a coach what he must teach his players during training sessions, and the following matches test that teaching. If players do not work during training on those areas that present the biggest problems for them in match competition, then their match performance will in all likelihood not improve, and the training sessions will have served little or no purpose.

Before taking a new group of players to train, a coach should always observe them first in a match situation to analyze where their strengths and weaknesses lie. Only then will he be able to plan training sessions properly and make the most of available time in an attempt to improve the players' problem areas and reinforce those things they do well.

A player wants to know what his shortcomings are. He also does not always know what position is best suited to him. These questions can be answered only through proper match analysis.

Problems in Analyzing Play

Besides having a sound knowledge of soccer, a coach must discipline himself and avoid becoming emotionally involved if he is to analyze play effectively. Too frequently inexperienced coaches become engrossed in a match and get emotionally involved because of their partisanship. This may cause them to lose sight of the important underlying factors that cause things to happen in a match. As a result they are unable to properly analyze the reasons for the success or failure of many situations during the match.

In addition to divorcing himself from emotional partisanship to properly determine where a team needs improvement and how to achieve it, a coach must also divorce himself from personal prejudices of technique and style. He must be as objective as possible in his analysis. This is the only way to recognize those factors that create problems for the players and that he must alter to bring about improvement.

When analyzing the breakdowns in match play such as the loss of ball possession from an intercepted pass, a coach must be certain that he determines what the *principal* cause of the breakdown was. He must be careful not to get distracted by secondary and related errors that are in reality merely ancillary problems.

For example, if the ball were passed improperly as a result of poor technique in striking the ball, does the player really not know how to pass the ball or was it a mental error? Quite often improper technique is a result of poor concentration brought on by the mental and physical pressures of match play rather than a lack of knowledge or the inability to contact a ball properly. Thus to correct the problem, the coach must determine the primary cause and either work with the player on learning the proper passing technique or place the player under match-related pressure during training and have him practice his technique under those circumstances.

On the other hand, if the ball were passed properly but was still intercepted, the error may have been either a physical one or a mental one and may be the fault of either the player making the pass or the one who was to receive it. The player passing the ball may have selected an improper time to pass or an improper space into which to pass. These would be mental errors, showing a lack of ability to read the game properly. If the selection of space and time to pass were correct, the interception may have occurred because the man who was to receive the ball did not run into the proper space at the right time. This could mean that the player who was to receive the ball is not reading the game properly, which would be a mental error, or not moving to receive passes because he is not fit, a physical problem. The important thing to remember when analyzing play is that a coach, like a physician, must first diagnose the problem correctly if he expects to cure it!

Analyzing Technique Through Tests

To determine the players' technical competency, a coach may establish a battery of tests. By exposing the players to exercises testing technical ability, players and coaches alike may well be surprised by the inaccuracy and limited proficiency of even the better players on a team. Quite often problems like poor shooting in match play are attributed to match pressure and a limited amount of time in which the players are allowed to play the ball. However, when the same players are allowed to simply roll the ball forward and shoot at an empty goal from the top of the penalty area without pressure from any opponent, an amazingly large proportion of their shots do not find their way into the goal. This should prove immediately that players need to work on their shooting technique. Other tests can be used to test all techniques used in playing a soccer ball. Each player must be given a minimum of 10 attempts in each test. Note that many training games listed in Chapter 4 can also be used to test soccer techniques. The following are examples of technique tests.

Tests for passing

1. The player stands 15 yd away from two markers placed 3 ft apart, and attempts to pass a stationary ball between them.

2. Same as exercise 1 except that the players receive the ball and must pass it first time without first attempting to stop it.

3. The player stands in the penalty area and tries to chip a stationary ball into the center circle.

4. Same as exercise 3 except that the player must hit a moving ball. He can dribble it and then chip it to the center circle, or he can receive a pass and chip it first time.

5. Same as exercise 4 except that players receive the ball in the air and must volley it. Less experienced players can throw the ball up in front of them and volley it after one bounce.

6. The player dribbles the ball down the touchline and attempts to hit a target man at the penalty mark spot.

Tests for shooting

1. The player pushes the ball forward and shoots on goal from outside

the penalty area. The goal can be left unattended at first, and later a goalkeeper can be brought in to require greater shooting accuracy.

2. The player stands at the penalty mark spot, alternately receives crosses from both wings, and shoots on goal as he receives the ball.

How to Spot Potential

Many people seem to believe that coaches who recognize potential stars at an early age possess some mystical attribute. They sometimes credit this to an instinctive ability. Some people do have an innate gift of being able to recognize young stars, especially when it comes to seeing a young player's determination to succeed. However, there is far more to the gift than instinct. It is an ability to analyze individual performance properly and know what to look for in a young player who could turn into one of world-class caliber.

There are three primary qualities a coach must examine when analyzing potential. (1) The first and most important is the player's ability to handle the ball and his soccer intelligence. (2) The second is the player's physical attributes, and (3) the third is his attitude towards the game. To determine whether or not a player possesses exceptional qualities, a coach must observe him in match play to determine his ability and talk to him on several occasions to form a justifiable opinion of his attitude. It is important that while observing a player perform in a match, a coach watch him constantly to see how he handles and distributes the ball as well as how he contributes to the game when he is not in possession of the ball.

One can easily recognize world-class players. They all look as though they feel at home on the soccer field and as though everything comes very naturally. Beckenbauer of West Germany, Cruyff of the Netherlands, Pelé of Brazil, and all the other greats stand out immediately when they handle the ball. They want the ball and look and feel at ease when they have it. So too must a young promising player. He must enjoy playing with the ball and yet have the intelligence to know when and where to pass it. When he has possession of the ball, he must exude confidence. He should be able to receive the difficult passes as well as the easy ones, move to meet the ball, and demonstrate, as he moves about, the head, shoulder, and body feints that come so naturally to all class players.

A player's soccer intelligence is not in any way reflected by his IQ or academic success. Many players who have been genuises on the soccer

Figure 7.1 Brazilian star Pelé, now playing with the New York Cosmos of the North American Soccer League. (Courtesy New York Cosmos)

field have fallen well short of that description in the academic area. Thus it is important not to confuse the two, for they are not related. Just as some people are mechanically gifted, so others are gifted with an intelligence for sport.

A coach can recognize soccer intelligence in the way a player reads the game and anticipates the play of others, the way he positions himself when without the ball, the way he makes use of available space on the field and creates new space, and in what he does with the ball when it is in his possession. Being an intelligent player is every bit as vital to a potential star as what he can do technically with the ball, for both ingredients are vital for playing efficiently on the soccer field.

The primary physical attributes to look for in a promising young player are speed, stamina, and strength. However, it is important to remember that physical attributes are related to a player's age and must be observed and evaluated in relationship to it. In addition, a coach should make allowances for those youngsters who are late bloomers with respect to physical maturity.

Once he has determined the degree of a player's ability and soccer intelligence and his physical potential, a coach must analyze his attitude towards the game and look at some psychological traits like courage and fear. One of the main differences between players who make it to the top and those who do not is the ability to withstand the mental and physical pressures that players must endure, especially at the professional level. To overlook making a judgment as to whether a young player is easily intimidated during play could be disastrous in evaluating his potential. Many players with extremely refined and polished ball-handling technique have never made it at the professional level because they fear physical punishment in match play. A player who can be intimidated because he fears physical challenges from the opposition will develop only up to a certain point and then stop. He will never leave a mark on the game of soccer at the top level!

This ability to endure mental and physical match pressure and punishment is probably the greatest single difference between those players who make the grade at the top and those who do not. Technique is the pure ability to handle the ball, but skill is the ability to apply this technique in match play under match pressure. There are many jugglers in the circus who have good technique with a ball, but they cannot put it to use in match conditions. A player can have excellent technique but limited skill, although all truly skillful players will have a high degree of technical ball-handling ability.

Finally a coach must talk to a prospect for stardom to determine his attitude towards the game itself. To make it to the top, a player must be dedicated to improving his ability and bringing it as close as possible to perfection. He must be willing to sacrifice and work hard. If, in fact, he passes this final test after receiving high marks in all the other areas, then he may make it. He may make it, that is, with a bit of luck, few serious injuries, and the hands of a capable coach who can help him develop his natural qualities. We must not forget that more than a few players with potential have lost their incentive and been discouraged after suffering under poor coaching and improper management.

Determine Proper Positions for Players

In modern soccer, forwards are required to fall back into defense and backs are called on to attack and even score goals. Thus players must understand the responsibilities not only of their own positions but also those of all their teammates.

"Total football" is considered the ultimate goal in soccer development, but even here where players seem to interchange positions at will with no specific positional assignment, each player still plays more in one area of the field than in others. Some players possess qualities that enable them to be more proficient at playing as strikers than as backs and vice versa. Players will never roam all over the field regardless of the style or system a team utilizes or its tactical schemes. Different positions do require specific qualities in players if they are to be played truly well.

Deciding what position a player is suited for is at best a difficult task. However, a coach must analyze the abilities of all his players and then place them in the positions where they can be most effective and in which they will benefit the team most.

UNDERSTANDING THE LEARNING PROCESS

It is imperative that every coach, if he wishes to be successful as a teacher, understand the learning process and how to bring about learning. The coach must have a working knowledge of the basic process of motor skill learning as well as some of the psychological aspects of learning in general. Since most people in the field of physical education have courses in their undergraduate curriculum that deal with these subjects, coaches with degrees in this field often have a slight edge over those who do not. However, coaches without physical education backgrounds can and should quickly bridge this gap by studying the learning process.

Motor learning is learning that involves the use of muscles. Individuals must acquire new muscular coordination as a mode of response to certain situations. In addition, motor learning also depends on learning to recognize available visual and verbal cues. Thus although verbal instruction preceding the performance of any action is helpful in learning motor tasks, complex tasks also require demonstrations. Coaches will generally acquire the best results by combining verbal instructions with demonstrations and presenting them simultaneously.

Motor learning also incorporates other, general aspects of learning such as perception, motivation, and reinforcement. Keeping instruction simple and easy to understand will facilitate learning by assuring that players understand the instruction. Positive teaching will enhance and quicken learning, for negative teaching, which would dwell constantly on pointing out errors and using punishment, will kill the players' spirit and reduce their enthusiasm. It is very important that a coach never point out mistakes to a player without also explaining how to correct them. It is also very helpful to mix criticism of a fault with praise of well-done actions, for reward in the form of praise is reinforcement that will motivate the players to work harder and learn faster.

PLANNING TRAINING SESSIONS

Just as any good classroom teacher has a lesson plan that outlines the areas to cover and the amount of time to devote to each topic, so a soccer coach must have a plan for each training session. Without a doubt, a well-organized and thoroughly planned training session is the only way to achieve maximum efficiency in training. However, the coach must be aware that some segments of each session may not always produce the desired results as quickly as anticipated and must be able to adapt and improvise in his training session just as a player has to do in a match. Problem areas not previously evident may arise and each session must be flexible enough to deal with them.

Proper training session planning is essential for the development of the players. It will force the coach to think ahead, ensuring the players' progressive development. It will also enable players to understand clearly why training is necessary and how it enables them to improve their performance. Especially in situations where a coach is confronted with a limited amount of time to prepare his team, planning is vital to avoid wasting time during practices.

Principles of preparation

1. *Progression* What to coach must be determined by the players' previous performances. For maximum efficiency, a coach must establish progressive work loads and rates. He can accomplish this only by determining the level of fitness or technique of the players and then applying the "overload" principle.

2. *Pressure and competition* Training must duplicate match situations as much as possible, including pressure from opponents and competition among players.

3. *Diversity* Training is hard work, and many exercises that incorporate repetition can become very boring. Every coach must attempt to make his training sessions as interesting as possible and use a variety of different exercises to stimulate interest among the players. It is also advisable to end all training sessions with a game. This will leave the players with a pleasant memory of the session since the last thing they did will stay with them most vividly. As the rule in show business says, "Leave them on a happy note and wanting more if you expect them to come back."

4. *Flexibility* Not only must the training schedule be flexible because progress may not come at the anticipated rate but it must also compensate for unexpected weather and for unexpected variations in the number of players present.

5. *Individuality* Training must also incorporate the specific needs of individual players as well as those of the entire team. Obviously, all the players are not on the same level, and to achieve maximum progress, specific needs must receive appropriate attention.

6. *Simplicity* All learning is more difficult when the material to be learned is complex. To facilitate learning progress, a coach must keep things as simple as possible. In tactics, for example, it is far better to teach one or two variations for specific situations than to offer players five or six options. It is far better to have players do a few things very well than to have them do many things but none of them very proficiently.

7. *Coaching example* Every coach is a model figure whose actions are emulated by his players. If he is prompt, the players will be prompt; if he is serious, the players will be serious; and if he is lackadaisical in his preparation, the players will react in the same manner towards the training.

Year-round Organization

To achieve maximum efficiency, coaches must plan programs for their players that cover the full year. This may be somewhat hampered depending on the level of competition, the specific situation (for example, schoolboy or club play), and the restrictions existing on what may or may not be done in the off season. However, even where restrictions prevent his active involvement, the coach should always provide some recommendations for off-season activity.

Coaches must devote preseason training to preparing the players for competition. Fitness training will always be an important aspect of this training since most players invariably permit their fitness level to deteriorate during the off season. Although all three areas of fitness, technique, and tactics must be covered during the period, a coach must give initial priority to fitness, then technique and skill, and finally tactics. As the season draws closer, the amount of time spent on each area will change so that just before the first match the priority order will have changed to tactics, technique and skill, and fitness.

Seasonal training must out of necessity be devoted primarily to preparation for upcoming matches, and the results of the matches will dictate priorities. Ideally it should be necessary only to maintain the fitness level, maintain and improve the level of skill, and improve on tactical play depending on its effectiveness during matches. Training loads should peak between matches so that on the days immediately preceding and following them, players will have the lightest work loads.

Off-season training may be hindered, as already mentioned, by specific restrictions existing on any program. However, it is most advisable to permit a total rest period immediately after the season. The remainder of the off season should be utilized for maintaining fitness, building strength and power through weight training and other techniques, and further developing individual technique and skills.

MOTIVATION

At many levels of sport, especially at the higher levels, there is little difference in the knowledge of the coaches or managers and a very limited impact that this knowledge can make on the result of the games. This is precisely why we see the game of "musical teams" played by professional coaches every year. It is fair to state that in a league of 20 teams, possibly two coaches are superior to the others, one or two are inferior, and the rest are all about the same. Thus few new faces appear each year, and the coaches fired by one team are hired by another even before they finish packing their bags.

For the most part the players are all prepared in the same way, and the personal influence of the coach in the form of tactical maneuvers or schemes is minimal. At best a coach can hope to influence one or two matches per season in such a way. Why then are some coaches more successful than others, and why will one team hire a coach who has just been fired by another? The reason is that different coaches get along better with different players, and some have a better ability to communicate with their players and motivate them to perform to the best of their abilities. Certainly superior players will usually win out over inferior ones, but the motivation a coach instills can make the difference when players of equal ability meet, and can sometimes overcome a team's deficiencies to enable them to defeat a superior opponent.

Besides the intangible factor of personality, which can either hamper or aid player-coach relationships, all coaches should apply several specific motivation factors.

1. *Incentive* Coaches should set specific goals for all players that are flexible and realistic. This will provide the players with targets to shoot for and a greater sense of awareness of what they should accomplish.

2. *Success* The goals set for players must be realistic and set progressively higher as training progresses. This will enable them to achieve various stages of success and will serve as encouragement to continue to work for improvement. Levels of success should constantly be pointed out to the players to help in enhancing their self-esteem. Certainly valid criticism is necessary at times, but the more positive the coaching, the more successful it will be. Everyone wants and needs praise to reinforce a sense of accomplishment; this is true especially when the work load is very demanding.

3. *Reinforcement* It is very important not to underestimate players' intelligence. They want to know not only *how* but also *why* specific steps are necessary to accomplish specific objectives. When players understand and accept the necessity of training, they are much more willing to dedicate themselves to hard work.

4. *Interest* As much as possible, the coach should make all exercises and training sessions interesting and innovative. Although this calls for a great deal of planning and forethought on his part, it pays high dividends in the form of more work from the players.

5. *Competition* It is very important to realize that all competition must be realistic. This is true of training as well as match scheduling. Competition is desirable only if there is a reasonable probability of success. Pitting a vastly superior player against a relatively inexperienced one will stifle the inferior player's desire to win because he will approach the competition with a defeatist attitude. The same is true when an entire

team is constantly mismatched against far superior competition. The players will not work hard and up to their maximum potential if they know in advance that there is no hope of winning.

6. *Individuality* Finally, it is imperative that every coach realize that a team is composed of individuals, each of whom needs unique treatment. Not only does a coach have to learn how to handle each player, for some need a harsher approach than others, but he also has to find out precisely what each player really wishes to achieve. A coach cannot assume that all players wish to become world beaters, and although the level of an individual's aspiration can be altered, knowing his present level is vital in determining the best way to motivate him.

REFERENCES

Cofer, R.N., and M.H. Appley. *Motivation: Theory and Research.* Wiley, New York, 1964.

Cramer, Dettmar. *United States Soccer Federation "Coaches Manual."* Four Maples Press, Minisink Hills, Pa., 1973.

Hall, J.F. *Psychology of Motivation.* Lippincott, New York, 1961.

Hughes, Charles F.C. *Tactics and Teamwork.* E.P. Publishing, Wakefield, England, 1973.

Millenson, J.R. *Principles of Behavioral Analysis.* Macmillan, New York, 1967.

Murray, E.J. *Motivation and Emotion.* Prentice-Hall, Englewood Cliffs, N.J., 1964.

Ruch, Floyd L. *Psychology and Life.* Scott, Foresman, Chicago, 1963.

Wade, Alan. *The FA Guide to Training and Coaching.* William Heinemann, London, 1967.

Winterbottom, Walter. *Soccer Coaching.* William Heinemann, London, 1952.

———. *Training for Soccer.* William Heinemann, London, 1960.

8

Coaching
Soccer Techniques

SINCE SOCCER is played with 22 players on the field and only one ball, the amount of time that any one player has possession of the ball is minimal. Generally, a player will not have the ball in his possession for more than 2 or 3 min during any match. As a result, each player must make the most of the time he has the ball and perform as efficiently as possible if the total team effort is to be successful. A breakdown in technical skill on the part of any player may cost his team the match, for he never knows when the ball is played whether this is the pass or shot that leads to the winning goal.

Regardless of what other attributes a soccer player may have, he cannot play the game well if he has not mastered the ball-handling techniques. Even though many of the techniques are not easy to master and require a great deal of timing and judgment, players must practice them until they are perfected to such a degree that they become automatic. The *instinctive* ability to handle a soccer ball will reveal itself very quickly when players have to perform in limited space, with very little time, and under opponent pressure in match play.

Especially at the schoolboy level in the United States where the playing season is relatively short overlooking techniques can be disastrous. A common error of many coaches when they are confronted by a lack of training is to push tactics ahead of technique. This error can only frustrate the players since their inability to perform various skills properly will break down the simplest of tactical combinations. Tactics must be geared to the skill level of the players, and imposing tactics that are too demanding for the players' skill level will simply make them revert to a kick-and-run form of soccer.

Even when players reach the professional level, it is amazing how poor some players' technique is. We expect professionals to perform all soccer skills well, but by simply putting them to a test such as shooting on an unattended goal from outside the penalty area, we can be amazed at the inaccuracy and technical deficiency of many professional players. If this is the case at such a high level of play, then most assuredly these deficiencies can be found in even greater abundance at lower levels.

By observing their players in match situations or by setting up skill tests, coaches can determine their technical deficiencies and concentrate their coaching and training in these areas. Players who can perform all the technical skills necessary for their positions may not need coaching in this area, but even they need to practice their techniques.

Good coaches will teach techniques on known principles proven through experience. However, when teaching techniques, coaches should bear in mind that the result is the most important thing. A coach need not be overly concerned if a player does not kick a ball exactly as it is shown in a textbook as long as the player accomplishes the task he set out to do. Some players have a natural style that may seem improper but may be quite effective.

We all want to develop two-footed players since this will obviously increase the effectiveness of every player. However, a player's weak foot should not be developed at the expense of his natural foot. Ferenc Puskas, perhaps the greatest inside left ever to play soccer, was predominately a left-footed player. Some felt that he used his right foot only to stand on, but his left was so dynamic and powerful that he became one of the greatest players ever to kick a soccer ball. When queried as to why he only used his left foot, he is reported to have replied, "I would rather have one world-class foot than two no-class feet." In teaching technique especially to beginners, a coach must find a happy medium between having the player work only on his natural foot and having him develop both feet at the expense of developing one very well. Certainly no one could argue with the fact that it is better to have a player pass 9 out of 10 balls accurately with one developed foot than pass only 4 out of 10 balls accurately using either foot.

STEPS IN TEACHING TECHNIQUES

The word "technique," as used in this book, refers to the pure ability to handle a soccer ball. The word "skill," on the other hand, refers to the player's ability to implement his technique under all the physical and mental pressures that accompany match play. In teaching soccer techniques, coaches should follow a specific pattern, starting with (1) pure technique training, which involves only making the proper contact with the ball and having it do whatever is desired; (2) technique training under match-related conditions, where movement and opponents are brought in to create varying degrees of pressure; and (3) technique training under match conditions, where opponent pressure would simulate what is experienced in actual match play.

In the introductory stage of technique training, coaches should place the sole emphasis on the proper execution of the desired technique and concentration. Speed should not be considered as a factor and the use of power should be discouraged. The player should first become accustomed to the proper motion and timing required like a professional dancer who first walks through various new dance steps to familiarize himself with the various body movements required before attempting actually to dance. It is best, especially with the more difficult techniques, to first break down the technique into steps so that all movements are perfectly clear to the player.

Once a player is familiar with the various movements required by a given soccer technique and has achieved some success, he can train at the normal speed and strength generally used for that particular technique. However, a coach should not be in a rush to bring in the second step of match-related training. Throughout the learning process, especially with young players, it is vital that the speed from one step to the next be directly related to the success achieved at the previous step. A coach must be careful that in his eagerness to train in match-type conditions he does not retard the player's progress by allowing him to become frustrated with his inability to perform certain techniques well.

When players are called on to play the ball in a game, they will be either walking, jogging, or running. Thus the first step in match-related technique training brings in motion. This in itself begins to simulate match conditions and increase the difficulty of technique performance. Then the coach must bring in opposition pressure which causes mental tension and makes concentration on technique performance more difficult. The role of opponents must be restricted greatly to allow the player practicing techniques adequate time to play the ball. However, opponents can be permitted to challenge for the ball if a player takes more than a reasonable amount of time to play it.

For example, place a defender 10 yd away from a man receiving the ball and practicing bringing it under control. The defender is not allowed to challenge until after the player receiving the ball has actually touched it. Thus the player bringing the ball under control should have sufficient time to do so and protect it with his body from the defender. At the same time he will now also be aware of an opponent and will have to consider him when bringing the ball under control.

The final step in technique training can actually be referred to as skill training. Now players are confronted by opponents exactly as in match situations and must execute soccer techniques under physical and mental pressures that tend to reduce the level of concentration, as well as limit the space and the time in which to play the ball. Once players can perform in such conditions, they have mastered the technique and converted it into skill.

When introducing and teaching a new soccer technique, it is important: (1) to know beforehand the competency level of the players, (2) to demonstrate the technique, (3) to explain where to use it and why it must be mastered, and (4) to make all exercises for practicing it as enjoyable and innovative as possible.

A demonstration is best when accompanied by an explanation. Young players especially are not interested in hearing lectures on the playing field, they come to play. Thus it is best to combine all explanations with demonstrations of the techniques, for the sake of both brevity and clarity.

Obviously, by assessing the competency level of his players, a coach can adjust the entire training session to suit them and have proper exercises ready for their particular level. This procedure also saves time because it eliminates wasting time on exercises that are either too elementary or too advanced for a specific group of players.

Finally, coaches must realize that, in general, technique exercises are inevitably somewhat boring and monotonous. Unfortunately, repetition is a necessary evil in the mastery of motor tasks for all of us. A coach can do much, however, to help make exercises more innovative and enjoyable as possible. Many of the training games in Chapter 4 can be used for technique training and will allow the players to enjoy themselves while practicing.

NECESSARY SOCCER TECHNIQUES

A soccer team consists of 10 field players and 1 goalkeeper. The goalkeeper is the only real specialist on the playing field and has his own set of techniques. The field players all need to master the same basic techniques, although some positions dictate a greater mastery of certain techniques than others. For example, a defender must be a good tackler while a striker needs competency in shooting.

There are seven technique areas that field players must master to be effective players. The following is a list of these technique areas and a breakdown of specific techniques necessary under each general heading.

I. *Ball Control*

   A. Controlling rolling balls

      1. Sole of the foot
      2. Inside of the foot
      3. Outside of the foot

  B. Controlling balls from the air

      1. Instep
      2. Inside of the foot
      3. Outside of the foot
      4. Thigh
      5. Chest
      6. Head

II. *Dribbling*

  A. Basic technique

      1. Protect the ball
      2. Use inside and outside of the foot

  B. Feints without the ball

      1. Change of speed
      2. Change of direction
      3. Body feints

  C. Feinting with the ball

III. *Passing*

  A. Passing short distances

      1. Inside of the foot
      2. Outside of the foot
      3. Instep
      4. Heel

  B. Passing for distance

  C. Volley and half-volley

  D. Outside of the heel

  E. Bending the ball

  F. Chipping balls

IV. *Heading*

  A. Two forms

1. Feet on the ground
2. Jumping into the air

B. Placement

1. Short
2. Long

C. Changing directions

D. Power heading

E. Diving headers

V. *Shooting*

A. Inside of the foot

B. Instep

C. Outside of the foot

D. Volley and half-volley

E. Bending the ball

VI. *Tackling*

A. Jockeying

1. Foot work
2. Body position
3. When to tackle (proper time to challenge)

B. From the side

C. From behind

D. Sliding

VII. *Throw-ins*

A. Hand positioning

B. Stationary throws

C. Running throws

D. Short throws

E. Long throws

BALL CONTROL

The term "ball control" refers to the technique of receiving a ball and bringing it under full control. It is used synonymously with the term "trapping," but where trapping generally denotes killing a ball such as wedging it between a foot and the ground, ball control also includes receiving a ball without completely stopping its motion and playing it after bringing it under control.

A player must be capable of controlling a ball that comes to him from any angle and at any speed. He must develop confidence in his ability to control balls quickly under all the pressures of\match play.

In the past, players had considerably more time to play the ball than they do in today's game. They used to receive the ball, control it, look around to evaluate the situation, and then play the ball. However, in modern soccer opponents pressure players far more than before, and thus the time and space a player has to control a ball have decreased tremendously. Thus players must not only bring the ball under control very quickly but must also know what they plan to do with the ball before they receive it.

After controlling the ball, a player has one of four options: (1) He can screen it from an opponent by positioning himself between the ball and the defenders; (2) he can pass the ball; (3) he can shoot it; or (4) he can dribble it. The time he has to do any of these will directly depend on how quickly and efficiently he controls the ball after he receives it.

Principles of Ball Control

There are certain principles that players must follow if they wish to be proficient at ball control. If a player is not going to move with the ball immediately after receiving it, he must adhere to the following principles:

1. It is imperative that whenever possible he position himself in the direct flight of the ball.

2. Especially when opponents are near him, he should move towards the ball to receive it.

3. He must maintain proper balance and concentrate on the ball.

4. He must decide as early as possible what part of his body he will use to control the ball.

Figure 8.1 The larger the surface of the body used to control the ball, the less the chance of error. (Courtesy St. Louis University and The Athletic Institute)

5. He must use the largest possible body surface to control the ball to lessen the chance of error (Figure 8.1).

6. Before he receives it, he must decide what he is going to do with the ball, depending on the specific circumstances.

7. He must relax the part of the body to receive the ball to provide a cushion that will absorb the speed of the ball and prevent it from rebounding.

When players wish to control and move with the ball immediately, they must adhere to the following principles:

1. Move into the proper position, if possible in the direct flight of the ball.

2. Move towards the ball to receive it.

3. Maintain proper balance and concentration.

4. Decide as early as possible what part of his body is to control the ball.

5. Use the largest possible surface to control the ball to lessen the chance of error.

6. Decide before receiving it what to do with the ball.

7. Turn the body part that is to receive the ball in the planned direction.

8. Do not relax the body part that is to receive the ball, but stiffen it instead so that it does not absorb the speed of the ball and the ball rebounds off the body.

9. Move the body part receiving the ball slightly in the direction intended for the ball to go.

10. The ball should now rebound in the desired direction.

Frequent Ball Control Errors

The following are some of the most frequent ball control errors that players make:

1. They do not move towards the ball to receive it.

2. They maintain improper body balance.

3. They fail to concentrate on the ball throughout the technique.

4. They do not sufficiently relax the part of the body receiving the ball and as a result it rebounds away upon contact.

Ball Juggling

Players like Pelé seem to have such total control over a soccer ball that it seems that they can talk to the ball and the ball obeys. Neither Pelé nor any other player who possesses such great ball control were born with this ability: It was acquired as a result of many hours of practice, and one of the means of developing ball control is ball juggling.

Ball juggling is nothing more than keeping the ball in the air with repeated touches of any part of the body other than the hands or arms. Some people have felt that it has no value since it cannot actually be used in match play. However, ball juggling can be of tremendous value to

Figure 8.2 (left) Ball juggling using the feet. (Courtesy St. Louis University and The Athletic Institute) **Figure 8.3** (center) Ball juggling using the thighs. (Courtesy St. Louis University and The Athletic Institute) **Figure 8.4** (right) Ball juggling using the head. (Courtesy St. Louis University and The Athletic Institute)

players. It can (1) develop ball control, (2) develop a touch on the ball that will enable a player to know just how much power he needs to project it various distances, (3) develop a player's weak foot, (4) develop proper balance and (5) concentration, and (6) possibly most important, build a player's confidence. A player who feels at ease with the ball will find that in a match situation, he will no longer worry about how or if he can control the ball but will be free to think about what he will do with it after he brings it under control (Figures 8.2, 8.3, and 8.4).

Many great players have developed their ball-handling techniques through juggling, and when they didn't have a soccer ball available, they would stuff a stocking with rags or sawdust and juggle it. Others have used small balls such as tennis balls to juggle with, and Pelé has even juggled a grapefruit to demonstrate his total mastery of ball control.

Perhaps one of the greatest advantages of juggling for developing ball control is that a player can do it all by himself. Whether in his own back yard or in a field somewhere, a player can juggle alone, in a pair, or in a group. Juggling also works as an immediate means of showing progress since the longer a player can keep a ball in the air, the better is his ball control.

Exercises for Ball Control Development

1. Pure technique exercises.

    a. Individual, pair, and group juggling (see Chapter 4, page 104–105).

    b. Two players face each other, using one ball, and one player serves the ball while the other brings it under control.

    c. Three players form a triangle, using one ball, and serve the ball from one player to the next, bringing it under control.

    d. Variation of exercises (b) and (c) is to have the server call out the part of the body to be used to bring the ball under control.

2. Match-related technique training.

    a. Two or three players jog in place while positioned about 10 yd from a server they are facing. The server throws the ball to one player at a time who must come to meet the ball, bring it under control, and pass it back to the server. The player serving changes with one of the players receiving the ball after a designated number of services.

    b. Same as exercise (a) except that when a player receives the ball, he must control it in the air and volley it back gently to the server before it touches the ground.

    c. Player *A* serves the ball to player *B* who is positioned 15 yd away. Player *C*, playing the role of an opponent, is positioned 5 yd beyond player *B* and is permitted to challenge for the ball as soon as player *B* touches it. Player *B* must control the ball and either shield it from his opponent or may use player *A* to pass the ball so that the opponent does not win it.

    d. Training games from Chapter 4.

        1) Soccer Volleyball, page 105.
        2) Soccer Tennis, page 106.

3) Circle Ball, page 109.

4) Bulls Eye, page 114.

3. Match condition technique training.

a. Some exercise may be used as exercise 2(c), except that the opponent is permitted to mark player *B* and can challenge for the ball at any time. Player *A* should not serve the ball until player *B* briefly frees himself of his opponent.

b. Playing a five-versus-five match, players are restricted to two consecutive touches of the ball: the first touch to bring the ball under control and the second to pass or shoot.

c. Same as (b) except the restriction is used in an 11-versus-11 match.

DRIBBLING

Dribbling involves moving a ball along the ground while jogging or running and having it under full control and taking on an opponent and beating him while still retaining possession of the ball. It is probably the most difficult technique of soccer, but it is the most spectacular of all soccer skills. Each player must develop his own particular style of dribbling since it is a very individual and personal thing.

In modern soccer dribbling is not as important a technique as passing or ball control since it is a much slower and generally less effective means of achieving attacking penetration than quick and accurate passing. However, there are times that passing opportunities are not available, and every player must be able to dribble a ball in order to move it up the field in such a situation.

Having the skill to take on an opponent and beat him while in possession of the ball can provide a player's team with a great advantage. Whenever an opponent is beaten by a man who is dribbling, the team in possession of the ball may often gain a numerical advantage in attack since the beaten opponent now finds himself behind the ball and temporarily out of the play. However, it is generally foolish to take on a second opponent since this will take time that can permit the first man beaten to recover and place him back in a defending position.

As a rule players should dribble only when good passing opportunities are not available. It is much harder to run with the ball than without it, and since a player cannot move up the field as quickly while dribbling as when running, the speed of a team's attack is considerably slowed down. Remember also that dribbling is a tiring skill since it requires a great deal of effort and concentration. On the other hand, a soccer ball never tires. Even if the game goes into extra time, the ball will not be fatigued, so why not pass it and let it do most of the work?

To take on and beat opponents while dribbling, a player must have the ability to manipulate the ball while moving at speed. He must master not only the technique of handling the ball while dribbling but also that of feinting with all parts of his body to deceive opponents. This takes a great deal of practice and time.

Throughout the years many outstanding dribblers have emerged who seemed to perform magic feats while dribbling a soccer ball. Players like Sir Stanley Mathews, George Best, and Pelé, to name just a few, will be forever remembered as dribbling magicians. All of them were masters of the two primary ingredients necessary to beat opponents: (1) the ability to quickly change directions and (2) the ability to quickly change their speed. Even without any other great assets, if a dribbler can effectively execute those two things, he will be a successful dribbler, able to beat opponents.

Quick changes of direction often can catch an opponent unbalanced and leave the dribbler with the opportunity to move past him, while sudden bursts of speed may well be more effective than overall running speed. Francisco Gento of Real Madrid was a true master of changing his speed while dribbling. His sudden starts and stops invariably created space for him to play in since his opponents never knew when they were coming, and these variations usually gained Gento one or two strides.

Principles of Dribbling

Although specific dribbling techniques are practically impossible to teach since their nature is so personal, there are certain basic principles of dribbling that all players must adhere to.

1. A player should incline his upper body slightly forward to lower his center of gravity.

2. He should run on the balls of his feet to enable quick direction changes.

Figure 8.5 Malcolm MacDonald of Newcastle United dribbles with his right foot to keep his body between the ball and his opponent. (By arrangement with Newcastle Chronicle and Journal Limited, England)

3. His entire body must be relaxed and well balanced.

4. A player must take short strides whenever near an opponent.

5. His eyes should be on the ball when making contact, but at all other times the player must look up to see how the play is developing in front and around him.

6. He should dribble the ball close to his feet and always within immediate playing distance. Precisely how close to keep it depends on the dribbler's ability and the proximity of other players.

7. The player's ankle should be loose on making contact with the ball so that he does not push it too far away.

8. The player must always position his body between the ball and an

opponent to shield the ball if the opponent is next to him. He should dribble the ball with his left foot if the defender is on the right side and with his right if the defender is on the left. (See Figure 8.5.)

9. A player must never dribble unnecessarily, too often, or too long!

Feinting

The ability to take on an opponent and beat him while dribbling requires a player to master many feinting techniques. Generally, the type of feints he uses will especially depend on whether the opponent is (1) in front of the man with the ball, (2) behind him, or (3) next to him. A player can use various techniques in these different situations to distract the opponent's attention from what he really intends to do with the ball and to get the opponent to commit himself in a given direction, thus allowing the dribbler space into which to take the ball and beat the defender.

Players can feint both with and without actually moving the ball. Experienced defenders are much more difficult to fool with mere body feints, and at the professional level it is often necessary to move the ball to beat a defender. However, all players, especially those with limited ball-handling proficiency, must remember that if a body feint without the ball is believable enough, an opponent may well buy it. The chances of error and the possibility of losing possession of the ball increase considerably when feints incorporate movement of the ball.

Players must follow certain basic principles when implementing feints with dribbling.

1. The object is to distract the opponent's attention from what a player really intends to do with the ball.

2. The primary objective is to get the opponent to move and commit himself so that the dribbler can move before the defender can recover.

3. Before feinting, a player must know what he will do next, depending on the defender's reaction.

4. All feints must be realistic and believable.

5. A dribbler must not become predictable—a good dribbler has a variety of feints.

6. Remember that speed and direction changes are the most important aspects of successfully dribbling past opponents.

The following are a few of the most frequent errors made by players learning dribbling techniques:

1. Not making proper contact while dribbling and pushing the ball too far ahead.

2. Disrupting the natural running rhythm while dribbling.

3. Constantly keeping the eyes fixed on the ball and not looking up to evaluate the playing situation in the nearby area.

When teaching dribbling, the coach's primary objective is to have the players adhere to the basic principles of dribbling and feinting. Once they are doing this, let the players find and develop their personal dribbling styles. Allow them to be creative and learn how to improvise.

Exercises for Developing Dribbling

1. Pure technique exercises.

a. Players dribble a ball the width of the field, keeping it close to them and moving it with the inside and outside of both the left and right feet.

b. Players dribble the ball with the inside of the foot, alternating feet with every touch and touching the ball with each step so that it moves back and forth between the left and right feet.

c. Hopping on one foot, players move the ball forward, to the side, and backward with the sole of the other foot.

d. *Shadow dribbling.* Two players follow a third, who leads the line at a jogging pace around an open area, changing directions frequently. The second player in the line dribbles a ball while following the leader. Upon the command "change," the dribbler leaves the ball for the man behind him, takes over the role as the leader, and the previous leader moves to the end of the line. (See Diagram 8.1.)

e. Players dribble in an open area, frequently changing speed and directions while maintaining full control of the ball.

Diagram 8.1 Shadow dribbling exercise.

2. Match-related technique training.

a. Each player has a ball, and all the players are placed in a confined area. They dribble within the area confines maintaining possession of the ball and avoiding all the other players. An entire team of 18 to 20 players could use the center circle for this exercise. This will help develop control while dribbling, and the presence of other players in a limited area will force the dribblers to look up to avoid other players and look for open space to move into. (See Diagram 8.2.)

b. Players dribble the width of the field with an opponent mildly harassing each dribbler on either the right or the left side. Players should alternate being the dribbler and the defender.

c. *Keep-away dribbling.* One player dribbles around while another attempts to win possession of the ball. Once the defender wins the ball, he must try to maintain possession.

d. Training games from Chapter 4.

  1) Team Ball Tag, page 102.
  2) Slalom Dribbling, page 117.
  3) Grid Dribbling, page 117.

3. Match condition technique training.

a. One versus One (see chapter 4, page 135).

b. Small-sided game (five versus five) with a restriction that no player may pass the ball before taking on and beating one opponent while dribbling.

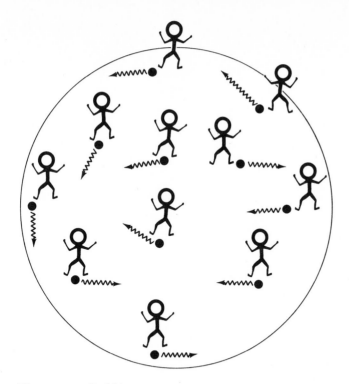

Diagram 8.2 Dribbling exercise.

Soccer is a team game that requires all the players on one side to work together as a collective unit. Achieving this necessitates accurate inter-passing. This is the reason why the technique of passing is the one most necessary to master before an individual can call himself a soccer player. A player who cannot pass a ball is simply not effective in a soccer game.

Passing is the ability to kick a ball to a teammate. Since accuracy is a vital element of a kick, it is best to refer to the technique of getting the ball from one player to another as "passing" instead of just kicking. This is also the reason why all training for kicking technique should incorporate a target for players to aim at.

In the defensive third of the field, it is sometimes necessary to clear the ball simply to gain time for the defense to reorganize. However, clearing the ball is only the first priority, and no player should ever forget that the next priority is to get the ball to a teammate. Since ball possession is the main principle of playing soccer, every time a player makes contact with a ball, he should do whatever he can to try to guarantee that his team will maintain possession of it.

Principles of Passing

There are several very important principles of all passing that players must remember:

1. Players must follow the attacking principle of penetration, making passes in the direction of the goal being attacked whenever possible. Square and back passes delay the attack and help the opposition by permitting them time to reorganize and establish their defense.

2. Players must pass the ball on a basis of percentages, recognizing that certain passes carry with them a greater chance of losing possession than others. The degree of risk permissible for each pass is directly related to what third of the field a player finds himself in at a given moment. In the defensive third of the field, a player should avoid a poor passing risk. As he moves towards the goal that he is attacking, poorer percentage passes are acceptable, especially in the attacking third of the field where a goal may result from a risky pass.

3. Players should know where to pass the ball before they receive it and should follow the sequence of looking first, controlling the ball, and then passing it.

4. Players should always attempt to pass accurately.

5. The speed of the ball should be correct to facilitate its control by the receiver.

6. Simple passes have the greatest chances of success.

7. Players should pass quickly and conceal the intended direction of the pass whenever possible.

8. To reduce chances of the loss of ball possession, a player should direct passes at a teammate's feet in the defensive third of the field, but may lead a teammate into space as play moves towards the attacking third of the field.

9. After every pass a player should run to support the player who receives the ball.

Figure 8.6 To achieve proper short passing technique, the player must strike the ball with the inside of his foot for greatest accuracy and make contact through the middle of the ball to prevent it from rising. (Courtesy St. Louis University and The Athletic Institute)

Most passes can be categorized into two types: (1) those that remain on the ground and (2) those that are lofted and passed through the air. Most of the passes made on the ground are used for short distances, and, with the exception of a short chip pass, those that are passed through the air are meant for covering long distances.

Principles of Short Passing (See Figure 8.6)

Players should adhere to the following principles when making short passes:

1. Players should keep the ball on the ground.

2. Players should make contact with the inside, outside, or heel of the foot.

3. Players should make contact through the middle of the ball to prevent it from rising.

4. On impact with the ball, the foot should be at the lowest point of its swing.

5. The nonkicking foot should be placed next to the ball.

6. The longer the follow-through of the kicking leg, the greater the accuracy.

7. Players must keep their eyes on the ball at contact.

Frequent Short Passing Errors

The following are some of the most frequent errors players make when making short passes:

1. They strike the ball with improper force, causing it to travel too slow or too fast.

2. They maintain poor balance and are thus susceptible to numerous technique errors.

3. They strike the ball too low, causing it to rise.

4. Their eyes are not on the ball at contact.

5. They place the nonkicking foot too far behind the ball.

6. The kicking leg does not go through the ball, but across it, causing it to spin off inaccurately.

Principles of Lofted Passing (See Figure 8.7)

Players should adhere to the following principles when making lofted passes:

1. The player makes contact with the instep of the foot with the ankle held firm.

2. He makes contact through the lower half of the ball, causing it to rise.

3. His last stride before kicking the ball should be a long one, permitting a long swing of the kicking leg to produce power.

4. He should plant the nonkicking foot slightly behind and to the side of the ball.

Figure 8.7 For a lofted pass the last stride prior to kicking the ball is a long one and the nonkicking foot is planted slightly behind and to the side of the ball. Contact is made with the instep and through the lower half of the ball. (Courtesy St. Louis University and The Athletic Institute)

5. He must keep his eyes on the ball at contact.

6. His kicking leg should go through a full follow-through in the direction the ball is intended to go—kick through the ball and not at it.

7. He should straighten his knee with power just prior to contact.

Frequent Lofted Pass Errors

The following are some of the most frequent errors players make when making a long lofted pass:

1. They concentrate too much on power and not enough on accuracy.

2. They have poor power because they do not kick through the ball.

3. They make contact too high on the ball, preventing it from rising.

Selecting the Type of Pass

The specific part of the foot used to make a pass should be determined by each specific situation and by an individual player's degree of skill. The more ways that a player can pass a ball accurately, the greater the chance is that he will make successful passes, and the easier it will be for him to disguise them.

It is important to allow players to improvise and pass in whatever manner seems natural to them. A young player who has received little or no coaching will probably take a ball coming from his side and often pass it on with the outside of his foot. This is a natural movement, and coaches must be careful not to stifle such instinct for the sake of seeing players utilizing "textbook technique."

Too frequently, coaches with limited experience will demand that players do all short passing with the inside of the foot. This is foolish since a player who can effectively use the outside of his foot and his heel can be more effective than one who passes with just the inside of the foot. It is, however, important to stress that players should make passes in the simplest manner, taking the fewest chances. There is no need to be fancy just to please the fans, unnecessarily chancing the loss of ball possession, and players should always use the technique that will assure them the highest chances for success.

Exercises for Developing Passing

1. Pure technique exercises.

   a. Using a pendulum ball, a player works by himself performing passing techniques. This type of repetition training will enable players to perfect the pure technique of proper contact with the ball necessary for successful passes.

   b. Players work in pairs, passing the ball back and forth and increasing the distance between them gradually until they are practicing lofted passes for distance.

   c. Same as exercise (b), except that three players work in a triangle.

   d. Three players stand in a straight line about 10 yd from one another. The player in the middle receives alternate passes from the other two, each of whom has a ball, and returns the ball to the man he receives it from. This is the same exercise described in Chapter 6 under pressure training.

2. Match-related technique training.

   a. A coach can use all the training games in Chapter 4 that incorporate passing, which are enjoyable as well as good training.

   b. All exercises pitting more attackers than defenders against each other, in a confined area such as a training grid, are extremely useful.

3. Match condition technique training.

   a. Small-sided games that increase the number of times each player handles the ball are excellent for passing practice.

   b. Same as exercise (a), except restrictions such as three-touch or two-touch are added to increase passing and reduce dribbling.

   c. Full 11-versus-11 matches, with restrictions such as three-touch or two-touch to increase the number of passes.

HEADING

The higher the caliber of a team's play, the less frequently they send the ball into the air. However, well-organized and sometimes "stacked" modern defenses often make it difficult if not impossible to move the ball on the ground in front of the goal to provide a shooting opportunity. Then players must put the ball into the air to create a scoring chance.

Regardless of the systems of play or the particular style a team uses, there will always be balls crossed in front of the goal to create scoring chances. For this reason teams will always need players who can successfully head balls out of danger in their defense and head balls on goal in attack. Poor headers will invariably find themselves at a great disadvantage at one time or another during a match.

Soccer is the only game where the players use their heads to play the ball. Unlike the technique of kicking, which all children practice by kicking rocks, cans, or what have you from the time they start to walk, heading is not a natural act. As a result, beginning players are usually apprehensive and afraid of getting hurt from heading a ball. This fear is the first thing coaches must address themselves to and the first thing players must overcome before they can master the technique of heading.

Figure 8.8 Heading the ball with the feet on the ground. As the ball approaches shift the weight to the back leg; make contact with the forehead; project the head through the ball and swing upper body and head forward to make contact. (Courtesy St. Louis University and The Athletic Institute)

Although any part of the head can be used to propel a soccer ball, the forehead is the area most frequently used. The thickest part of the skull is the frontal bone that forms the greatest part of the forehead; thus no pain accompanies striking the ball with the forehead. In addition, the forehead is the flattest area of the head and permits the greatest accuracy when heading a ball.

When introducing the technique of heading, the following progression sequence is recommended:

1. Have the players hold the ball in their hands and hit themselves in the forehead with it. At first they should do this lightly and then progressively harder. This will help them to understand that there is no pain involved when they head the ball properly.

2. It is a normal and involuntary act for the eyes to blink on contact, but coaches must stress that players must keep their eyes open as long as

Figure 8.9 Heading a ball after jumping into the air. Make contact with the ball at the apex of the jump, creating power by using the entire body weight. (By arrangement with Newcastle Chronicle and Journal Limited, England)

possible or else they could strike the ball improperly, which can be painful. Players can head accurately only if they keep their eyes open.

3. Have the players toss the ball a short distance into the air and make contact with the forehead.

4. Finally, a coach can introduce training exercises for heading after explaining and demonstrating the principles of proper heading techniques.

There are two primary heading techniques. Players head a ball either (1) while they are on the ground as in Figure 8.8 or (2) they will have to jump and head the ball in the air as in Figure 8.9. Both heading techniques have certain basic principles that must be followed.

Principles of Heading While on the Ground

The following principles should be adhered to when heading a ball while on the ground:

1. Spread the feet at a comfortable distance to provide proper balance, and bend the legs at the knees with one leg in front of the other.

2. Keep the weight on the balls of the feet to enable quick adjustment of body position.

3. As the ball approaches shift the body weight to the back leg, and bend the upper body backward.

4. Just prior to contacting the ball, shift weight to the front leg, and swing the upper body and head forward from the hips for greater power than when using only the head. The power is greater because a larger portion of the body weight is now used in striking the ball.

5. Keep eyes open and watch the ball until contact.

6. Bend the chin down and tighten the neck muscles just prior to contact.

7. Project the head through the ball for maximum power.

8. Extend the arms comfortably to help provide balance.

Principles of Heading While in the Air

The following principles should be adhered to when heading a ball in the air:

1. Whenever possible precede jumping into the air with a short run. This will help the body overcome inertia and permit a higher jump.

2. Make the take-off of the jump off one foot to achieve maximum height.

3. Upon take-off straighten the leg and push the body upward off the sole of the foot.

4. Bend the leg not used for take-off at the knee and swing it upward to help the body rise.

5. Also swing the arms upward on take-off to assist in the momentum of the jump.

6. Bend the upper body and head backward in anticipation of striking the ball.

7. Bend the chin down and tighten the neck muscles.

8. Just prior to contact swing the upper body and head forward.

9. Keep eyes open and watch the ball until contact is made.

10. Make contact through the ball with head at the apex of the jump, and with the power created by the force and weight of the entire upper body.

11. Time the jump carefully for proper accuracy and power.

Frequent Heading Errors

The following are some of the most frequent errors players make when heading a ball:

1. They allow the ball to hit the head instead of striking through the ball with the head and the force and weight of the entire upper body. This tremendously reduces the power of heading.

2. They close their eyes before contact, creating improper and sometimes painful contact with the ball resulting in poor accuracy.

3. Their poor balance prevents proper execution of heading technique.

4. Poor timing in jump-heading prevents the player from striking the ball at the apex of his jump, and greatly reduces his power and accuracy.

Special Heading Situations

Some heading situations necessitate altering the normal technique slightly. For example, when a player wishes to head a ball a short distance to a teammate's feet, less power is called for and the player need not utilize the weight and force of impact of the entire upper body. A snap of his head will generally suffice, and if the ball is coming very fast, he might just let it hit his forehead and rebound in the proper direction or even withdraw his head slightly on contact to take some of the pace off the ball.

Another situation that calls for altering normal heading technique is when a player can strike an approaching ball only by diving and making contact with his head. When teaching diving headers, it is imperative to stress the proper technique of landing after contact. The hands must be thrust out immediately after striking the ball so that the arms absorb most of the impact when the body hits the ground. As a player makes contact in a dive-header, his body should be almost parallel to the ground and he should throw its entire weight into the contact to achieve maximum power.

Exercises for Developing Heading

1. Pure technique exercises.

   a. Head juggling.

   1) Each player tries to see how many repetitive head balls he can perform without having the ball touch the ground or any other part of his body.

   2) In pairs, players head the ball back and forth.

   3) Two-touch heading in pairs. Same as exercise 2 except that each player must make two consecutive touches with his head.

   b. Ring heading. (See Chapter 4, page 115.)

   c. Pendulum heading. (The same exercises can be performed in pairs with one player serving the ball to the other if a pendulum is not available.)

   1) Repetitive heading in a standing position.

   2) Repetitive heading in a sitting position to accentuate the necessity of bending the upper body for power.

   3) Heading in a standing position, but after each header, players bring the ball under control and stop it with their heads.

   4) Repetitive jump heading.

   5) Same as exercise 3, except that players use jump-heading technique.

   6) Jump-heading with a short approach run added.

2. Match-related technique training.

   a. Pendulum exercises in pairs. (See Chapter 6, page 194.)

   b. Soccer Volleyball with heads only. (See Chapter 4, page 105.)

   c. Circle Ball with heads only. (See Chapter 4, page 109.)

   d. Distance Heading. (See Chapter 4, page 116.)

Diagram 8.3 Heading exercise.

e. In pairs, players face each other and remain about 5 yd apart. One player serves the ball while the other jogs forward and backward. The player heading the ball must return it to the server's hands. Services can be head high or higher for jump-heading training. (See Diagram 8.3.)

f. Two players stand one in front of the other facing the server. The player closest to the server jumps up only as a distraction and does not head the ball; the player behind him must time his jump to head the ball back to the server over the opponent.

3. Match condition technique training.

a. Head Goal Handball. (See Chapter 4, page 122.)

b. Goals From Heads Only. (See Chapter 4, page 119.)

SHOOTING

Whenever a player kicks a soccer ball, he does so to accomplish one of two things: (1) He wishes to pass it to a teammate, or (2) he wants to hit a shot on goal. All the kicking techniques mentioned in the section on passing technique are applicable for shooting on goal. The objective in shooting is very similar to that in passing since in both instances the player wishes to propel the ball with accuracy to a specific spot (Figure 8.10).

To achieve the greatest accuracy and power, players should use the instep kicking technique. The instep is a hard bony area with a relatively large surface that can provide considerable accuracy and power. However, different circumstances will dictate other kicking techniques for shooting on goal and the technique a player uses must be dictated by the specific situation.

Figure 8.10 Proper use of shooting technique brings about both accuracy and power. (By arrangement with Newcastle Chronicle and Journal Limited, England)

Players must be able to shoot well if they expect to apply the principle of finishing in attack. A coach cannot expect to win matches, regardless of what other proficiencies his team possesses, unless the players are able to finish scoring opportunities with good shots on goal. Without the ability to score, the most beautiful build-up play is wasted. It is useless for a player to move the ball beautifully from his own defensive third of the field up to the opponent's penalty area, if when he gets there no one can finish the play with a shot on goal that scores.

It is a fact that the ratio of goals that result from shots on goal is very poor. In general, a team may be satisfied if one out of every nine shots on goal results in a score. This fact must make it perfectly clear that no team that wishes to score goals can afford to pass up any respectable shooting opportunities. The more shots on goal a team takes, the greater is their chance of scoring goals and winning matches.

The biggest mistake made by players in attack is not to take a shot when the opportunity presents itself. Some players pass up shooting chances because they fear they will not score, while others try to be unselfish and pass to a teammate who might have a better chance to score. In either case players must be encouraged not to pass up shots, and every coach should try to find strikers who want to shoot and score whenever they get a chance.

To score goals, players need quick reactions to respond when shooting opportunities present themselves and the skill to shoot well. This skill includes the mastery of shooting techniques when kicking the ball under severe pressure from opponents, little time for reacting, and very limited space in which to play the ball. Players who expect to be good shooters must learn first-time shooting. It is better to hit 10 shots first-time, even if all of them fail to score, than to try to set up a perfect shot by bringing the ball under control and then fail to get even one shot off because of pressure from defenders. Remember that in the time that an attacking player brings a ball under control, an opponent will generally be able to run a distance of about 5 yd. Since it is rare to find enough space in front of the opponent's goal where there is no defender within 5 yd, defenders can always prevent shots if the attackers first try to bring the ball under control before attempting a shot on goal.

Shooting consists of two major components, accuracy and power. It is very important that coaches stress the importance of accuracy over power. Too many young players get carried away with the importance of power in shooting and as a result fail to concentrate on accuracy. Attacking players must try to make the job of the opponent's goalkeeper as difficult as possible. Thus all shots should be on target. Any ball that does not score and is not saved is not a good shot! The same holds true if a player is passing a ball to a teammate. Simply that he kicked it well does not mean it was a good pass, especially if possession of the ball is lost because the ball did not hit its target.

The lower the shot, the better it is because it will be more difficult for a goalkeeper to save. Whenever possible, players should direct shots towards the side of the goal opposite the goalkeeper and swerved away from him. Such shots are always more difficult to save, and if the goalkeeper does stop them from scoring they are most difficult for him to catch and hold. As a result, they will often provide the attacking side with a second shot on goal if the initial one is saved.

The importance of concentration on the part of the player shooting cannot be stressed too much. More often than not, when a shot on goal is poor, it is more a result of poor concentration than of poor kicking ability. The greatest physical and mental pressure of the match comes down on the players while they attempt to shoot and score. For this reason, they must practice shooting under match-type conditions as much as possible.

Whenever a shooting opportunity arises, a player must keep his head about him and not be nervous. This is even more true when the defense has been beaten and an attacking player finds himself with the ball and only the opponent's goalkeeper to beat. In this instance, the attacking player should shoot low and to the far corner as a general rule, although specific situations may dictate other methods such as chipping the ball over the keeper or dribbling around him to score.

Exercises for shooting are of little value if they do not reflect the type of shooting the players do in match situations. For example, the only time a player gets the opportunity to shoot a still ball is for a direct or indirect kick after a foul. These shots are usually delegated to one or two specialists on the team. If this is the case, then the majority of the players get an opportunity to shoot only moving balls. Why in the world, then, would any coach allow players to shoot on goal balls that are not moving?

In addition, at least 50 percent of the shots taken come from balls that are generally difficult to handle. These balls bounce, come at the players from all angles, and often come down from above. Therefore, 50 percent of all shooting exercises must reflect this type of shooting. Also, players rarely take shots without pressure from opponents so that once they have reasonably mastered the kicking technique, they should practice shooting under pressure and with little time to prepare for the shot.

Principles of Shooting

The following are some basic principles that players should apply when shooting on goal:

1. Use the simplest and most basic kicking technique whenever possible, combined with accuracy and power for best shooting results.

2. Remember that accuracy is more important than power in shooting.

3. Shoot quickly, concentrate on technique, and remain calm.

4. Shoot low, to the far post, and bend balls away from the goalkeeper.

Frequent Shooting Errors

The following are some of the most frequent errors players make when shooting:

1. Lack of concentration as a result of pressure.

2. The use of improper kicking technique.

3. Too much concentration on power and not enough on accuracy.

4. Fear to shoot because of the possibility of failing to score.

5. Rushing the shot from lack of patience and poise in front of the goal.

Exercises for Developing Shooting

1. Pure technique exercises.

   a. All exercises for kicking a ball, especially those stressing accuracy, prior to introducing shooting at a goal.

   b. Exercises for kicking with the use of a pendulum ball.

   c. Target shooting. (See Chapter 4, page 113.)

   d. Shooting at goal from outside the penalty area. The age and strength of the players determine the specific distance to practice shooting. While still acquiring the proper kicking technique, players may shoot both stationary and moving balls.

2. Match-related technique training.

   a. The shooter positions himself about 12 to 15 yd out from the goal and receives varied services of the ball to shoot on goal. A defender is positioned 5 yd away from the shooter and challenges as soon as the shooter receives the ball. First-time shooting should be stressed whenever possible. (See Diagram 8.4.)

   b. Two attacking players start from 35 yd out from goal with one ball. They must beat one defender who opposes them and get a good shot on goal.

   c. Same as exercise (b) except that three attackers try to beat two defenders.

   d. Four-wall soccer. (See Chapter 4, page 117.)

   e. Pin Soccer. (See Chapter 4, page 112.)

3. Match condition technique training.

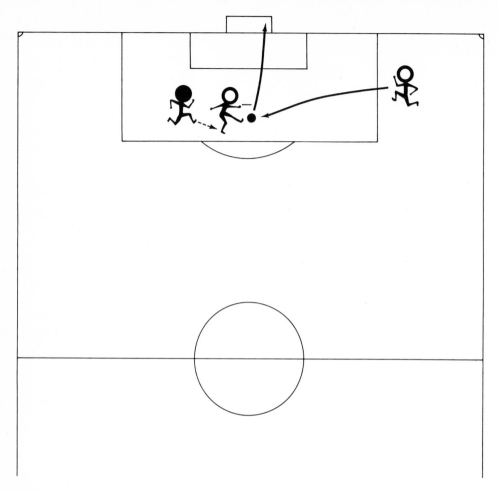

Diagram 8.4 Shooting exercise.

a. Small-sided games with full goals and goalkeepers will increase the frequency of shots per team as well as per player.

b. Four-goal soccer. (See Chapter 4, page 129.)

c. Two-way soccer. (See Chapter 4, page 126.)

d. Half-field soccer. (See Chapter 4, page 131.)

e. Attack versus Defense. (See Chapter 4, page 133.)

"Tackling" refers to taking the ball from an opponent. It is one of the most effective ways of winning the ball, and a player does not need to be a giant to be an effective tackler. He must simply master all the aspects of tackling and challenge for the ball in a determined manner.

Unfortunately, especially at the professional level, players have used tackling to inflict pain on opponents and intentionally disabling them so that they cannot continue to play. Such brutal tactics have been used far too frequently by defenders, especially against top strikers. A prime example is the brutal mauling of Pelé during the 1966 World Cup competitions in England, where he was fouled badly under the guise of a tackle in two matches and could not continue to play. The loss of his play was a key factor in the elimination of the Brazilian National team in the first round of the competition. Certainly soccer is a physical and aggressive game, but there is no room in the sport for outright brutality and the intentional crippling of opponents.

Improper tackling can also hurt and injure the tackler. As a result, correct tackling is a technique that must be properly taught, just as heading, so that players will perform without the fear of pain. Many poor tacklers are simply reluctant to tackle because of a painful experience while they were first learning the technique. Nonetheless, it is a technique that all players must master, especially in modern soccer where players interchange positions frequently and attacking players often find themselves in the role of defenders.

Unlike many other soccer techniques, successful tackling requires as much tactical play on the part of a player as it does proper technique of the tackle itself. Unsuccessful tackles are more often a result of improper preparation and tackling at the wrong time than of improper technique.

Jockeying

Jockeying a player with the ball, by giving ground and maneuvering him in preparation for tackling, is a most important aspect of attempting to win the ball. Proper defensive jockeying can take the advantage away from the player with the ball. By feinting properly when about to tackle, a defender can take the offensive and the dribbler, instead of concentrating on how he is going to beat the defender, will have to worry about the upcoming tackle. In addition, proper jockeying can maneuver the

Figure 8.11 Proper jockeying technique is essential to being effective in defense. (Courtesy St. Louis University and The Athletic Institute)

dribbler towards another defender or near a touchline where the limited space will increase the chances of a successful tackle. (See Figure 8.11.)

When jockeying an opponent, the defender must take short steps, maintain good body balance with knees slightly bent, and keep his weight on the balls of his feet to enable quick changes of direction. He should never jockey facing the opponent directly, for the opponent could dribble past on either side. Instead, the defender should jockey at an angle giving the dribbler space in the area where the defender wishes him to move. By moving the opponent around, the defender can also force him to control the ball with his weakest foot, since he will be forced to shield it. This will also increase the chances of a successful tackle.

It is important for all defenders to utilize the initial stages of a match to familiarize themselves with the strong and weak points of their opponents' play. Every player prefers to use one foot more than another, and most forwards will favor some feinting techniques over others. The more a defender knows about the play of the various opponents he faces, the greater the likelihood of executing successful tackles and generally minimizing their effectiveness.

Challenging for the Ball

Besides gaining the ability to jockey well, defenders must understand when it is most advantageous to commit themselves to a tackle. This requires precise timing, and more often than not will determine whether the tackle will be successful.

An opponent can be challenged for the ball either (1) when he is about to control a ball he is receiving or (2) while he is dribbling it. If he is receiving the ball, the ideal time to tackle is just as he is attempting to bring it under control. At that moment he is concentrating on ball control and a challenge for the ball will force him to worry about the defender as well. Thus not only does he not have the ball under full control yet but he also may misplay the ball as a result of the defender's pressure.

If a player is dribbling, the proper time to challenge is at the moment the dribbler pushes the ball forward. Even if the ball is close to him, it will be moving away and towards the defender, providing the optimum chance for a successful tackle.

Types of Tackling Technique

There are several different forms of tackling technique, depending on the position of the defender with regard to the player with the ball. The most frequently used is the block tackle, which is implemented when the two players are facing each other. The other tackling techniques are a block tackle from the side, a tackle from behind, and a slide tackle. It is most important for players to familiarize themselves with all the techniques so that they will be able to use whatever tackle a given situation calls for.

Principles of Block Tackling

The following are some basic principles that players should apply for block tackling:

1. Move in close to the opponent in preparation for the tackle.

2. Whenever possible, wait for defensive support prior to committing yourself to tackling.

3. Position nontackling foot to the side and behind the ball.

4. Bend knees to absorb impact and for balance.

5. Raise toe of the tackling foot slightly, the knee turned out, and hold the ankle tight.

6. Make the block with the inside of the foot at the center of the ball.

7. Put the entire body weight into the tackle, directing the force through the center of the ball.

8. Tackle aggressively and with determination to win the ball.

9. Try to win the ball by dragging it over the opponent's foot or pushing it between his legs after making the block.

Frequent Block Tackling Errors

The following are some of the most frequent errors players make when block tackling:

1. Improper timing.

2. Not tackling with determination.

3. Leaning away from the ball during the contact.

4. Placing all of the body weight on the tackling foot.

5. Holding the ankle of the tackling foot too loosely, resulting in injury.

Tackling an opponent from behind is legal but difficult since a player must be certain of first making contact with the ball. This is a dangerous tackle to use in a player's own penalty area because a slight breakdown in timing or technique could result in a costly foul, leading to a penalty kick for the opposition.

Principles of Sliding Tackling

The sliding tackle can be a very helpful technique, but players should not use it too freely and must consider it a desperation measure. This is because the defender attempting it will be completely out of the play if his tackle is unsuccessful since he will be lying on the ground in no position to recover and help in defense.

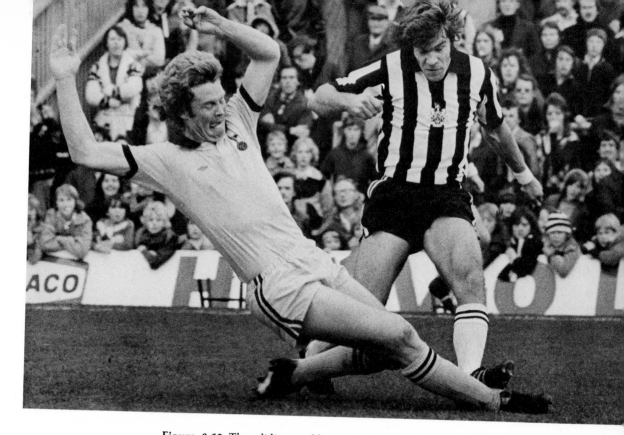

Figure 8.12 The sliding tackle can be effective but should be used only in desperation when attempting to dispossess an opponent of the ball. (By arrangement with Newcastle Chronicle and Journal Limited, England)

Players should apply the following principles in sliding tackles (see Figure 8.12):

1. Get as near the player with the ball as possible before starting the slide.

2. Use proper timing.

3. Use the leg farthest from the opponent as the tackling leg.

4. Make the slide on the side of the nontackling leg.

5. Make the tackle as the opponent pushes the ball forward and away from himself.

Diagram 8.5 Tackling exercise.

6. Variations of this sliding-tackle technique such as making contact on the ball with the leg used to slide on can also be used effectively.

Exercises for Developing Tackling

1. Pure technique exercises.

   a. Two players position themselves facing each other and 1 ft away from a ball placed between them. Simultaneously they approach the ball and practice proper techniques of block tackling. (See Diagram 8.5.)

   b. Same as exercise (a), except after blocking the ball, each man tries to win it.

   c. Individual players practice making proper contact for tackling by placing a ball near a wall and blocking it into the wall.

2. Match-related technique training.

   a. One player dribbles the ball while another practices various tackling techniques. The dribbler should provide a limited amount of resistance.

   b. Grid Dribbling. (See Chapter 4, page 117.)

3. Match condition technique training.

   a. One versus One. (See Chapter 4, page 135.)

   b. Small-sided games (three versus three up to six versus six) with a restriction that no player may pass the ball prior to taking on and beating an opponent while dribbling. This will create many tackling opportunities.

The throw-in is the simplest soccer technique to master and execute properly, and yet too frequently possession of the ball is lost because of an improper throw. Since it is a restart situation, the player throwing the ball is not exposed to the physical pressures of normal match play, and as long as he knows the proper technique and concentrates on what he is doing, there is no reason for him to commit a foul throw.

Unfortunately, however, because it is such an elementary technique, many coaches ignore it in training and place little emphasis on having players practice it. Yet it can be a very useful attacking tool since every throw-in is an opportunity to initiate an attacking thrust.

Chapter 5, which deals with restarts, covered the tactical aspects of throw-ins in depth. In this chapter, therefore, we will cover only the specific technique required for proper execution of throw-ins.

The technique variations for throw-ins are quite limited by the laws of soccer, and unlike other soccer techniques, throw-ins allow little room for individuality. The laws clearly state that the ball must be thrown by a player facing the playing area, with his feet on or outside the touchline. Part of each foot must be on the ground, and the player must throw the ball from over his head, using both hands.

Principles of Throwing the Ball

Coaches must stress the following principles of throwing the ball into play:

1. Hold the ball with both hands, fingers spread comfortably, thumbs near each other, and apply equal force from both hands during the throw.

2. Keep the feet either in a straddle position or with one foot slightly in front of the other, spread a comfortable distance (Figures 8.13 and 8.14).

3. Lift the ball over the head with the arms bending at the elbows.

4. Arch the trunk and head back and bring the ball behind the head, bending the knees for balance.

5. Straighten the arms and knees as you throw the ball forward in one

Figure 8.13 When throwing the ball into play, the ball must be brought over the head, using the entire force of the upper body, and thrown with one smooth motion. (Courtesy St. Louis University and The Athletic Institute)

full motion, bringing the trunk forward to utilize maximum body weight and force.

6. Release the ball when it is over the head or in front of the body, and use a full follow-through with the arms and trunk for power as the body weight is shifted to the balls of the feet if in a straddle position, or to the front leg if one foot is in front of the other.

7. Make certain to maintain contact with the ground with both feet. It may be necessary to drag the back foot if throwing from a position where one foot is in front of the other.

In addition to the specific principles of technique, players must concentrate on the following points:

Figure 8.14 Throw-ins may be made with the feet straddled or with one foot in front of the other. It is imperative that both feet are in contact with the ground when the ball is released for the throw-in to be legal. (Courtesy St. Louis University and The Athletic Institute)

1. Throwing the ball quickly whenever possible, not allowing the opponents to organize their defense fully.

2. Throwing the ball accurately and making it as easy as possible to control.

3. Throwing the ball to an unmarked man whenever possible.

4. Throwing the ball forward whenever possible to apply the principle of penetration in attack.

Frequent Throwing Errors

The following are some of the most common errors players make while throwing the ball into play:

1. Lack of concentration on proper technique.

2. Feet spread too wide resulting in poor balance.

3. Ball held with hands too far apart.

4. Throwing the ball without the support of body weight.

5. Throwing the ball with the force of one hand instead of with the equal force of both.

6. Raising the rear leg off the ground during the throw.

7. Bringing the ball over the head and dropping it instead of throwing with a full follow-through.

Exercises for Developing Throw-ins

Since throw-ins come about in restart situations, the only pressure on the player throwing the ball is mental. Therefore as long as players master the proper technique of throwing the ball and concentrate on it in match play, they should never commit a foul throw.

Exercises for learning the technique involve simple imitation, throwing the ball at a target such as a wall or another player. All technique exercises that require the ball served to a player can have the server utilize the proper throw-in technique.

GOALKEEPING

The goalkeeper is the only real specialist on a soccer field and thus has his own unique techniques to master because he is the only player on the field who uses his hands.

Unfortunately, because a team consists of 10 field players and only 1 goalkeeper, coaches often fail to devote sufficient time to training their goalkeeper and never establish a specific training program for him. This can be a disastrous oversight! The goalkeeper is every bit as important as any other player, more important, in fact. A good keeper can often make a season successful and a poor one can, through just a few errors, have a terrible effect on the outcome of a match.

Whenever possible one coach should be assigned to oversee the training of a team's goalkeepers. It is far more important, if a team has more than one coach, to assign one coach to the goalkeepers than to have an assistant working with the field players.

A goalkeeper can make few errors that are not punished by the opponents' scoring a goal. As a result, to be successful a keeper must master all the necessary techniques required of his position and practice them extensively so that he can execute them as flawlessly as possible in match competition.

Personal Qualities of Goaltenders

Above all else a goalkeeper must have sure hands that will enable him to catch and hold on to the ball. Agility and quick reactions are also vital qualities. All other things being equal, it is preferable to have a fairly tall goalkeeper, 6 ft or perhaps an inch or two taller. However, although height may give a goaltender greater range for collecting balls in the air, it should not be preferred to the agility of a slightly shorter man.

The best goalkeeper is the one who prevents opponents from taking shots. This is the top priority in performing his primary task, which is to prevent goals. Only if he is unable to prevent a shot should he rely on making saves off the goal line.

Since the goalkeeper is the only one in the penalty area permitted to use his hands, he must make the most of this advantage and attempt to collect as many balls as possible, especially those in the air. The keeper who always stays on the goal line as if he were nailed or glued to it gives up this great advantage and must try to save many shots that might otherwise never have been taken. As a result he is bound to concede more goals simply because as the number of shots taken increases, so does the probability that one will get to the back of the net.

Because the penalty area is usually crowded with players, a goalkeeper must be strong enough to withstand the physical punishment he is exposed to. Even though the laws of the game protect goalkeepers from physical abuse, invariably they will be forced to go after balls where contact with opponents is imminent. They must be confident to the point of cockiness and courageous almost to the point of insanity.

Many people have said that a goalkeeper has to be at least a little crazy. After all, what sane person would want a job where he is bombarded with shots, must fly through the air to make saves and then land on the ground, dive at the feet of opponents to win balls, and be in a position where one human error could make people forget all the brilliant saves during a match and label him the buffoon who lost the match for his team?

Crazy or not, the goalkeeper is perhaps the most important player on a team. He must do far more than just prevent goals. A good goalkeeper, because of his unique vantage point for observing the play in front of him, must be the director of the defense, a tactician positioning his defenders in the most advantageous places, and a vitally important initiator of an attacking thrust after a save.

Defensive Principles of Goalkeeping

Like the techniques of field players, the techniques a goalkeeper must use have special principles that he needs to adhere to for their proper execution. Naturally the most important techniques of goalkeeping are those used in defense to perform the keeper's number one role— preventing goals.

The goalkeeper must be familiar with proper positioning before he proceeds to master the techniques of making saves. Thus the two areas of defensive principles of goalkeeping are his positioning without the ball and his handling of the ball.

The principles of (1) basic positioning, (2) reducing shooting angles, and (3) challenging opponents for the ball are the three positioning areas goalkeepers must familiarize themselves with. The second area of defensive principles of goalkeeping deals with the technique of making saves by catching, punching, or deflecting the ball. The ball may come in high, medium, or low, and every goalkeeper must master the techniques necessary to handle and save balls regardless of their height, speed, or angle.

Principles of basic goalkeeper positioning

The following basic principles of the goalkeeper's ready position must be adhered to (see Figure 8.15):

1. The position must ready the keeper to make a save.

2. He straddles the feet comfortably and bends them slightly at the knees for balance.

3. He keeps his body weight on the balls of his feet to allow quick changes of direction.

4. He bends his trunk slightly forward for balance.

5. He keeps his arms close to his body, bent at the elbows, with the

Figure 8.15 The goalkeeper in ready position must be prepared to move in any direction to make a save. (Courtesy St. Louis University and The Athletic Institute)

palms of his hands open and the fingers slightly spread, pointing a little upward.

6. He fixes his eyes on the ball and the players around it.

Principles of reducing shooting angles

To reduce the likelihood that a shot will score and to make the task as difficult as possible for the opposing forwards, goalkeepers must position themselves in the spot where they stand the greatest chance of catching the ball, and covering the greatest area of the goal. This is referred to as reducing the shooting angles and is accomplished by adhering to the following principles (see Diagrams 8.6 and 8.7):

1. The goal line between the posts should be considered the base of a triangle.

2. The vertex of the triangle is the position of the ball and is therefore constantly changing.

3. The goalkeeper, as a general rule, should position himself so that when he dives, he could save any ball between the imaginary sides of the triangle.

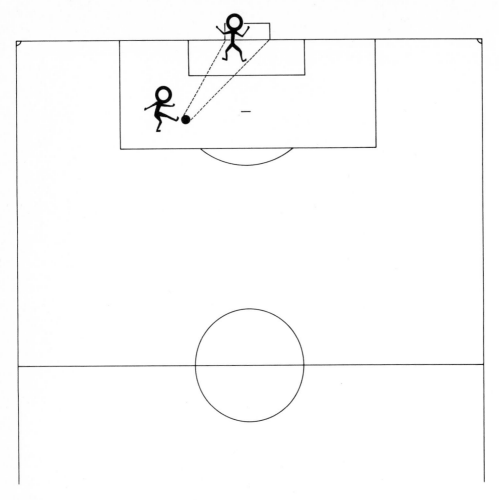

Diagram 8.6 Goalkeeper reducing the shooting angle.

4. When it is not possible for the goalkeeper to comply with principle 3, he should always make certain that he can save all balls to the goalpost nearest him and sacrifice limited space to the far post.

Principles of challenging opponents for the ball

Sometimes an opposing forward with the ball beats the last defender and advances towards the goal with only the goalkeeper left to beat. If the goalkeeper is certain that none of his defenders will be able to recover

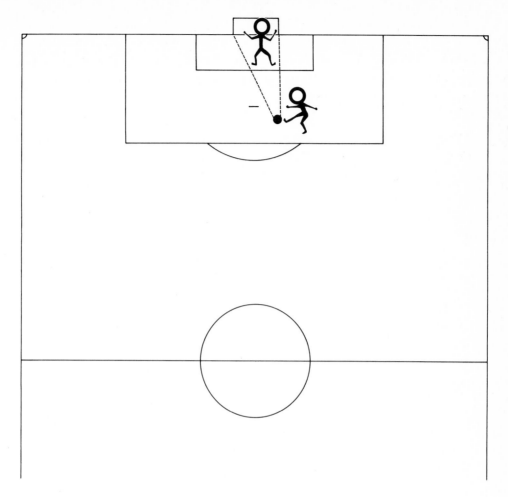

Diagram 8.7 Goalkeeper reducing the shooting angle.

before the forward shoots, he must advance to challenge the player with the ball and not permit him to pick his own shooting spot. To a great extent, he must take the attitude of a defender jockeying an opponent and become the aggressor rather than the victim. By coming out, the goalkeeper will distract the forward with the ball and force him to concentrate on the movements of the keeper as well as where and how to shoot. This small edge may help the keeper prevent a goal.

In some cases it will be necessary for the goalkeeper to go down to the ground in an attempt either to win the ball or to block the shot off the

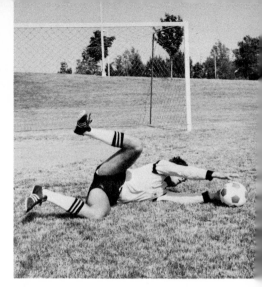

Figure 8.16 When a goalkeeper has to win or save a ball from an opponent's feet, he must go down on his side, reach for the ball with his hands, and produce the largest area that may block a shot. (Courtesy St. Louis University and The Athletic Institute)

forward's feet, as in Figure 8.16. When this situation arises, the goalkeeper should remember the following principles:

1. He should go down on his side with his feet first, as a baseball player would slide into a base.

2. He should direct his upper body and hands in the direction where the player with the ball is heading, in order to gather in the ball if the dribbler plays it too far in front.

3. He must try to produce the largest and longest surface to block the shot, and take care that the ball cannot squeeze between his body and the ground as he slides.

4. If the slide is properly timed, it could block a shot since it will be difficult for the forward to shoot a ball that rises over the keeper's outstretched body.

Principles of catching high balls

The main difficulty that arises in executing these techniques is deciding when to leave the goal mouth to go after a ball and what technique to use

Figure 8.17 When catching a ball in the air, the goalkeeper must try to catch it at the apex of his jump. (By arrangement with Newcastle Chronicle and Journal Limited, England)

at a given moment. The answers can only come from experience since they all depend on individual judgment based on individual capabilities. One thing is certain, however, and that is that the goalkeeper must gather in all balls in the 6-yd box in front of the goal.

The following are principles for catching high balls (see Figure 8.17):

1. Face the direction from which the ball is coming, and keep eyes on the ball.

2. Call for the ball when going after it so that teammates can get out of the way.

3. Jump into the air from a one-footed take-off to gain maximum height.

4. Catch the ball at the apex of the jump, with both hands, arms outstretched, and fingers comfortably spread.

5. As soon as the ball is caught, bend the elbows and bring the ball down in front of the body, holding it tightly.

Figure 8.18 To catch a medium-high ball, the goalkeeper should allow it to come into his chest or stomach and then curl his arms under and around it. (Courtesy St. Louis University and The Athletic Institute)

Principles of catching medium-height balls

The following principles are for catching medium-height balls (see Figure 8.18):

1. Face the ball and keep eyes on it.

2. As the ball approaches, get the body behind it.

3. Allow the ball to come into the chest or stomach depending on its height, and retract that part of the body to absorb some of the impact.

4. Curl the arms under the ball, and on contact tighten the fingers around the ball.

Principles of catching low balls

The following principles for catching low balls must be adhered to:

1. Face the ball and keep eyes on it.

2. As the ball approaches, get the body behind it.

Figure 8.19 When collecting a ground ball, with the feet together the goalkeeper must bend down to pick up the ball and then curl his arms around it. (Courtesy St. Louis University and The Athletic Institute)

3. Bend down from the waist with the feet together and place the hands, with palms up, to gather in the ball. (See Figure 8.19.)

4. Some goalkeepers prefer to turn and kneel on one leg as the ball approaches, as in Figure 8.20. The important thing is to be certain that the ball cannot go between the legs.

5. As the ball rolls into the hands, curl the arms under it and bring it up to the chest.

Principles of punching balls

Whenever a goalkeeper is unable to catch a high ball—for example, when several other players are also jumping for it—he must either punch it away or deflect it over the goal. However, every goalkeeper must try to *catch* the ball if he can, for if he punches it away, chances are that the opposition may retain ball possession.

The following principles for punching balls must be adhered to (see Figure 8.21):

1. Approach the jump for the ball the same way as when jumping to catch a high ball.

Figure 8.20 Some goalkeepers prefer to use a half-kneeling position when collecting ground balls. (By arrangement with Newcastle Chronicle and Journal Limited, England)

2. At the start of the jump, bend the arms at the elbow and punch the ball with the fists at the apex of the jump.

3. Extend the arms during the jump to aid in overcoming inertia and to make contact with the greatest possible force.

4. Whenever possible, punch the ball with both fists to provide the largest and flattest surface area possible for maximum accuracy and general safety.

5. When punching with one fist, use the hand farthest away from the direction in which the ball is intended to go. This presents a natural overarm swing and provides maximum power.

6. Punch the ball in a direction away from where it came.

Principles of deflecting balls

When a goalkeeper is near the goal mouth and cannot catch the ball, he may wish to deflect it either over the crossbar or around the uprights.

Figure 8.21 Punching the ball is another method goalkeepers use to make a save. (By arrangement with Newcastle Chronicle and Journal Limited, England)

Goalkeepers use this technique most often when punching the ball may not clear it out of danger. Although it will concede a corner kick to the opposition, it is still an effective method of saving a goal.

The following principles for deflecting balls must be adhered to:

1. Use the fingers and the part of the palm nearest the fingers to tip the ball.

2. Since power is not necessary, use the arm nearest the ball to deflect.

3. Above all else, tip balls in a manner that is most natural and effective even if it deviates from textbook principles.

Principles of diving

The last opportunity available to a team to prevent its opponents from scoring is for the goalkeeper to save a shot off the goal line. In general, the techniques he uses for this are the same as catching, punching, or deflecting balls. However, in addition, the goalkeeper must master the technique of diving in the event that a shot is not within easy reach of his body but is within reach of the hands.

A goalkeeper can dive to save balls regardless of the height of their flight. The principles of diving will vary slightly depending on where the ball is, but, in general, goalkeepers should adhere to the following principles:

1. Take up the normal ready position.

2. If the ball is quite far away, take one or two preliminary sideways steps.

3. The take-off foot is the one closest to the direction of the dive.

4. Transfer weight to the take-off leg, which is bent at the knee.

5. As soon as the foot leaves the ground, swing the arms upward to reach for the ball and help overcome inertia.

6. Straighten the take-off leg during take-off, and bend the other leg at the knee, swinging the knee upward.

7. Bend both legs slightly while in the air.

8. Bend the arms reaching for the ball slightly at the elbows.

9. Fix the eyes on the ball the entire time.

10. If there is any chance that the ball cannot be caught and held, punch or deflect it away.

11. The dive is lateral, with the body facing the field of play. (See Figure 8.22.) This permits landing on the side.

12. Soften the landing by making contact on the ground first with the leg closest to it, then the arms, and finally the side of the body. When the upper body comes down first, make initial contact with the arm nearest the ground.

13. Draw the ball into the body as soon as possible for protection, with the arms wrapped around it.

The most common fault in diving by novices is that they tend to fall instead of really becoming airborne. In addition, they dive with their

Figure 8.22 When diving to make a save, the goalkeeper should dive with his body facing the field. (By arrangement with Newcastle Chronicle and Journal Limited, England)

bodies facing the ground. This can be very dangerous both because it is more difficult to catch the ball this way and because when landing they could be seriously injured.

Attacking Principles of Goalkeeping

As with any other player on a team, as soon as the goalkeeper wins possession of the ball, he becomes an attacking player. It is vital that every goalkeeper realize this since often he can be instrumental in generating an attacking thrust at the opposition's goal through proper distribution of the ball.

There are only two ways a goalkeeper can distribute the ball to his teammates. He can use his hands and throw or roll the ball out, or he can kick the ball, using a volley or drop-kick technique. Regardless of the method he selects, it is imperative that he be as accurate as possible and always try to get the ball to an unmarked teammate in the best position to penetrate the defense of the opposition. The most important priority, however, is to maintain ball possession, and if the ball might be lost, then it should be lost as far away from the goal as possible. The goalkeeper, like any attacking player, must remember that the degree of risk he can take is directly related to how far the ball is from his goal.

Throwing or rolling the ball out will give the goalkeeper greater accuracy than kicking it. However, most goalkeepers can kick a ball much farther than they can throw it, and the depth of penetration a long kick achieves may sometimes be worth the loss of some distribution accuracy.

Rolling a ball out to a teammate is quite similar to bowling. The important thing is to make certain that the ball rolls along the ground with sufficient speed to reach the intended player without being intercepted.

The goalkeeper can throw a ball using either the over-the-head technique used in throwing a baseball or a slingshot technique preferred by many goalkeepers. In the slingshot technique the goalkeeper holds the ball more in the base of his palm, brings it over his head and flings it forward using his entire arm as a catapult. In the baseball-type throw, he bends the elbow of his throwing arm and extends it forward as he throws with a whipping motion of the hand and forearm.

When kicking the ball to start an attack, the goalkeeper may either drop it to his foot and volley it with the instep, or drop it to the ground and half-volley kick it with the instep just as the ball starts to bounce back up. The drop-kick or half-volley technique will usually enable the goalkeeper to keep the trajectory of the ball lower and his teammates to bring it more easily under control. In addition, any kick that goes high into the air is a free ball since members of either team will be able to get into position to receive it; thus the chances of maintaining possession are reduced to 50–50. Every goalkeeper should always try to distribute balls so that his team can maintain possession of them. Otherwise he will find the ball back in his area again very soon, possibly necessitating another save.

Goalkeepers' Circuit

The following goalkeepers' circuit was compiled by Gary Hindley, soccer coach at Trenton State College. Basically a preseason or in-season workout, it incorporates all the necessary skills of net play in a match-type situation. Goalkeepers should follow it every day, except possibly the day before a game.

The entire circuit, with two or three goalkeepers rotating for each drill, should take approximately 20 to 25 min. Each goalie, while in the net, should give 100 percent concentration and effort. A coach should be present for the first five or six workouts to ensure that the goalies are doing the exercises properly. Also, the goalkeepers should perform the entire circuit in an isolated goal area away from the rest of the team.

1 *Warm-up Exercise.*   Kick balls lightly at the goalie from 12–15 yd out; kicks should be directly at him, moderately high, moderately low, several to the right and left; no diving or overextending; 12 to 15 kicks.

2. *Warm-up Exercise.*   Same as exercise 1, but kick from 15–18 yd out and much harder; 12 to 15 kicks.

3. *Upper body reaction exercise.*   Have the goalie kneel on the goal line directly in the center of the goal; kick balls directly at him—some high, some low, some on the ground, some just to the right and left; kicks should be progressive from soft, to moderate, to moderately hard; 12 to 15 kicks.

4. *Turn exercise.*   Have the goalie stand in a ready position with his toes on the goal line, facing directly towards the net; a kicker should position himself near the center of the penalty area and about 15–18 yd out; just before the kicker attempts his kick, he must shout *"turn"*; on the command the goalie turns quickly and attempts to save the ball, which by this time has been kicked; the kicker should mix up his kicks—some high, low, soft, right, left, hard, etc.; 12 to 15 kicks.

5. *Tipping exercise.*

a. The goalie stands about 3 yd from the midpoint of the goal line and in front of it; the kicker (or tosser) should be about 12–15 yd out; the tosser attempts to hit the crossbar with the ball on a looping toss; the goalie must tip the ball over the bar; six to eight tips. (*Note*: the ball should be caught whenever possible.)

b. Same as exercise (a), but the goalie moves out 5 or 6 yd; six to eight tips.

c. Same as exercise (a), but the goalie moves out 12–15 yd; four to six tips.

6. *Diving exercise.*   Have the goalie lie directly on the goal line on his stomach with his arms fully extended so that his fingers are touching the inside of the post (his feet are pointing towards the other post); the kicker is about 15 yd from the goal; on the command *"up,"* the goalie bounces up, takes one large step, and dives to save the ball which the kicker has kicked in the direction of the far post; the same action is repeated, with the goalie facing the other post; 10 to 12 dives.

7. *High ball contact exercise.*   The goalie kneels on all fours, looking at the ground at approximately the penalty mark; the kicker stands directly behind him, punts the ball into the air, and shouts *"up"*; as the goalie attempts to get up and go after the ball for the save, the kicker attempts to harass, hold, or bump, the goalkeeper; 8 to 10 saves.

8. *Crosses and corner kick obstruction and contact exercise.*   Goalie assumes his normal position for deep crosses and corner kicks; the kicker is out deep in the wing or corner area; another player (most likely one of the other goalkeepers) positions himself alongside or in front of the goalie; on the cross, he attempts to deliberately obstruct, harass, bump, or hold, the goalkeeper attempting the save; four to six crosses from each side.

9. *Reaction exercise.*   The goalie positions himself just in front of the goal line and shades toward one post; two kickers, each with a ball, are about 10 yd out and directly in line with each post; each in turn kicks a moderately rolling ball towards his goal post. As soon as the goalie has made one save and returned the ball with a roll, the other player kicks towards the other post, and so on; 16 to 20 kicks.

10. *Offensive Exercise.*

> a. *Kicking exercise* (punts or drop kicks)   Kick into the net from approximately 8–10 yd out; 12 to 15 kicks with the dominant leg and 2 to 3 kicks with the opposite leg.
>
> b. *Rolling exercise.*   Practice a quick release roll towards a stationary and a moving player; six to eight rolls.
>
> c. *Short throw or sling exercise.*   Practice the short release towards a stationary and a moving player; 8 to 10 throws.
>
> d. *Long throw exercise.*   Practice the long release towards a stationary and a moving player; 8 to 10 throws.

e. *Four-man save and release exercise.* The goalie positions himself in the goal mouth according to the position of the ball to be played; two players, each with several balls, position themselves on the right side of the field approximately 35–40 yd out; another pair, also with several balls, position themselves on the left side; one player in the group on the right lofts or shoots a ball towards the goal; the goalie makes the save and releases towards one of the players on the left side who has moved to receive the release pass (either short for roll, medium for sling or throw, or long for kick or throw). After the release the other player on the left then shoots the ball towards the goal, the goalie makes the save, and releases towards a moving player on the right; the sequence then repeats itself; six to eight releases each side.

11. *Situations exercises.* A few different players each day should be assigned to work with the goalies on specific situations; several things they should cover are angles, lobs, spinning shots, coming out, one on one, penalty kicks, walls, and so on.

It is extremely important that a coach teach his goalkeepers the proper techniques of playing in the goal before he places them in this circuit. Without the knowledge, understanding, and proper execution of these skills, the circuit will only help develop bad habits.

REFERENCES

Allison, Malcolm. *Soccer for Thinkers.* Pelham Books, London, 1967.

Cramer, Dettmar. *United States Soccer Federation "Coaches Manual."* Four Maples Press, Minisink Hills, Pa., 1973.

Csanadi, Arpad. *Soccer.* Corvina, Budapest, 1965.

Gardner, Paul. *Pelé: The Master and His Methods.* Pepsi Co., Purchase, N.Y., 1973.

Greaves, Jimmy. *Soccer Techniques and Tactics.* Pelham Books, London, 1966.

Hughes, Charles F.C. *Tactics and Teamwork.* E.P. Publishing, Wakefield, England, 1973.

Jones, Ken and Pat Welton. *Football Skills and Tactics.* Marshall Cavendish, London, 1973.

Smith, Stratton and Eric Batty. *International Coaching Book.* Souvenir Press, London, 1966.

Vogelsinger, Hubert. *The Challenge of Soccer.* Allyn and Bacon, Boston, 1973.

Wade, Alan. *The FA Guide to Training and Coaching.* William Heinemann, London, 1967.

Wilson, Bob. *Goalkeeping.* Pelham Books, London, 1970.

Winterbottom, Walter. *Soccer Coaching.* William Heinemann, London, 1952.

———. *Training for Soccer.* William Heinemann, London, 1960.

9

Coaching
Soccer Tactics

FITNESS, technique, and tactics make up the foundation for match performance in soccer. Ideally players should be competent in all three areas, but unfortunately this is not always the case. Thus the less capable a player is in one area, the more he needs the other two to make up for the deficiency.

Tactics are the application of technique in match play by using fitness and thinking. Thus it is imperative that coaches devise tactics for players to suit their ability level. If this is not done and tactics are pushed ahead of technique, the players will be unable to implement them in match play and will simply become frustrated.

It is wisest to keep tactics as simple as possible to ensure their success, for the more complex the tactics, the greater the chance that the players will be unable to apply them successfully. Proper application of tactics will mold individual players into a cohesive and effective team unit.

Players of limited skill can greatly enhance their value to a team by being sound and intelligent tacticians, especially since players implement much of their individual tactics without the ball. During a match a player is without the ball for 97 percent of the time, and it is during this time that proper positioning, support of teammates, and intelligent running to make use of and create space can turn a player with average skills into a very valuable asset.

Tactics are the implementation of the principles of play in matches. They include the development of systems of play, but only as a means of helping to determine specific responsibilities for the players. Ideally a coach determines the best tactics for his team by taking the best of all he has seen or heard, improving on this by adding his own ideas, and then adapting all this knowledge to his own players.

The match itself will test the effectiveness and soundness of a coach's tactics. The match will clearly show what is working and what is not and will thus dictate what he must change or stress in the training sessions. This is true of the team as a whole as well as of individual players, for it will become quite clear which players understand and which do not what is expected of them in every possible situation.

Just as coaching techniques has a series of steps leading up to the implementation of technique under match conditions, so also does the coaching of tactics follow a progressive build-up pattern. Tactics fall into the three categories: individual tactics, group tactics, and team tactics. These three areas must be coached progressively, but even after a coach has gone into team tactical work, the players must practice the other two areas constantly since all three are integral parts of match tactics as a whole.

The game of soccer invariably boils down to one-versus-one confrontations. In attack a player with the ball will have to beat his opponent by dribbling, passing, or shooting, and when he is without the ball, he will have to go on runs to free himself of the opponent marking him to place himself in a position to receive the ball. In defense a player must limit the effectiveness of his opponent by preventing him from making good penetrating passes or taking a shot if he has the ball and through tight marking prevent him from receiving the ball. Possession of the ball is won and lost by individual players, and the more refined the tactics of individuals are, the more frequently and longer a team will have possession of the ball.

Much of individual tactics deals with the proper implementation of personal technique into match play. The exercises for this sort of training would be the same as those used in match condition technique training.

FUNCTIONAL TRAINING

Although modern soccer requires a great deal of interchanging positions, each player still spends a major portion of the match in one particular position. Every position on a team has its own particularly characteristic skills. Thus it is only sensible to have players practice their skills in situations related to and characteristic of their specific positions. This form of training is called *functional* training.

It is also wise to have players perform functional training in other positions in which they might find themselves during a normal match. This will not only make them aware of the needs of these positions, but it will also make them more aware of and sympathetic to the difficulties confronting their teammates who normally play in these spots.

Functional Exercises for Backs

1. Attack

   a. Combination play with wingers and midfielders and interchanging of positions.

   b. Overlap runs.

   c. Hitting long and accurate passes to forwards.

d. Free kick placement.

e. Attacking during corner kicks.

f. Attacking during free kicks.

g. Throw-in restarts.

h. Providing support in attack.

2. Defense

a. Handling crosses in the penalty area.

b. Chasing through passes and playing them back to the goal-keeper.

c. Chasing through passes and controlling them.

d. Handling overload situations when there is an extra opponent, such as two versus one and three versus two.

e. Containing opponents with the ball.

f. Recovering after being beaten by a forward.

g. Covering on the goal line when the goalkeeper is out of the net.

h. Defending during corner kick situations.

i. Defending during free kick situations.

j. Defending against throw-ins.

k. Playing opponents offsides.

l. Volley kicking as a desperation clearance.

m. Providing cover in defense.

Functional Exercises for Midfielders

1. Attack.

a. Controlling goal kick.

b. Controlling clearances from the goalkeeper.

c. Combination play with wingers, strikers, and other midfielders; interchanging positions.

d. Overlap runs.

e. Hitting accurate through passes to wings and strikers, including crosses.

f. Free kick situations.

g. Corner kick situations.

h. Kick-off restarts.

i. Throw-in restarts.

j. Combination play near penalty area.

k. Providing support in attack.

l. Shooting long shots from outside the penalty area.

2. Defense.

a. Handling overload situations when there is an extra opponent.

b. Containing and delaying opponents with the ball.

c. Recovering after being beaten by a forward.

d. Chasing through passes and playing them back to a teammate.

e. Defending during corner kick situations.

f. Defending during free kick situations.

g. Defending against throw-ins.

h. Providing cover in defense.

Functional Exercises for Wingers

1. Attack

a. Controlling goal kicks.

b. Controlling clearances from the goalkeeper.

c. Dribbling down the touchline, beating a back, and crossing the ball.

d. Running down the touchline, receiving a long pass and crossing it.

e. Dribbling the ball in from the touchline to the goal line in the penalty area and passing the ball back to strikers for shots.

f. Centering low and hard crosses from the wing.

g. Dribbling in from the wing to shoot.

h. Combination play with strikers and midfielders; interchanging positions.

i. Combination play in the penalty area.

j. Corner kick situations.

k. Free kick situations.

l. Throw-in restarts.

m. Dummy runs to create space in the penalty area for teammates.

n. Shooting crosses from other wing.

o. Overload situations where there are more attackers than defenders.

p. One-on-one situations with the goalkeeper.

2. Defense.
   a. Immediate chase and delaying opponent's attack after losing possession of the ball.

b. Recovering and containing opponent after being beaten.

c. Marking wing back of opposition during defense.

d. Corner kick situations.

e. Free kick situations.

f. Throw-in restarts.

Functional Exercises for Strikers

1. Attack.

   a. Controlling goal kicks.

   b. Controlling clearances from the goalkeeper.

c. Combination play with midfielders, wingers, and other strikers; interchanging positions.

d. Wall passing in and near the penalty area.

e. Runs to use available space and free self of defensive marking.

f. Dummy runs to create space in the penalty area for teammates.

g. All possible shooting situations.

h. Corner kick situations.

i. Free kick situations.

j. Throw-in restarts.

k. Dribbling to beat a back and shoot.

l. Overload situations where there are more attackers than defenders.

m. Runs to receive long passes directed behind the last line of defense coming from the defensive third of the field.

n. One-on-one situation with the goalkeeper.

o. Ball control and dribbling under tight marking.

p. Opportunism in the penalty area near the goal.

q. Dealing with offside traps.

2. Defense
a. Immediate chase and delaying opponent's attack after losing possession of the ball.

b. Recovering and containing opponent after being beaten.

c. Positioning during corner kicks.

d. Free kick situations.

e. Throw-in restarts.

The functional exercises listed will help improve individual positional play, and in turn as individual team members improve, so will the total effectiveness of the team. Additional exercises for each position can be devised, as the aforementioned are merely examples of functional training and by no means constitute all possible exercises that incorporate specific match situations for various positions.

The functional exercises for the goalkeeper can be the same as those exercises listed in the goalkeeping circuit in Chapter 8. Also some tactical schemes are devised that deviate from normal positions, and these may very well need specific functional exercises. Such is the case for teams that use a free back or sweeper.

Free Back

The sweeper back provides cover for the last line of defenders and relieves them of the responsibility of defensively covering each other. This enables these defenders to concentrate on marking their specific opponents and usually permits a team to mark all opposing attackers while still having defensive cover. If the opponents attack with three forwards, the defense has a back line of three men with one sweeper. When the opponents attack with four forwards, the defense will have four in the back line and a fifth back playing the role of the sweeper, as in the Italian catenaccio system. (See Diagrams 9.1 and 9.2.) In addition to providing defensive cover and marking the vital space in front of the goal, the sweeper is also responsible for picking up and challenging any opponent who comes through unmarked. This will happen occasionally when an opponent comes into the attack on a run from behind the main attacking thrust, as is the case with attacking fullbacks.

The sweeper back has been widely used throughout the world, and his flexibility has been determined by the personal qualities of the player playing the position. Those who have exceptional ability to anticipate and read the game, like Franz Beckenbauer of West Germany, have even added a new dimension in attack by occasionally rushing into the attack, leaving the opposition totally unprepared for such a surprising run.

Functional Exercises for Sweepers

1. Attack.

a. Same as all backs.

b. Coming through into the attack from his deep-lying position.

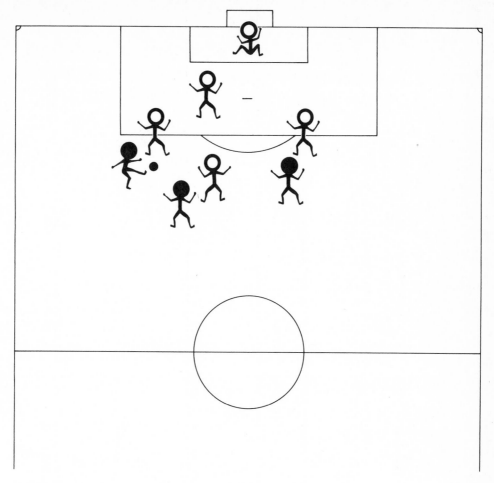

Diagram 9.1 Catenaccio defense versus three attacking forwards.

2. Defense.

    a. Same as all backs.

    b. Providing defensive cover for all the backs as the ball moves from one side of the field to the other.

    c. Challenging forwards who beat one of the backs.

    d. Picking up opponents who come through unmarked.

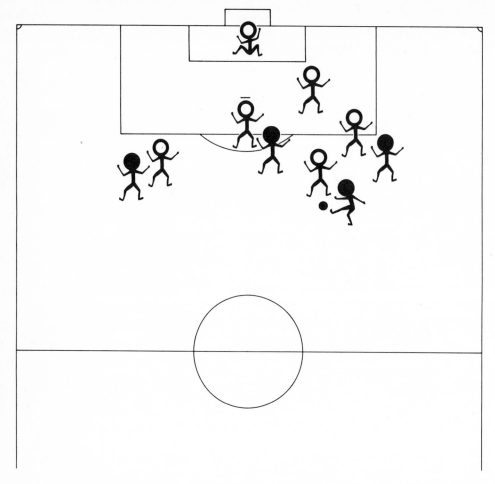

Diagram 9.2 Catenaccio defense versus four attacking forwards.

GROUP TACTICS

One of the primary ways to adhere to the main principle of soccer, maintaining ball possession, is to attempt to have numerical superiority over the opposition whenever possible. This necessitates working in pairs or groups of players who provide cover in defense and support in attack. The more defenders a team has in the area of the ball, the greater is their chance of winning possession, and the more attackers in the area of the ball, the greater the number of passing opportunities, which increases the likelihood of maintaining possession of the ball.

Group tactics refers to the play of two or more teammates. It must be an integral part of most training sessions, for the players must work together frequently to learn each other's strengths and weaknesses and to be able to anticipate each other's moves. The more familiar the players become with each other's game, the more efficiently they will play together through anticipation of their teammates' actions and through the knowledge of their teammates' preferences.

Exercises for Developing Group Tactics

To make training for group tactics most realistic, it is best to have the players perform in restricted space directly proportional to the number of players involved. During a match the full soccer field is used by 22 players, so any training done on a full field with fewer numbers provides the players with more time and space than they would have under match conditions. This is all right for match-related training when a coach first introduces a tactical concept, but the space and time should be realistic once the players grasp the idea of what they must accomplish. For example, a grid 10 yd square is excellent for playing two versus one, three versus one, or three versus two as in the Keep Away game in Chapter 4, and the team can play small-sided games of three versus three or four versus four in larger but still confining areas. A section of Chapter 4 is devoted to games that help develop tactics. Many of these are applicable to group tactical training.

One of the most difficult tactical concepts to teach, especially to beginning players, is the proper use of available space and how to create new space in attack. The following sequence of exercises has proven quite successful in helping young players grasp this concept and learn to look for the best passing opportunities, which may not always be forward towards the goal being attacked.

1. Team Passing game. (See Chapter 4, page 101.)

2. Two groups of five players each are intermingled in an area about 30 yd square. Each group has one ball, and the players are numbered 1 through 5. The players pass the ball within their own group in succession so that No. 1 always passes to No. 2, No. 2 always passes to No. 3, and so on with No. 5 always passing to No. 1 to recommence the pattern. Coaches should stress several points:

a. The player receiving the pass must move into an open space to receive the ball, calling for it from the man who is to pass it.

b. The player with the ball may not pass it over another player and must see clearly the man he is passing to.

c. To force movement of players, a restriction should be placed on the exercises, dictating that a ball may only be received by a moving player.

d. The passes are made with the hands so that the players can concentrate on moving into proper space to receive the ball; they need not worry about their passing technique as normally used in soccer.

3. Same as exercise 2 but now the players use their feet to pass the ball. Coaches should stress these points:

a. Same as (a) in exercise 2.

b. All passes must be on the ground.

c. Each player must control the ball, stop it, and then make an accurate pass. This reduces the number of inaccurate passes.

4. The same groups as for exercise 2 remain in the confined area, but now they use one ball. One team defends while the other attacks by attempting to make five consecutive passes using their hands. Coaches should emphasize certain restrictions and rules:

a. See Numbers Passing game in Chapter 4, page 121.

b. In the event that the players have difficulty in scoring points, reduce the number of consecutive passes necessary to score.

5. Same as exercise 4, but now the restriction of passing in sequence is eliminated, and the players may pass to any member of their team. Double the number of passes necessary to complete for a point, since it will be easier to complete greater numbers of passes. See No-goal Handball game in Chapter 4, page 121.

6. Same as exercise 4 but now the players pass with their feet. All the passes should be on the ground, and the coach must stress accuracy. If players begin to dribble too much, impose a restriction on the number of consecutive touches per player.

7. Head-goal Handball as in Chapter 4, page 122.

8. Small-sided games with goals, but to encourage more passing award two points for a goal and one point for every five consecutive passes.

9. Full-field games with the same scoring system as in exercise 8.

Additional exercises for group tactics would incorporate attacking the goal. Coaches can give an advantage to either the attackers or defenders by providing one side with an extra man, to make a two versus one, three versus two, or four versus three situation, with a goalkeeper in the goal.

TEAM TACTICS

Once the number of players grows too large to be referred to as one group such as six versus four, six versus five, or six versus six, we are now involved with multiple group, or *team*, tactics. The difficulty here is simply that a greater number of players need to work together as one large unit. Accomplishing this is no easy task, and it clearly makes the difference between teams that are successful and those that are not.

Communication Between Players

It will be virtually impossible for 11 players on a team to work as a cohesive unit without proper communication. The importance of clear, loud, concise, and positive talk among the players of a team from the youth level all the way through to the international level of professional players cannot be overemphasized. Quite often when two teams of equal ability meet, the difference between success or failure lies in the ability of the players to communicate properly.

Unfortunately, ill-informed coaches have often discouraged young players from talking frequently during a match because they believe that they are fostering team discipline. Nothing could be further from the truth, for even at the highest levels, a soccer player cannot play with his mouth shut.

It is vital that players understand what kind of talking is proper and what kind is not. Negative criticism of teammates' play and useless chatter are certainly deterrent factors. The laws of the game themselves prohibit some forms of talk: (1) Players are not permitted to use foul or abusive language during a match, and (2) a player may not seek to gain an unfair advantage over an opponent through the use of misleading calls such as *"I got it,"* meant to call an opponent off the ball. Such verbal tactics obviously have no place in soccer.

However, giving advice to a teammate in possession of the ball and informing teammates of what is happening behind them or on their "blind sides" can be a tremendous asset in team play. Some players are just not capable of reading the game well or fast enough, and advice on where the best passing opportunities lie or what to do with the ball can greatly increase their effectiveness. Many inexperienced players have a tendency to overwatch the ball or dribble while constantly looking at it. Although these deficiencies must certainly be corrected, in the meantime proper communication from teammates can compensate for them.

It is most advisable for the members of a team to develop a common vocabulary that is concise and clear so that each player will know what the others mean. When players pass, they can shout "square" for a ball to be passed to the side, "back" for a pass to be dropped behind the man with the ball, or "through" for a forward penetrating pass. When a player receives the ball with his back to the goal being attacked, a quick shout of "turn" can inform him that he is not tightly marked and has space and time to turn with the ball and face the direction of the attack. A call such as "man on" can inform a player that he is tightly marked and must shield the ball. Other calls such as "leave it," "hold it," "carry it," and "settle it" or "control it" are simple and clear instructions that can be of great assistance.

Players must also realize that at times it is unwise to call for the ball when they want to receive it since such a call will not only catch the attention of their teammate with the ball but also that of the defenders and could permit a defender to intercept the ball since he can anticipate the pass. However, "decoy calls," such as those used in restart plays, can be quite helpful in drawing defenders away from the space into which the pass is really intended. The player in possession of the ball must always be aware that all his teammates' calls are merely advice and that he must still evaluate the situation and choose the alternative he feels is best.

Because of the tremendous amount of position interchanging in modern soccer, proper communication among players is more important than ever before. It is vital that players let each other know when they are changing positions so that the balance, support, and depth of the team is not seriously disrupted. Proper position interchanging necessitates good talking and can be disastrous without it.

The goalkeeper is the one player on the team who can see the entire field of play in front of him. Because of this great vantage point, he can be of tremendous assistance to his teammates through good directions and advice. Especially in the defensive third of the field, a goalkeeper who takes the role of a general directing his men can greatly enhance the efficiency of his defense.

The goalkeeper must also be aware of the fact that when he comes out for a ball, a clear shout of "goalie" or "keeper" will alert his teammates that he is going for the ball. This will not only permit them to get out of his way and leave the ball for him but will also alert them that someone must cover the goal line for the keeper. Poor communication between the goalkeeper and his backs has often led to serious problems, even to the extent of conceding a goal when a back plays the ball while the goalkeeper is coming out to collect it. It is also vital that the goalkeeper take the initiative and call for all balls that should be played back to him, for if a ball is played back and he is not prepared, he could easily concede a goal to the opposition.

Inexperienced goalkeepers sometimes have a tendency to call for the ball by shouting "I got it." Not only is this confusing to his teammates since they may not be certain of who is calling for the ball, but it is also against the laws of the game since it may deceive an opponent who was about to play the ball and may lead to an indirect free kick for the opposition. Shouting "goalie" or "keeper" is just as easy, more clear to all, and above all is permissible by the laws of the game.

Rhythm of Play

Every team can develop a rhythm and pace of play, which to a great extent is dictated by their ability level and the manner of play that is natural to the players. Establishing the pace of a match and preventing opponents from settling into a rhythm that is natural to them can be a vital factor in determining the outcome of a game.

Changing the pace of play during a match can often disrupt the opposition's defense and work to a team's advantage. The Brazilians are masters of this sort of thing. They play the ball around slowly and deliberately with individual players holding and dribbling it, because of their tremendous ball control and dribbling ability. This sort of play seems aimless at times, but like a tiger who decoys his prey by pretending to be asleep before he attacks, so the Brazilians play slowly, slowly, and suddenly burst into an attack at the opponents goal with quick one-touch play. Their rhythm is almost like a dance, slow-slow-quick, and whenever they have been permitted to assert their style on a match, they have had resounding success.

The key to disrupting the rhythm of a team's natural style is pressure. When the ball and supporting players are pressured, the opposition is forced into playing at a quicker pace. By forcing the opponents to play more quickly than they wish, it is possible to reduce their control and greatly damage their confidence in their own style of play.

Many teams at the professional and international levels, especially those of South America, even resort to gamesmanship to destroy the rhythm and pace of their opponents. Many a player has gone down in seeming agony to enable the team trainers to come onto the field and have the game stopped. After stopping the play, providing at least temporary relief of the opponent's pressure, the injured players miraculously bounce back up and return to the match at full strength once again.

No team can work fast for the full 90 min of a match, but it can learn to change the speed of the play in training. A coach can allow players three or four consecutive touches while playing and then quickly restrict them to two- and one-touch play. Working first in small-sided games and then building up to full-side matches can help develop a team's ability to change the pace of play frequently. These rhythmic changes will make a team less predictable and far more difficult for opponents to anticipate.

Coaching Tactics in Progressive Thirds of the Field

An excellent means of working on team tactics is to use two full teams, with one acting as the attacking side and the other as the defending one. The players work on taking the ball from their own goal and moving it all the way through to finishing shots under the direct supervision of the coach.

To start, the ball should be served to the goalkeeper, who initiates the attack by distributing the ball. The initial aim is only to work the ball successfully out of the defensive third of the field. This will be accomplished by applying the principles of attack such as having the backs run wide as soon as the goalkeeper gets the ball to create attacking width. The coach should stop the play whenever major errors are committed and indicate the problem areas as well as how to correct them. It may also be helpful to make players freeze wherever they are when play is stopped so that improper positioning, available space, and passing opportunities can be clearly seen.

Once the players are able to move the ball repeatedly through their defensive third of the field, the coach should instruct them to bring the ball through the midfield third as well. Play still starts with the ball being served to the goalkeeper, but now the attacking side must successfully work it through two thirds of the field.

The midfield third of the field is a vital area. The team that controls the midfield will have possession of the ball most frequently during a match and more often than not will come out the winner. Thus the team must spend adequate time in midfield tactics during training.

After the players work the ball repeatedly through two thirds of the field successfully, then they should work it all the way through to a finishing shot. Again, however, the ball is started with distribution by the goalkeeper, thus constantly reinforcing the work done previously.

It is important that this sort of training does not develop into a scrimmage situation. The coach must constantly intervene when players make major errors, and the play is restarted with the goalkeeper whenever the attacking side loses possession of the ball. The coach must constantly stress the application of the principles of play and offer concise, clear directions on how to correct errors. The defenders' pressure may be reduced initially below that of actual match conditions if the attacking players are having major difficulties. However, it should be brought up to match condition pressure as soon as possible to provide the most realistic training.

Coaching Tactics Through Restrictions

Some players are more difficult to coach than others. This is especially true when the level of play gets higher and the players feel that they have mastered the game. At this level suggestions, requests, and even orders may often go unheeded. An excellent way to overcome this difficulty is by placing restrictions on play in training. This will circumvent the necessity of asking players to accomplish certain things such as dribbling less or making more short passes and will get some to believe they are accomplishing the necessary movements of their own volition and not as a result of coaching orders.

The restrictions imposed on the play in training will depend on what needs to be accomplished. For example, if the players are dribbling too much, the coach need not ask them to stop dribbling but can simply impose a restriction on the number of consecutive touches permitted each player such as in One-Touch Soccer (Chapter 4, page 118). Other games listed in Chapter 4 place different restrictions on play to accomplish specific things such as Goals from Heads (page 119), to develop more play on the wings, Low-Ball Soccer (page 119), to develop more short passing, and Goals from Back Passes (page 120), to develop more attacking support from behind the player with the ball. Many other restrictions can be placed on games that will force players to perform in the desired manner to accomplish specific tactical goals without directly instructing them.

Additional exercises

1. Man versus Man (see Chapter 4, page 120), to help develop defensive marking.
2. Half-field Soccer (see Chapter 4, page 131), to develop attacking and defensive play near the goal.
3. Attack versus Defense (see Chapter 4, page 133), to develop attacking and defensive play near the goal and for starting attacks out of the defensive third of the field.
4. Additional training of six attackers versus four defenders, six versus five, or six versus six can permit concentration on specific attacking and defensive tactics near the goal. Even when the purpose of training is primarily to develop finishing tactics, it is important to provide the defenders with target players in the middle third of the field, to whom they must attempt to get the ball after they win possession of it. It is unrealistic training and reinforcement of poor tactics to permit the defenders simply to clear the ball out immediately after gaining possession of it.

REFERENCES

Allison, Malcolm. *Soccer for Thinkers.* Pelham Books, London, 1967.

Batty, Eric. *Soccer Coaching the Modern Way.* Faber and Faber, London, 1969.

Cramer, Dettmar. *United States Soccer Federation "Coaches Manual."* Four Maples Press, Minisink Hills, Pa., 1973.

Csanadi, Arpad. *Soccer.* Corvina, Budapest, 1965.

Greaves, Jimmy. *Soccer Techniques and Tactics.* Pelham Books, London, 1966.

Hughes, Charles F.C. *Tactics and Teamwork.* E.P. Publishing, Wakefield, England, 1973.

Jones, Ken, and Pat Welton. *Football Skills and Tactics.* Marshall Cavendish, London, 1973.

Smith, Stratton, and Eric Batty. *International Coaching Book.* Souvenier Press, London, 1966.

Wade, Alan. *The FA Guide to Training and Coaching.* William Heinemann, London, 1967.

Winterbottom, Walter. *Soccer Coaching.* William Heinemann, London, 1952.

———. *Training for Soccer.* William Heinemann, London, 1960.

Glossary

acceleration The rate of increase in velocity.

aerobic Occurring in the presence of oxygen.

aerobic capacity The relative ability to supply oxygen during the contraction of a muscle, referring to the maximum oxygen consumption. It is considered the most reliable measurement of a person's endurance.

agility The ability to shift direction of the body or its parts quickly.

anaerobic Occurring in the absence of oxygen.

artery A vessel that transports blood away from the heart.

atrium Either of the two chambers of the heart that receive the blood from the veins and force it into the ventricles. Also referred to as *auricle*.

balance The defensive principle of play that provides for defenders to be spread out over most of the width of the field, so that proper marking of all vital space is assured.

cardiac muscle The muscle of the heart. An involuntary muscle since its contractions are not normally controlled by a person's will.

cardiac output The amount of blood pumped by the heart per minute.

cardiovascular endurance The type of endurance that enables a person to sustain activity in many of the large muscles of the body. Also referred to as *general endurance*.

catenaccio The Italian word for "bolt." The term given to the super defense system devised by the Italians during the 1950s.

center A pass that sends the ball from near the touchline to the middle of the field.

center back The defender who plays in the middle of the last line of defense.

center circle The circle, 10 yd in radius, at the center of the field.

center forward The principle attacking player, positioned in the center of the forward line. Now referred to as *striker.*

center halfback Originally the player in the middle of the three-player halfback line. Later the center halfback was withdrawn into the last line of defense and was referred to as the *stopper back* playing between the two fullbacks.

center line The line that divides the field into two equal parts. It runs straight across the width of the field and connects the two touchlines.

central nervous system The portion of the nervous system that includes the brain and the spinal cord.

charging To run into an opponent. The only legal method to charge another player is shoulder to shoulder with at least one foot on the ground.

chip Lofting a ball into the air by striking it with a jabbing motion at the lowest possible point.

circulatory system The body system responsible for transporting blood to all the body parts. It comprises the heart and all the blood vessels.

clearance Kicking the ball, usually over a reasonably great distance, so that it is no longer in a position where it poses a threat to the defense.

concentration The defensive principle of play that provides for defenders to concentrate in the danger area as the ball approaches their goal. This enables defenders to restrict the space from which their opponents could score goals.

contain To limit the effectiveness of an opponent by restraining him and keeping him in a given area.

contraction The shortening of the muscle fibers.

control The defensive principle of play that keeps defenders from committing themselves too quickly or rashly.

coordination The act of several muscles working together smoothly, producing several individual movements that result in one smooth action.

corner kick A direct free kick taken from the 1-yd arc at the corner of the field. A corner kick is awarded to the attacking team after the ball goes over the goal line, last touched by a defending player.

counterattack Immediately initiating an attack after winning the ball from the opposition.

cover To provide support for a teammate either on attack or defense. Sometimes also used as a synonym for "mark" or "guard" when a player is defending.

cramp Spasmodic and painful involuntary contraction of a muscle or muscles, generally resulting from overuse, insufficient oxygen, and too much lactic acid.

cross Passing the ball from one touchline to the center of the field or the other side of the field.

danger area The space in front of the goal from where a player's shot on goal could generally score a goal.

dead ball A ball that is no longer in play because it has gone out of bounds, or a goal has been scored, or play has been stopped by the referee for an infraction of the rules or other reason.

delay The defensive principle of play that directs defenders to attempt to slow down the attack of the opposition after the opponents have gained possession of the ball to provide the defense time to withdraw and organize the defensive structure.

deoxygenated blood Blood that has had its oxygen withdrawn.

depth A synonym for *support* when referring to both attacking and defending play.

direct free kick A free kick awarded to a team after a personal foul such as tripping or intentional use of hands to play a ball is committed by an opponent. The player taking the kick can score a goal directly from the free kick.

dribbling The technique of moving the ball along the ground using the feet and keeping the ball under control.

drop ball The means used to put the ball back into play after play is stopped by the referee but no team is awarded possession of the ball.

endurance Ability to delay the onset of fatigue, sustain intense activity for a prolonged period of time, and then recover quickly after fatigue.

fatigue A feeling of being tired that prevents a player from continuing an activity.

feint A movement made by a player in an attempt to deceive his opponent.

finishing The act of shooting on goal. The attacking principle of play that directs attacking players to shoot on goal.

first-time To kick the ball, whether to pass or shoot, without first bringing it under control.

fitness *See* physical fitness.

flexibility That quality of muscles that permits full range of motion of body parts: pliability.

forward Any player who primarily plays one of the positions on the front line of the attack.

free back A player who is positioned behind the last line of defenders and is responsible for providing them with cover, marking vital defensive space in front of the goal, and picking up to mark any attacking player who comes through unmarked. Also referred to as the *sweeper* or *libero*.

fullback A defender in the last line of a team's defense.

funneling The retreat of defenders who are spread out the width of the field to form a concentrated group in their danger area in an attempt to limit the attacking space available to their opponents.

general endurance Cardiovascular endurance.

glycogen The chief storage carbohydrate, a major energy-yielding food in animals. Its breakdown into lactic acid is the source of energy produced in the anaerobic process.

goal area The area directly in front of the goal, 6 by 20 yd, from which all goal kicks are taken.

goal kick An indirect free kick taken by the defending team after the ball goes out of bounds over the goal line, last touched by an attacking player. The kick is taken from anywhere within that half of the goal area closest to where the ball went out of bounds.

goal line The out-of-bounds line at both ends of the field.

goal side The position taken by a defending player when he is between the ball and the goal he is defending.

grid A series of confined areas used in training. Generally 10-yd squares.

halfback Players in the middle line of a team formation. Also referred to as *midfielders* or *linkmen*.

half-volley Playing the ball the instant it starts to bounce up after having hit the ground.

heading The technique used in projecting the ball with the head, usually the forehead.

heart rate The number of times that a heart contracts (beats) in 1 min.

hypertrophy An increase in the overall size of a tissue such as a muscle due to an enlargement of its constituent cells.

improvisation The attacking principle of play that directs players to adapt to all situations as they occur and react according to the circumstances.

indirect free kick A kick awarded for unintentional violations such as being offside that cannot score a goal unless touched by one other player besides the one taking the kick.

inside forward The player positioned in the middle of the attacking line of a team on either side of the center forward. In modern formations the players positioned in the middle of the front line are more commonly referred to as *strikers*.

inswinger A ball that swings in towards the goal, usually coming from near the touchlines or from a corner kick.

interval training Fitness training that requires brief periods of rest between activities.

involuntary muscle A muscle such as the cardiac muscle whose contractions are not generally controlled by the will.

isometric An attempted muscle contraction in which muscle tension increases but the muscle does not shorten since it does not overcome the resistance: static contraction.

isotonic Muscular contraction in which muscle fibers shorten as a result of stimulus: dynamic contraction.

jockey Containing an opponent, sometimes giving ground, while waiting for an opportunity to challenge for the ball.

kick-off The starting of play from the middle of the field at the beginning of each period and after a goal has been scored.

lactic acid The end product of the breakdown of glycogen in the anaerobic process. A fatigue toxin, a build-up of which is associated with muscle impairment.

libero The Italian term for the *free back* or *sweeper*.

ligament Tough connective tissue that forms joints by binding bones together.

link Another term for *midfielders*; players who *link* the attack and defense of a team together.

lob A high pass made without any great force, utilized to project the ball over opposing players.

local endurance The ability of a single muscle or a localized group of muscles to sustain or repeat contraction.

mark The act of guarding or covering an opponent.

maximum oxygen consumption The maximum amount of oxygen a person can take into the body every minute and use for oxidation; aerobic capacity.

metabolism The sum total of all the chemical processes of the body.

midfielder The player positioned between the forward line and the defending back line whose job is to link the two together. He has both defending and attacking responsibilities and must be a capable all-around player possessed of a high level of fitness.

mobility The attacking principle of play that provides for movement of attacking players to make use of existing space and create new space in attack to develop passing opportunities.

muscle boundness A condition brought about by improper training that causes the joints to lose some of their range of motion due to hypertrophied muscles.

nerve A bundle of nerve fibers connecting parts of the nervous system with other organs and conducting nervous impulses.

offside A player who is in an offside position when the ball is played to him or one who is in an offside position seeking to gain an advantage in attack.

offside position When a player is ahead of the ball before a member of his team plays it unless: (1) He is in his own half of the field, (2) there are two opponents nearer their own goal than he is, (3) the ball is last touched by an opponent, or (4) he receives the ball directly from a corner kick, goal kick, throw-in, or drop ball.

overlap A player coming from behind the man in possession of the ball and running past and in front of him to receive a pass.

overload principle To achieve improvement in strength or endurance the intensity, for strength, or the duration, for endurance, must exceed those levels previously attained.

oxidation The process of combining with oxygen.

oxygen debt The amount of oxygen used during recovery after effort, especially anaerobic, over and above the amount that would have been used at rest normally.

oxygenated blood Blood that is carrying oxygen.

penalty area The area 18 by 44 yd in front of the goal in which the goalkeeper is permitted to use his hands.

penalty kick A free kick awarded to the attacking team after a defending player commits a personal foul within his penalty area. The kick is taken from a spot 12 yd in front of the goal.

pendulum An apparatus with suspended soccer ball that is utilized in technique training.

penetration The attacking principle of play that provides for moving the ball forward as quickly as possible, using the fewest number of passes possible to get the ball deep into the opposition's defense and in a position from which attackers can score goals.

physical fitness A state of the body, not necessarily related to skill or motor ability, in which all systems are operating at near optimum levels.

power The ability to exert force at a rapid rate. The product of force times velocity.

pressure training A form of endurance training where players are required to perform specific soccer techniques. Players must perform a specified number of repetitions in a given period of time.

range of motion The amount of movement that can occur in a joint.

reaction time The amount of time between a stimulus signal and the beginning of the response.

reading the game The act of analyzing the play and the ability to anticipate forthcoming action.

reflex A response to a stimulus that bypasses the thought process.

respiratory system A system of organs that permits the body to breathe, supplying oxygen to the body for metabolism and relieving it of carbon dioxide.

restart The starting of play in a game at its beginning or after any suspension of play during the game.

RM (repetitions maximum) The maximum number of repetitions in weight training that a player can perform with a given weight.

rupture The tearing apart of a tissue.

save Preventing the ball from entering the goal. Usually performed by the goalkeeper by catching, deflecting, or punching the ball.

skeletal muscle The muscle responsible for limb movement and body support. Also referred to as *voluntary muscle* since it can be directly controlled by a person's will.

skill The ability to perform tasks requiring neuromuscular coordination and dexterity. The ability to perform soccer techniques under the physical and mental pressures of match competition.

smooth muscle Involuntary muscles found in the blood vessels, digestive tract, and certain other body organs.

spasm A sudden involuntary muscular contraction.

speed The velocity with which a limb may be moved; the ability to run fast.

sprain A sudden twist of a joint with tearing of ligaments.

square pass A pass sent directly to either side of a player.

stimulant Something that excites or increases functional activity.

stimulus Energy that excites or irritates a cell.

strain A sudden twist of a joint that causes stretching of ligaments.

strength The ability of an individual to apply force with a part of his body.

striated muscle Another term for *voluntary skeletal muscles,* so named because it has a striped appearance when viewed under a microscope.

striker The principal attacking player, positioned in the center of the forward line.

stroke volume The amount of blood pumped out by the heart through the left ventricle with each contraction.

support The defensive and attacking principle of play that provides for a concentration of players around the ball to assist the one player most involved with its playing.

tackle The technique used by a defender to dispossess an opponent of the ball.

technique The ability of a player to perform with a ball.

tendon The tough tissue that connects muscle to bone.

through pass A forward pass, usually one that penetrates the opponent's defense.

throw-in The technique used to put the ball back into play after it goes out of bounds over the touchline.

touchline The side boundaries of the field.

trap The technique of bringing the ball under control and then stopping it.

vascular Pertaining to the blood vessels.

velocity The rate at which an object travels.

ventricle Either of the two chambers of the heart that receive the blood from a corresponding atrium and send it into the arteries.

vital capacity The greatest amount of air a person can exhale after inhaling the greatest volume possible.

voluntary muscle A muscle that can be directly controlled by the will of a person.

width The attacking principle of play that provides for the use of the maximum amount of field width in attack in order to force the defense to spread out and create more attacking space in front of the goal.

winger The attacking player who is most often positioned near either touchline.

Index

Budai, Laszlo, 14
Bukovi, Martin, 13–14
Bulls Eye, 114–115, 265, diag. 114

Cardiff City Football Club, 10
Cardiovascular endurance, *see* General endurance
Cardiovascular system, 195–196, diag. 196
Catenaccio, 11, 20–24, 29, 324, diag. 21, 325, 326
Chapman, Herbert, 7–11 *passim*
Charlton, Bobby, 221
Circle Ball, 109–110, 265, 282, diag. 110
Circuit training, 205–213, 230–231, diag. 207
Clodoaldo, 31
Coaching
  and the learning process, 246–247
  methods of, 239–240
  and motivation, 249–251
  and planning, 247–249
  play analysis, 240–246
  principles of, 238–251
  see also Tactics coaching; Technique coaching
Combination defense, 80, 92
Concentration in defense, 46, 49, 87–90, diag. 88, 89
  in area of ball, 90
  danger area, 87–88, diag. 88
  funneling, 88–90, diag. 89
  how to develop, 90
Conditioning, *see* Training games
Control, 96–98
  communication and, 97–98
  how to develop, 98
  mental discipline and, 96–97
Corner kick, 157–172
  attack alignment for, 160–163, diag. 161, 162
  defending against, 157–160, diag. 158
  inswinger, 163–164, diag. 161, 164
  long, 163–165, diag. 161, 162, 164
  outswinger, 163, 165, diag. 162
  position of goalkeeper during, 158–159, diag. 159
  short, 165–172, diag. 166–171
Corso, Mario, 23
Counterattack, 13, 23, 66
Cruyff, Johan, 32, 35, 240, 243, fig. 33
Czibor, Zoltan, 14

Danger area, 87–88, diag. 88
Dean, Dixie, 9, fig. 10
Defense
  combination, 80, 92
  during corner kick, 157–160
  during free kick, 172–174
  during goal kick, 150
  during kick-off, 147
  during throw-in, 156–157
  forms of defensive structure, 75–91
  man-to-man, 75–77, 91
  primary objectives of, 74–75
  support/depth in, 77–78, 82–87
  zone, 77–80
  see also Principles of defense
Delay, 80–82
  how to develop, 82
  jockeying, 80–82, 289–291, fig. 81, 290
De Lorme, Thomas, 224
Del Sol, Louis, 18
De Vries, Herbert, 201
Deyna, Kazimierz, 35
Diagonal running, 57–58
Didi (Waldin Pereira), 18–19, 28, 218
Distance Heading, 116–117, 282, diag. 116
Di Stefano, Alfredo, 17–18, 29, 67, 194–195
Do Nascimento, Edson Arantes, *see* Pelé
Dos Santos, Manoel Francisco, *see* Garrincha
Drake, Ted, 9
Dribbling, 67–69, 258, 265–271, fig. 267
  exercises for developing, 269–271, diag. 270, 271
  feinting, 67, 268
  frequent errors, 269
  and improvisation, 67–68
  options, 68–69
  primary ingredients of, 266
  principles of, 266–268
Dutch Whirl, 31–32

Eintracht Football Club, 17
Endurance, 194–216
  circuit training, 205–213, 230–231, diag. 207
  exercises, 201–216
  general, 195–197, 200–201
  interval training, 201–203, diag. 202
  local, 197–200
  methods of improving, 198–216